CRE▲TIVE
HOMEOWNER®

COUNTRY&
FARMHOUSE
HOME PLANS

CREATIVE HOMEOWNER®, Upper Saddle River, New Jersey

COPYRIGHT © 2004

CREATIVE
HOMEOWNER®

A Division of Federal Marketing Corp.
Upper Saddle River, NJ

VP/Business Development: Brian H. Toolan
VP/Editorial Director: Timothy O. Bakke
Production Manager: Kimberly H. Vivas

Home Plans Publishing Consultant: James D. McNair III
Editorial Assistant: Jennifer Doolittle

Design and Layout: Arrowhead Direct (David Kroha, Cindy DiPierdomenico, Judith Kroha)

Cover Design: David Geer

Current Printing (last digit)
10 9 8 7 6 5 4 3 2 1

Country & Farmhouse Home Plans
Library of Congress Control Number: 2004103756
ISBN: 1-58011-221-8

CREATIVE HOMEOWNER®
A Division of Federal Marketing Corp.
24 Park Way
Upper Saddle River, NJ 07458
www.creativehomeowner.com

Printed in China

Note: The homes as shown in the photographs and renderings in this book may differ from the actual blueprints. When studying the house of your choice, please check the floor plans carefully.

PHOTO CREDITS

Front cover: *center* CH/131027, page 286; *bottom row (from right to left)* CH/211069, page 146; CH/181151, page 220; CH/131027, page 286; CH/121040, page 77 **back cover:** *top* CH/121045, page 96; *center* CH/141036, page 290; *bottom right* CH/131030, page 214; *bottom center* CH/131029, page 271; *bottom left* CH/131030, page 214 **page 4:** CH/111043, page 152 **page 5:** CH/321054, page 277 **page 6:** *top* CH/331003, page 280; *bottom* CH/331001, page 94 **page 7:** CH/331002, page 210 **page 52:** courtesy of Maine Cottage Furniture **pages 53–58:** George Ross/CH **page 59:** courtesy of Maine Cottage Furniture **pages 60–61:** George Ross/CH **page 62:** courtesy of Maine Cottage Furniture **page 63:** George Ross/CH **page 64:** courtesy of Maine Cottage Furniture **pages 65–67:** George Ross/CH **pages 108–109:** George Ross/CH **page 110:** Mark Samu/CH **page 111:** *all* George Ross/CH **page 112:** courtesy of Hunter Douglas **page 113:** *both* illustrations by Janet Kroenke/CH **pages 114–115:** *all* Mark Samu/CH **pages 158–164:** George Ross/CH **page 165:** courtesy of Waverly **pages 166–167:** George Ross/CH **pages 168–169:** Tina Basile/CH **page 200:** courtesy of Osram Sylvania **page 201:** courtesy of Maine Cottage Furniture **page 202:** *left* courtesy of Kraftmaid Cabinetry; *right* courtesy of Maine Cottage Furniture **page 203:** *top* courtesy of Sharp Electronics Corp.; *bottom* courtesy of Maine Cottage Furniture **pages 204–207:** *all* George Ross/CH, designer: Lyn Peterson **pages 244–251:** *all* illustrations by Steve Buchanan/CH **page 292:** George Ross/CH, designer: Lyn Peterson **page 293:** courtesy of Kohler Co. **page 294:** George Ross/CH, designer: Lyn Peterson **page 295:** courtesy of Motif Designs, designer: Lyn Peterson **page 296:** courtesy of Kohler Co. **page 297:** *top* courtesy of American Standard; *bottom* courtesy of Motif Designs, designer: Lyn Peterson **page 298:** *both* courtesy of Motif Designs, designer: Lyn Peterson **page 299:** George Ross/CH; designer: Lyn Peterson

Photographers & Manufacturers: American Standard, Piscataway, NJ; 800-442-1902. George Ross, Montclair, NJ; 973-744-5171. Hunter Douglas, Upper Saddle River, NJ; 800-789-0331. Kohler Co., Kohler, WI; 800-456-6422. Kraftmaid Cabinetry, Middlefield, OH; 440-632-5333. Maine Cottage Furniture, Yarmouth, ME; 207-846-1430. Motif Designs, New Rochelle, NY, 914-633-1170. Osram Sylvania, Danvers, MA; 978-777-1900. Mark Samu, Saratoga Springs, NY; 518-581-7026. Sharp Electronics, Mahwah, NJ; 800-237-4277. Waverly, New York, NY; 212-213-7900.

Contents

Getting Started

Maybe you can't wait to bang the first nail. Or you may be just as happy leaving town until the windows are cleaned. The extent of your involvement with the construction phase is up to you. Your time, interests, and abilities can help you decide how to get the project from lines on paper to reality. But building a house requires more than putting pieces together. Whoever is in charge of the process must competently manage people as well as supplies, materials, and construction. He or she will have to

- Make a project schedule to plan the orderly progress of the work. This can be a bar chart that shows the time period of activity by each trade.
- Establish a budget for each category of work, such as foundation, framing, and finish carpentry.
- Arrange for a source of construction financing.
- Get a building permit and post it conspicuously at the construction site.
- Line up supply sources and order materials.
- Find subcontractors and negotiate their contracts.
- Coordinate the work so that it progresses smoothly with the fewest conflicts.
- Notify inspectors at the appropriate milestones.
- Make payments to suppliers and subcontractors.

You as the Builder

You'll have to take care of every logistical detail yourself if you decide to act as your own builder or general contractor. But along with the responsibilities of managing the project, you gain the flexibility to do as much of your own work as you want and subcontract out the rest. Before taking this path, however, be sure you have the time and capabilities. Do you also have the

Every job will have a budget, even the finish work, above.

Building a new home, opposite, also involves the need to schedule inspections at the appropriate milestones.

time and ability to schedule the work, hire and coordinate subs, order materials, and keep ahead of the accounting required to manage the project successfully? If you do, you stand to save the amount that a general contractor would charge to take on these responsibilities, normally 15 to 30 percent of the construction cost. If you take this responsibility on but mismanage the project, the potential savings will erode and may even cost you more than if you had hired a builder in the first place. A subcontractor might charge extra for having to return to the site to complete work that was originally scheduled for an earlier date. Or perhaps because you didn't order the windows at the beginning, you now have to pay for a recent cost increase. (If you had hired a builder in the first place he or she would absorb the increase.)

Hiring a Builder to Handle Construction

A builder or general contractor will manage every aspect of the construction process. Your role after signing the construction contract will be to make regular progress payments and ensure that the work for which you are paying has been completed. You will also consult with the builder and agree to any changes that may have to be made along the way.

Leads for finding builders might come from friends or neighbors who have had contractors build, remodel, or add to their homes. Real-estate agents and bankers may have some names handy but are more likely familiar with the builder's ability to complete projects on time and budget than the quality of the work itself.

The next step is to narrow your list of candidates to three or four who you think can do a quality job and work harmoniously with you. Phone each builder to see whether he or she is interested in being considered for your project. If so, invite the builder to an interview at your home. The meeting will serve two purposes. You'll be able to ask the candidate about his or her experience, and you'll be able to see whether or not your personalities are compatible. Go over the plans with the builder to make certain that he or she understands the scope of the project. Ask if they have constructed similar houses. Get references, and check the builder's standing with the Better Business Bureau. Develop a short list of builders, say three, and ask them to submit bids for the project.

Contracts

Lump-Sum Contracts

A lump-sum, or fixed-fee, contract lets you know from the beginning just what the project will cost, barring any changes made because of your requests or unforeseen conditions. This form works well for projects that promise few surprises and are well defined from the outset by a complete set of contract documents. You can enter into a fixed-price contract by negotiating with a single builder on your short list or by obtaining bids from three or four builders. If you go the latter route, give each bidder a set of documents and allow at least two weeks for them to submit their bids. When you get the bids, decide who you want and call the others to thank them for their efforts. You don't have to accept the lowest bid, but it probably makes sense to do so because you have already honed the list to builders you trust. Inform this builder of your intentions to finalize a contract.

Cost-Plus-Fee Contracts

Under a cost-plus-fee contract, you agree to pay the builder for the costs of labor and materials, as verified by receipts, plus a fee that represents the builder's overhead and profit. This arrangement is sometimes referred to as "time and materials." The fee can range between 15 and 30 percent of the incurred costs. Because you ultimately pick up the tab—whatever the costs—the contractor is never at risk, as he is with a lump-sum contract. You won't know the final total cost of a cost-plus-fee contract until the project is built and paid for. If you can live with that uncertainty, there are offsetting advantages. First, this form allows you to accommodate unknown conditions much more easily than does a lump-sum contract. And rather than being tied down by the project documents, you will be free to make changes at any point along the way. This can be a trap, though. Watching the project take shape will spark the desire to add something or do something differently. Each change costs more, and the accumulation can easily exceed your budget. Because of the uncertainty of the final tab and the built-in advantage to the contractor, you should think twice before entering into this form of contract.

Contract Content

The conditions of your agreement should be spelled out thoroughly in writing and signed by both parties, whatever contractual arrangement you make with your builder. Your contract should include provisions for the following:

- The names and addresses of the owner and builder.
- A description of the work to be included ("As described in the plans and specifications dated . . .").
- The date that the work will be completed if time is of the essence.
- The contract price for lump-sum contracts and the builder's allowed profit and overhead costs for changes.
- The builder's fee for cost-plus-fee contracts and the method of accounting and requesting payment.
- The criteria for progress payments (monthly, by project milestones) and the conditions of final payment.
- A list of each drawing and specification section that is to be included as part of the contract.
- Requirements for guarantees. (One year is the standard period for which contractors guarantee the entire project, but you may require specific guarantees on

When submitting bids, all of the builders should base their estimates on the same specifications. Once the work begins, communicate with your builder to keep the work proceeding smoothly.

Inspect your newly built home, if possible, before the builder closes it up and finishes it.

certain parts of the project, such as a 20-year guarantee on the roofing.)

- Provisions for insurance.
- A description of how changes in the work orders will be handled.

The builder may have a standard contract that you can tailor to the specifics of your project. These contain complete specific conditions with blanks that you can fill in to fit your project and a set of "general conditions" that cover a host of issues from insurance to termination provisions. It's always a good idea to have an attorney review the draft of your completed contract before signing it.

Working with Your Builder

The construction phase officially begins when you have a signed copy of the contract and copies of any insurance required from the builder. It's not unheard of for a builder to request an initial payment of 10 to 20 percent of the total cost to cover mobilization costs, those costs associated with obtaining permits and getting set up to begin the actual construction. If you agree to this, keep a careful eye on the progress of the work to ensure that the total paid out at any one time doesn't get too far out of sync with the actual work completed.

What about changes? From here on, it's up to you and your builder to proceed in good faith and to keep the channels of communication open. Even so, changes of one sort or another beset every project, and they usually add to its cost.

Light at the End of the Tunnel.

The builder's request for a final inspection marks the end of the construction phase—almost. At the final inspection meeting, you and the builder will inspect the work, noting any defects or incomplete items on a "punch list." When the builder tidies up the punch list items, you should reinspect. Sometimes, builders go on to another job and take forever to clean up the last few details, so only after all items on the list have been completed satisfactorily should you release the final payment, which often accounts for the builder's profit.

Some Final Words

Having a positive attitude is important when undertaking a project as large as building a home. A positive attitude can help you ride out the rigors and stress of the construction process.

Stay Flexible. Expect problems, because they certainly will occur. Weather can upset the schedule you have established for subcontractors. A supplier may get behind on deliveries, which also affects the schedule. An unexpected pipe may surprise you during excavation. Just as certain, every problem that comes along has a solution if you are open to it.

Be Patient. The extra days it may take to resolve a construction problem will be forgotten once the project is completed.

Express Yourself. If what you see isn't exactly what you thought you were getting, don't be afraid to look into changing it. Or you may spot an unforeseen opportunity for an improvement. Changes usually cost more money, though, so don't make frivolous decisions.

Finally, watching your home go up is exciting, so stay upbeat. Get away from your project from time to time. Dine out. Take time to relax. A positive attitude will make for smoother relations with your builder. An optimistic outlook will yield better-quality work if you are doing your own construction. And though the project might seem endless while it is under way, keep in mind that all the planning and construction will fade to a faint memory at some time in the future, and you will be getting a lifetime of pleasure from a home that is just right for you.

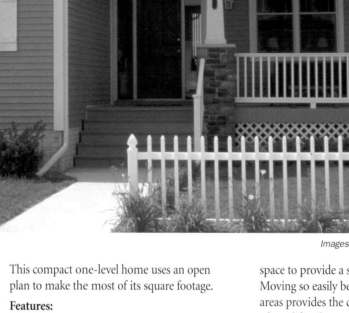

Plan #121012

Dimensions: 40' W x 48'8" D
Levels: 1
Square Footage: 1,195
Bedrooms: 3
Bathrooms: 2
Foundation: Basement
Materials List Available: Yes
Price Category: B

Images provided by designer/architect.

This compact one-level home uses an open plan to make the most of its square footage.

Features:

- Ceiling Height: 8 ft.
- Covered Porch: This delightful area, located off the kitchen, provides a private spot to enjoy some fresh air.
- Open Plan: The family room, dining area and kitchen share a big open

space to provide a sense of spaciousness. Moving so easily between these interrelated areas provides the convenience demanded by a busy lifestyle.

- Master Suite: An open plan is convenient, but it is still important for everyone to have their private space. The master suite enjoys its own bath and walk-in closet. The secondary bedrooms share a nearby bath.
- Garage: Here you will find parking for two cars and plenty of extra storage space as well.

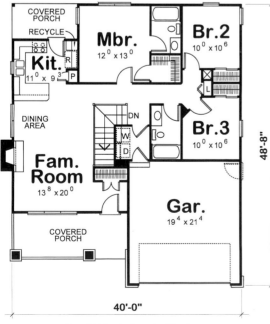

Copyright by designer/architect.

SMARTtip
Painting Doors

To protect the door finish while working, cover the sawhorses with towels or carpet scraps. Be sure to allow sufficient time for the door to dry before flipping it over.

To paint both sides of the door at one time, drive a pair of 16d nails into the top and bottom edges of the door, and then rest the door on the sawhorses, as shown below. After painting one side, simply flip the door over to paint the other side. (Note: This method may not work quite as well with very heavy wood or steel doors.)

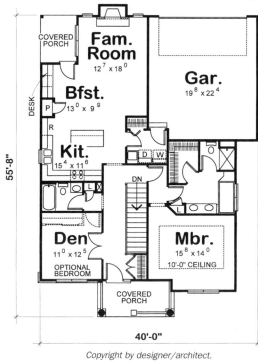

Plan #121013

Dimensions: 40' W x 55'8" D
Levels: 1
Square Footage: 1,375
Bedrooms: 1
Bathrooms: 2
Foundation: Basement
Materials List Available: Yes
Price Category: B

Images provided by designer/architect.

This convenient open plan is well-suited to retirement or as a starter home.

Features:

- Ceiling Height: 8 ft., unless otherwise noted.

- Den: To the left of the entry, French doors lead to a den that can convert to a second bedroom.

- Kitchen: A center island doubles as a snack bar while the breakfast area includes a pantry and a desk for compiling shopping lists and menus.

- Open Plan: The sense of spaciousness is enhanced by the large open area that includes the family room, kitchen, and breakfast area.

- Family Room: A handsome fireplace invites family and friends to gather in this area.

- Porch: Step through the breakfast area to enjoy the fresh air on this secluded porch.

- Master Bedroom: This distinctive bedroom features a boxed ceiling. It's served by a private bath with a walk-in closet.

SMARTtip

Paint Color Choices for Your Home

Earth tones are easy to decorate with because they are neutral colors. Use neutral or muted tones, such as light grays, browns, or greens with either lighter or darker shades for accenting.

Use bright colors sparingly, to catch the eye. Painting the front door a bright color creates a cheerful entryway.

Investigate home shows, magazines, and houses in your area for color ideas. Paint suppliers can also give you valuable tips on appropriate color schemes.

Colors that look just right on a color card may need to be toned down for painting large areas. If in doubt, buy a quart of paint and test it.

Copyright by designer/architect.

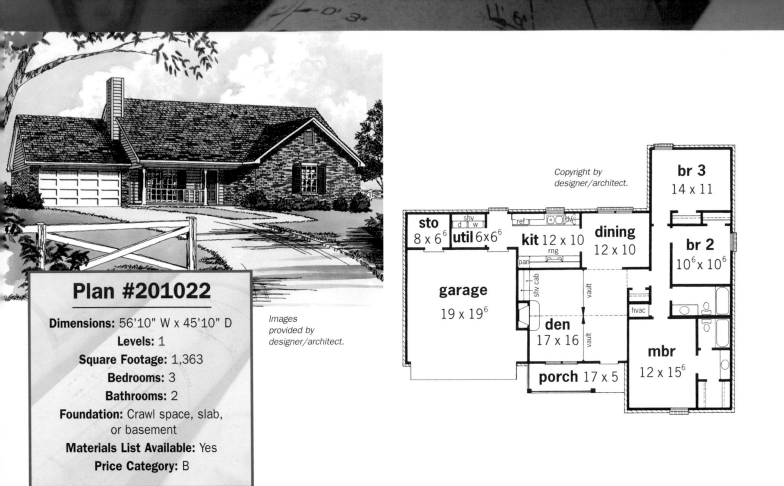

Plan #201022

Dimensions: 56'10" W x 45'10" D

Levels: 1

Square Footage: 1,363

Bedrooms: 3

Bathrooms: 2

Foundation: Crawl space, slab, or basement

Materials List Available: Yes

Price Category: B

Images provided by designer/architect.

Copyright by designer/architect.

sto 8 x 6⁶

util 6x6⁶

kit 12 x 10

dining 12 x 10

br 3 14 x 11

br 2 10⁶ x 10⁶

garage 19 x 19⁶

den 17 x 16

mbr 12 x 15⁶

porch 17 x 5

Plan #181152

Dimensions: 43' W x 34' D

Levels: 1

Square Footage: 1,339

Bedrooms: 3

Bathrooms: 1

Foundation: Basement

Materials List Available: Yes

Price Category: B

Images provided by designer/architect.

Copyright by designer/architect.

DECK

COV. PORCH

DINING RM 9' CLG 11'-0"x 15'-4"

KITCHEN 9'-0"x 10'-0"

OPTIONAL TWO CAR GARAGE 20'-0" x 20'-0"

BEDRM #3 11'-4"x 10'-0"

BATH #2

GREAT RM 10' CLG 20'-0"x 15'-4"

LAUN RM

UTIL

WICL

MSTR BATH

BEDRM #2 11'-4"x 12'-4"

COV. PORCH

MSTR BEDRM TRAY CEIL 12'-0"x 16'-4"

Copyright by designer/architect.

Images provided by designer/architect.

Plan #131014

Dimensions: 48' W x 43'4" D

Levels: 1

Square Footage: 1,380

Bedrooms: 3

Bathrooms: 2

Foundation: Basement, crawl space, or slab

Materials List Available: Yes

Price Category: C

Rear Elevation

FUTURE EXPANSION 20'-0"x 15'-4"

Bonus Room

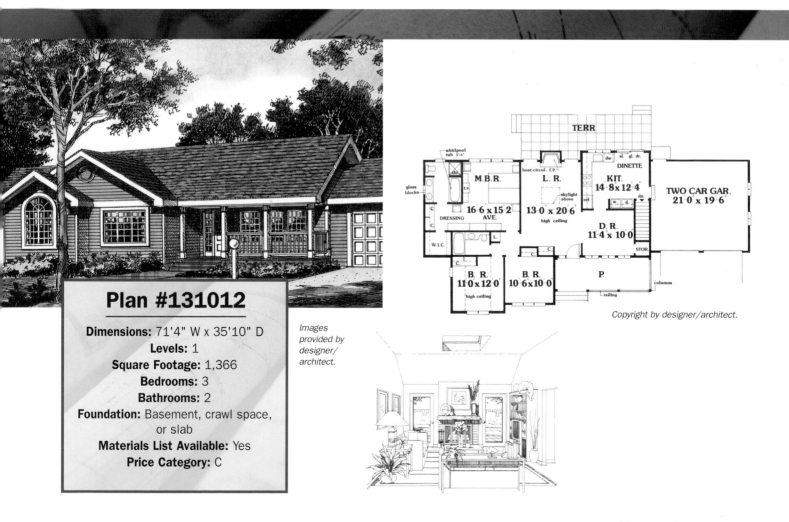

TERR

M.B.R. 16'-6 x 15'-2 AVE.

L.R. 13'-0 x 20'-6 high ceiling

KIT. 14'-8 x 12'-4

TWO CAR GAR. 21'-0 x 19'-6

whirlpool tub 5'-6"

glass blocks

heat-circul. f.p.

DRESSING

W.I.C.

DINETTE

D.R. 11'-4 x 10'-0

B.R. 11'-0 x 12'-0 high ceiling

B.R. 10'-6 x 10'-0

P.

Copyright by designer/architect.

Plan #131012

Dimensions: 71'4" W x 35'10" D

Levels: 1

Square Footage: 1,366

Bedrooms: 3

Bathrooms: 2

Foundation: Basement, crawl space, or slab

Materials List Available: Yes

Price Category: C

Images provided by designer/ architect.

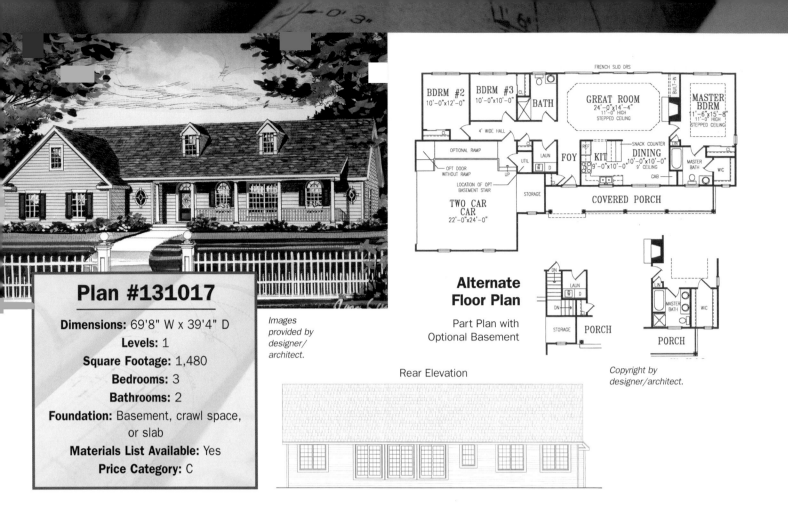

Plan #131017

Dimensions: 69'8" W x 39'4" D

Levels: 1

Square Footage: 1,480

Bedrooms: 3

Bathrooms: 2

Foundation: Basement, crawl space, or slab

Materials List Available: Yes

Price Category: C

Images provided by designer/architect.

Alternate Floor Plan

Part Plan with Optional Basement

Rear Elevation

Copyright by designer/architect.

Plan #201012

Dimensions: 51'10" W x 40'10" D

Levels: 1

Square Footage: 1,221

Bedrooms: 3

Bathrooms: 2

Foundation: Crawl space, slab, or basement

Materials List Available: Yes

Price Category: B

Images provided by designer/architect.

SMARTtip

Kitchen Cabinet Styles

You may not need to purchase expensive kitchen cabinetry to get fine-furniture quality details. Try adding crown molding to the top of basic cabinets and replacing the hardware with reproduction polished-brass door and drawer pulls to achieve a traditional look.

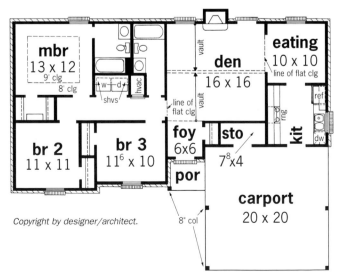

Copyright by designer/architect.

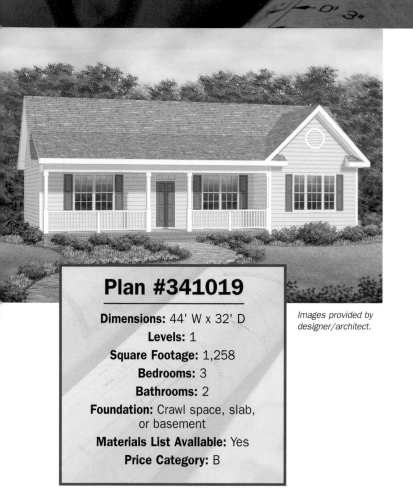

Plan #341019

Dimensions: 44' W x 32' D

Levels: 1

Square Footage: 1,258

Bedrooms: 3

Bathrooms: 2

Foundation: Crawl space, slab, or basement

Materials List Available: Yes

Price Category: B

Images provided by designer/architect.

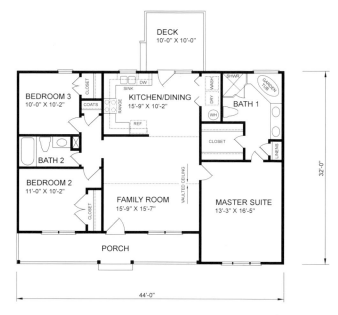

Copyright by designer/architect.

Plan #211016

Dimensions: 44'6" W x 59' D

Levels: 1

Square Footage: 1,191

Bedrooms: 3

Bathrooms: 2

Foundation: Slab

Materials List Available: Yes

Price Category: B

Images provided by designer/architect.

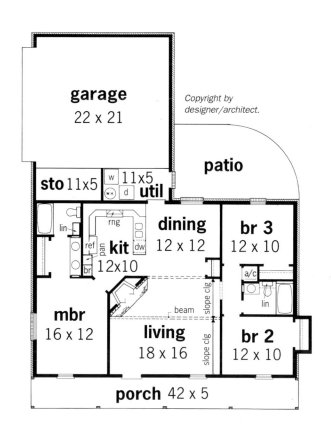

Copyright by designer/architect.

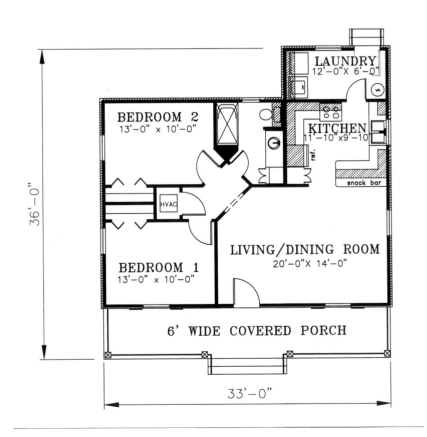

Plan #191030

Dimensions: 33' W x 36' D

Levels: 1

Square Footage: 864

Bedrooms: 2

Bathrooms: 1

Foundation: Crawl space or slab

Materials List Available: No

Price Category: A

Images provided by designer/architect.

Enjoy the view from the spacious front porch of this cozy cottage, which is ideal for a retirement home, vacation retreat, or starter home.

Features:

- Porch: This 6-ft.-wide porch, which runs the length of the home, gives you plenty of space to set up a couple of rockers next to a potted herb garden.

- Living/Dining Room: This huge living and dining area gives you many options for design. The snack bar that it shares with the kitchen is a practical touch.

- Kitchen: The first thing you'll notice in this well-planned kitchen is how much counter and storage space it offers.

- Laundry Room: Opening to the backyard, this room also features ample storage space.

- Bedrooms: Both rooms have good closet space and easy access to the large, luxurious bath.

Copyright by designer/architect.

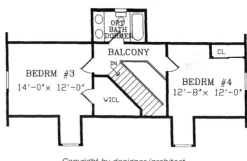

Plan #131034

Dimensions: 40' W x 32' D
Levels: 2 (Upper unfinished)
Square Footage: 1,040
Bedrooms: 5
Bathrooms: 2½
Foundation: Crawl space, slab, or basement
Materials List Available: Yes
Price Category: C

Images provided by designer/architect.

You'll love the versatility this expandable ranch-style home gives, with its unfinished, second story that you can transform into two bedrooms and a bath if you need the space.

Features:

- **Porch:** Decorate this country-style porch to accentuate the charm of this warm home.

- **Living Room:** This formal room features a wide, dramatic archway that opens to the kitchen and the dining room.

- **Kitchen:** The angled shape of this kitchen gives it character, while the convenient island and well-designed floor plan make cooking and cleaning tasks unusually efficient.

- **Bedrooms:** Use the design option in the blueprints of this home to substitute one of the bedrooms into an expansion of the master bedroom, which features an amenity-laden, private bathroom for total luxury.

Optional Main Level Floor Plan

Main Level Floor Plan

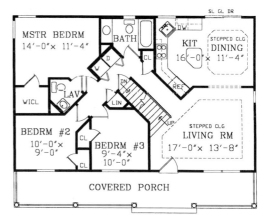

Kitchen

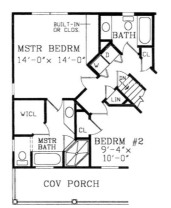

Upper Level Floor Plan

Copyright by designer/architect.

Plan #341025

Dimensions: 50' W x 32' D

Levels: 1

Square Footage: 1,392

Bedrooms: 3

Bathrooms: 2

Foundation: Crawl space, slab, or basement

Materials List Available: Yes

Price Category: B

Images provided by designer/architect.

Copyright by designer/architect.

KITCHEN 13'–11"X9'–6"

PORCH

BATH 1

LINEN

CLOSET

BEDROOM 2 12'–9"X11'–5"

BATH 2

DINING AREA

WASH

DRY

CLOSET

LIVING ROOM 15'–0"X23'–2"

BEDROOM 1 12'–5"X13'–5"

BEDROOM 3 11'–2"X11'–5"

COATS

CLOSET

PORCH

50'–0"

32'–0"

Plan #211018

Dimensions: 40' W x 64' D

Levels: 1

Square Footage: 1,266

Bedrooms: 3

Bathrooms: 2

Foundation: Crawl space

Materials List Available: Yes

Price Category: B

Images provided by designer/architect.

Copyright by designer/architect.

garage 22 x 21

sto 10x6

dining 12 x 10

util

br 3 11 x 10

br 2 12 x 11

kit 17 x 8

living 18 x 18

mbr 15 x 11

foy

porch 40 x 6

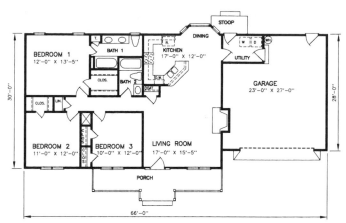

Images provided by designer/architect.

Plan #341005

Dimensions: 66' W x 30' D

Levels: 1

Square Footage: 1,334

Bedrooms: 3

Bathrooms: 2

Foundation: Crawl space, slab, or basement

Materials List Available: Yes

Price Category: B

Copyright by designer/architect.

Images provided by designer/architect.

Plan #341028

Dimensions: 40' W x 32' D

Levels: 1

Square Footage: 1,248

Bedrooms: 3

Bathrooms: 2

Foundation: Crawl space, slab, or basement

Materials List Available: Yes

Price Category: B

Copyright by designer/architect.

Plan #341023

Dimensions: 72'7" W x 34' D

Levels: 1

Square Footage: 1,469

Bedrooms: 3

Bathrooms: 2

Foundation: Crawl space, slab, or basement

Materials List Available: Yes

Price Category: B

Images provided by designer/architect.

Plan #341031

Dimensions: 50' W x 50' D

Levels: 1

Square Footage: 1,400

Bedrooms: 3

Bathrooms: 2

Foundation: Crawl space, slab, or basement

Materials List Available: Yes

Price Category: B

Images provided by designer/architect.

Copyright by designer/architect.

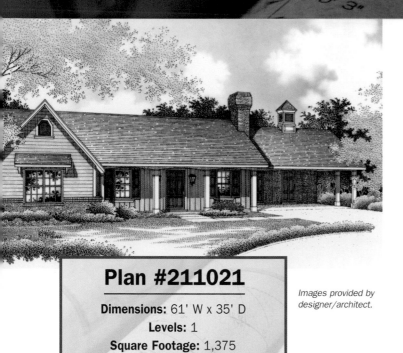

patio

| mbr 15 x 14 | kit | dining 13 x 10 | util | sto 9 x 10 |

rng · dw · pan · ref · clo · shvs · HEAT & AC

living 20 x 15
cathedral ceiling

br 3 12 x 10
beam

carport 21 x 20

br 2 13 x 11

porch

Copyright by designer/architect.

Images provided by designer/architect.

Plan #211021

Dimensions: 61' W x 35' D
Levels: 1
Square Footage: 1,375
Bedrooms: 3
Bathrooms: 2
Foundation: Slab
Materials List Available: Yes
Price Category: B

SMARTtip

Creating Built-up Cornices

Combine various base, crown, and cove moldings to create an elaborate cornice that is both imaginative and tasteful. Use the pattern throughout your home to establish a unique architectural element having the appearance of being professionally designed.

SMARTtip

Basic Triangle-Kitchens

Draw up your kitchen plan in this order: sink, range, refrigerator. Once you have the basic triangle located, add the other appliances, such as wall ovens and a dishwasher, and then the cabinets, counters, and eating areas.

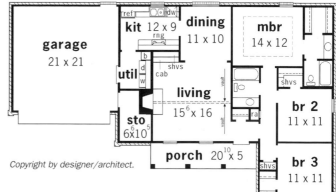

| garage 21 x 21 | kit 12 x 9 | dining 11 x 10 | mbr 14 x 12 |

ref · dw · rng · b · shvs · cab

util d w

sto 6×10⁵

living 15⁶ x 16
vault

br 2 11 x 11

porch 20¹⁰ x 5

br 3 11 x 11

Copyright by designer/architect.

Plan #201015

Dimensions: 63'10" W x 38'10" D
Levels: 1
Square Footage: 1,271
Bedrooms: 3
Bathrooms: 2
Foundation: Crawl space, slab, or basement
Materials List Available: Yes
Price Category: B

Images provided by designer/architect.

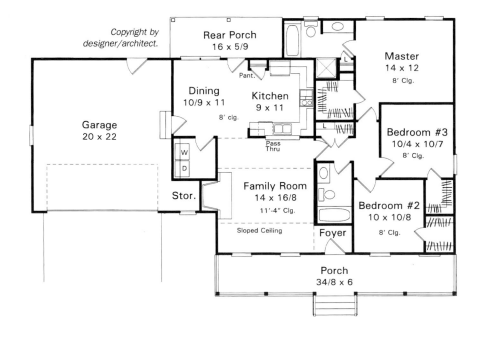

Plan #251001

Dimensions: 61'3" W x 40'6" D
Levels: 1
Square Footage: 1,253
Bedrooms: 3
Bathrooms: 2
Foundation: Crawl space, basement
Materials List Available: Yes
Price Category: B

Images provided by designer/architect.

This charming country home has a classic full front porch for enjoying summertime breezes.

Features:

- Ceiling Height: 8 ft.

- Foyer: Guests will walk through the front porch into this foyer, which opens to the family room.

- Screened Porch: A second porch is screened and is located at the rear of the home off the dining room, so your guests can step out for a bit of fresh air after dinner.

- Family Room: Family and friends will be drawn to this large open space, with its handsome fireplace and sloped ceiling.

- Kitchen: This open and airy kitchen is a pleasure in which to work. It has ample counter space and a pantry.

- Master Bedroom: This master bedroom features a large walk-in closet. It has its own master bath with a single vanity, a tub, and a walk-in shower.

- Garage: This attached garage provides plenty of extra storage space, as well as parking for two cars.

Copyright by designer/architect.

Rear Porch 16 x 5/9

Dining 10/9 x 11 — 8' clg.

Kitchen 9 x 11

Pant.

Pass Thru

Master 14 x 12 — 8' Clg.

Bedroom #3 10/4 x 10/7 — 8' Clg.

Garage 20 x 22

Stor.

W D

Family Room 14 x 16/8 — 11'-4" Clg.

Sloped Ceiling

Foyer

Bedroom #2 10 x 10/8 — 8' Clg.

Porch 34/8 x 6

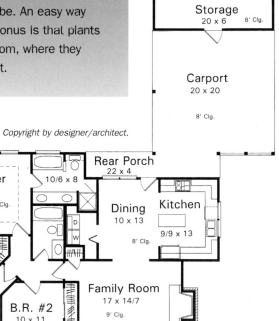

Plan #251002

Dimensions: 55'6" W x 64'3" D
Levels: 1
Square Footage: 1,333
Bedrooms: 3
Bathrooms: 2
Foundation: Crawl space, slab
Materials List Available: Yes
Price Category: B

Although compact, this farmhouse has all the amenities for comfortable modern living.

Features:

- Ceiling Height: 8 ft. unless otherwise noted.

- Foyer: This gracious and welcoming foyer opens to the family room.

- Family Room: This inviting family room is designed to accommodate all kinds of family activities. It features a 9-ft. ceiling and a handsome, warming fireplace.

- Kitchen: Cooking in this kitchen is a real pleasure. It includes a center island, so you'll never run out of counter space for food preparation.

- Master Bedroom: This master bedroom features a large walk-in closet and an elegant 9-ft. recessed ceiling.

- Master Bath: This master bath offers a double vanity, a tub, and a walk-in shower.

- Garage: This attached garage provides plenty of extra storage space, as well as parking for two cars.

Images provided by designer/architect.

SMARTtip

Arts and Crafts Style

The heart of this style rests in its earthy connection. The more you can bring nature into it, the more authentic it will be. An easy way to do this is with plants. A bonus is that plants naturally thrive in the bathroom, where they enjoy the humid environment.

Copyright by designer/architect.

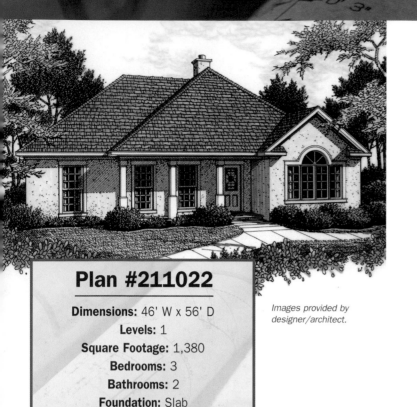

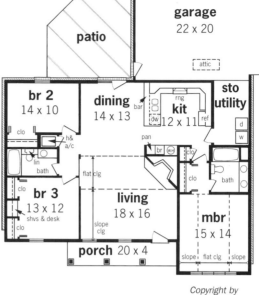

Plan #211022

Dimensions: 46' W x 56' D

Levels: 1

Square Footage: 1,380

Bedrooms: 3

Bathrooms: 2

Foundation: Slab

Materials List Available: Yes

Price Category: B

Images provided by designer/architect.

Copyright by designer/architect.

Plan #211024

Dimensions: 61' W x 44' D

Levels: 1

Square Footage: 1,418

Bedrooms: 3

Bathrooms: 2

Foundation: Slab

Materials List Available: Yes

Price Category: B

Images provided by designer/architect.

Copyright by designer/architect.

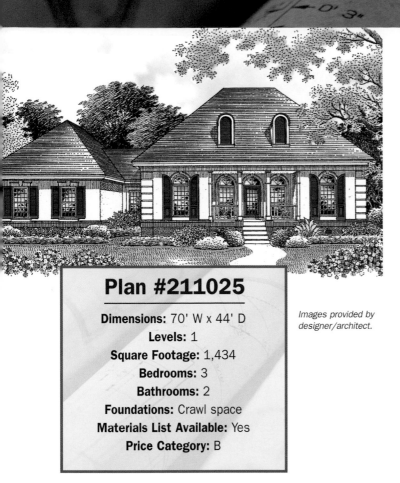

Plan #211025

Dimensions: 70' W x 44' D
Levels: 1
Square Footage: 1,434
Bedrooms: 3
Bathrooms: 2
Foundations: Crawl space
Materials List Available: Yes
Price Category: B

Images provided by designer/architect.

Kitchen Peninsulas & Islands

If a peninsula or island separates the kitchen work area from the eating or living area in a great room, consider installing a 48-inch-high snack bar along the dividing line and standard height counters everywhere else. The high counter will help keep dirty dishes, pots, and pans out of sight while you are dining.

Copyright by designer/architect.

Copyright by designer/architect.

Creating Built-up Cornices

Combine various base, crown, and cove moldings to create an elaborate cornice that is both imaginative and tasteful. Use the pattern throughout your home to establish a unique architectural element having the appearance of being professionally designed.

Plan #211021

Dimensions: 61' W x 35' D
Levels: 1
Square Footage: 1,375
Bedrooms: 3
Bathrooms: 2
Foundation: Slab
Materials List Available: Yes
Price Category: B

Images provided by designer/architect.

Plan #211019

Dimensions: 73' W x 37' D

Levels: 1

Square Footage: 1,395

Bedrooms: 3

Bathrooms: 2

Foundation: Slab

Materials List Available: Yes

Price Category: B

Images provided by designer/architect.

Copyright by designer/architect.

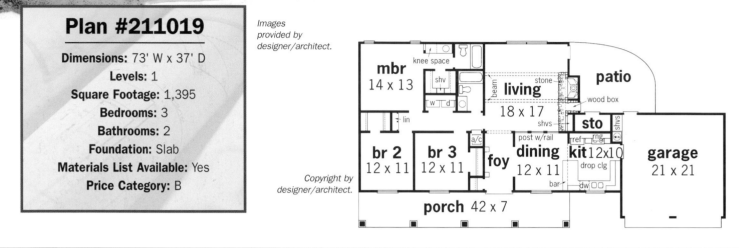

Plan #341034

Dimensions: 50' W x 38'2" D

Levels: 1

Square Footage: 1,445

Bedrooms: 3

Bathrooms: 2

Foundation: Crawl space, slab, or basement

Materials List Available: Yes

Price Category: B

Images provided by designer/architect.

Copyright by designer/architect.

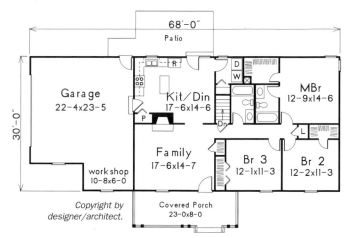

Copyright by designer/architect.

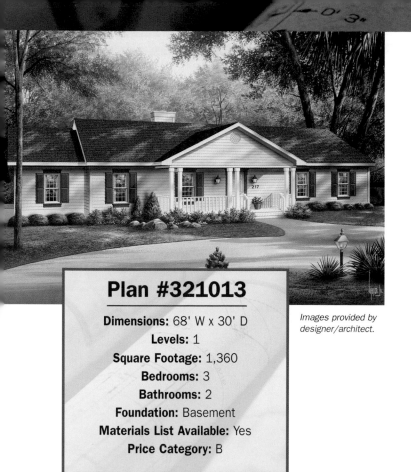

Plan #321013

Dimensions: 68' W x 30' D
Levels: 1
Square Footage: 1,360
Bedrooms: 3
Bathrooms: 2
Foundation: Basement
Materials List Available: Yes
Price Category: B

Images provided by designer/architect.

SMARTtip

Glass Doors and Fire Safety

Professionals recommend keeping glass doors open while a fire is burning. When the doors are left completely open, the burning flame has a more realistic appearance and the glass doesn't become soiled by swirling ashes. When the doors are closed, heat from a large hot fire can break the glass.

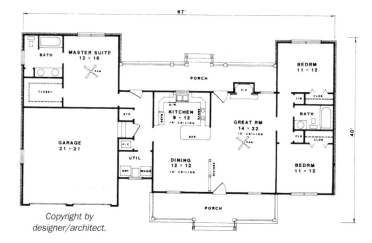

Copyright by designer/architect.

Plan #171002

Dimensions: 67' W x 40' D
Levels: 1
Square Footage: 1,458
Bedrooms: 3
Bathrooms: 2
Foundation: Slab, crawl space
Materials List Available: Yes
Price Category: B

Images provided by designer/architect.

SMARTtip

Accent Landscape Lighting

Accent highlights elements in your landscape. It creates ambiance and helps integrate the garden with the deck. Conventional low-voltage floodlights are excellent for creating effects such as wall grazing, silhouetting, and uplighting.

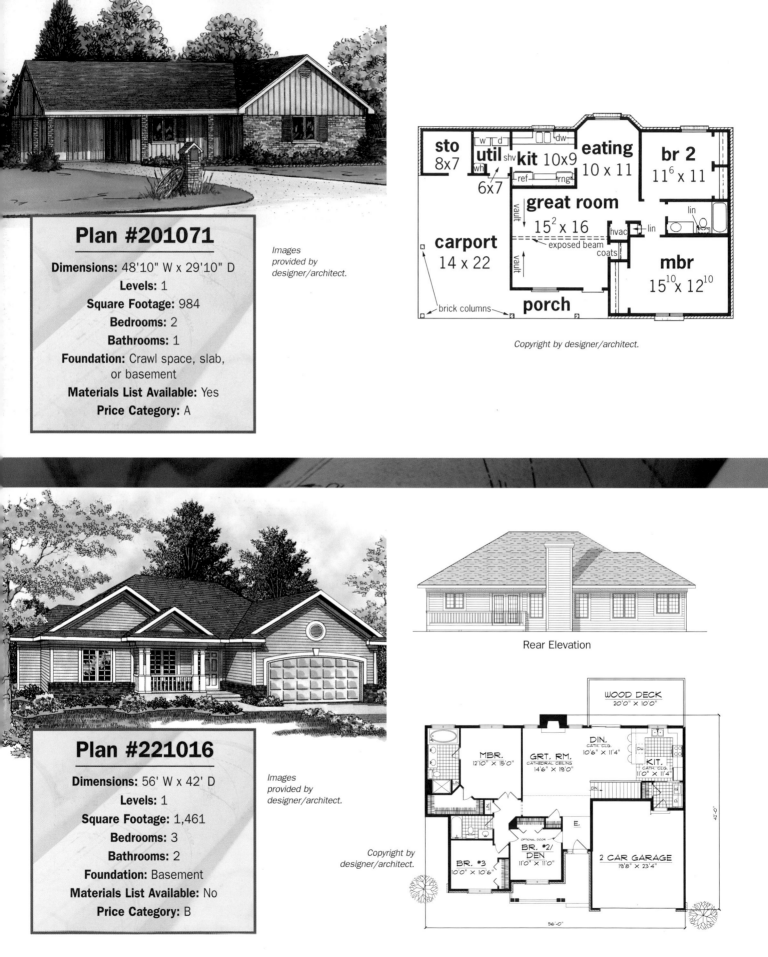

Plan #201071

Dimensions: 48'10" W x 29'10" D

Levels: 1

Square Footage: 984

Bedrooms: 2

Bathrooms: 1

Foundation: Crawl space, slab, or basement

Materials List Available: Yes

Price Category: A

Images provided by designer/architect.

sto 8x7

util 6x7

kit 10x9

eating 10 x 11

br 2 11⁶ x 11

great room 15² x 16

carport 14 x 22

exposed beam

mbr 15¹⁰ x 12¹⁰

brick columns

porch

Copyright by designer/architect.

Plan #221016

Dimensions: 56' W x 42' D

Levels: 1

Square Footage: 1,461

Bedrooms: 3

Bathrooms: 2

Foundation: Basement

Materials List Available: No

Price Category: B

Images provided by designer/architect.

Rear Elevation

WOOD DECK 20'0" X 10'0"

MBR. 12'10" X 15'0"

GRT. RM. CATHEDRAL CEILING 14'6" X 19'0"

DIN. CATH. CLG. 10'6" X 11'4"

KIT. CATH. CLG. 11'0" X 11'4"

BR. #2/ DEN 11'0" X 11'0"

BR. #3 10'0" X 10'6"

2 CAR GARAGE 19'8" X 23'4"

Copyright by designer/architect.

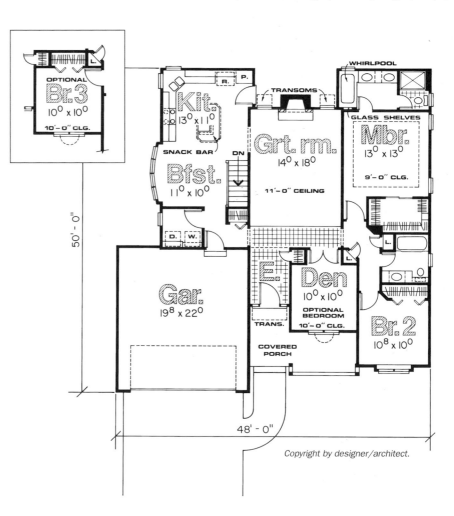

Plan #121056

Dimensions: 48' W x 50' D
Levels: 1
Square Footage: 1,479
Bedrooms: 2
Bathrooms: 2
Foundation: Basement
Materials List Available: Yes
Price Category: B

This home is ideal if the size of your live-in family is increasing with the addition of a baby, or if it's decreasing as children leave the nest.

Features:

- **Entry:** This entry gives you a long view into the great room that it opens into.

- **Great Room:** An 11-ft. ceiling and a fireplace framed by transom-topped windows make this room comfortable in every season and any time of day or night.

- **Den:** French doors open to this den, with its picturesque window. This room would also make a lovely third bedroom.

- **Kitchen:** This kitchen has an island that can double as a snack bar, a pantry, and a door into the backyard.

- **Master Suite:** A large walk-in closet gives a practical touch; you'll find a sunlit whirlpool tub, dual lavatories, and a separate shower in the bath.

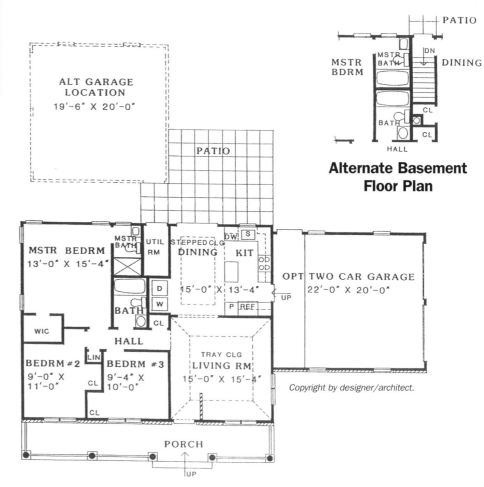

Plan #131004

Dimensions: 59'4" W x 35'8" D
Levels: 1
Square Footage: 1,097
Bedrooms: 3
Bathrooms: 2
Foundation: Basement, crawl space, or slab
Materials List Available: Yes
Price Category: C

You'll love the extra features you'll find in this charming but easy-to-build ranch home.

Features:

- **Porch:** This full-width porch is graced with impressive round columns, decorative railings, and ornamental moldings.

- **Living Room:** Just beyond the front door, the living room entrance has a railing that creates the illusion of a hallway. The 10-ft. tray ceiling makes this room feel spacious.

- **Dining Room:** Flowing from the living room, this room has a 9-ft.-high stepped ceiling and leads to sliding glass doors that open to the large rear patio.

- **Kitchen:** This kitchen is adjacent to the dining room for convenience and has a large island for efficient work patterns.

- **Master Suite:** Enjoy the privacy in this bedroom with its private bathroom.

Alternate Basement Floor Plan

PATIO
MSTR BDRM
MSTR BATH
DN
DINING
BATH
CL
CL
HALL

ALT GARAGE LOCATION
19'-6" X 20'-0"

PATIO

MSTR BEDRM
13'-0" X 15'-4"
MSTR BATH
UTIL RM
STEPPED CLG DINING
15'-0" X 13'-4"
KIT
DW
S
D
W
BATH
CL
WIC
HALL
LIN
BEDRM #2
9'-0" X 11'-0"
CL
BEDRM #3
9'-4" X 10'-0"
CL
TRAY CLG LIVING RM
15'-0" X 15'-4"
P REF
UP
OPT TWO CAR GARAGE
22'-0" X 20'-0"
PORCH
UP

Plan #251003

Dimensions: 42' W x 42' D

Levels: 1

Square Footage: 1,393

Bedrooms: 3

Bathrooms: 2

Foundation: Crawl space, slab

Materials List Available: Yes

Price Category: B

Images provided by designer/architect.

Copyright by designer/architect.

Plan #321022

Dimensions: 44' W x 27' D

Levels: 1

Square Footage: 1,140

Bedrooms: 3

Bathrooms: 2

Foundation: Basement

Materials List Available: Yes

Price Category: B

Images provided by designer/architect.

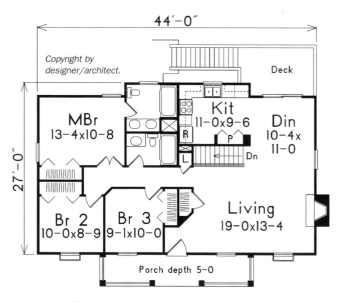

SMARTtip

Basement Moldings

Keep moldings simple in a basement with lower ceilings. Elaborate moldings around the ceiling or floor can shorten the height of the room.

Plan #181015

Dimensions: 58' W x 28'4" D
Levels: 1
Square Footage: 1,776
Bedrooms: 3
Bathrooms: 1
Foundation: Basement
Materials List Available: Yes
Price Category: B

A pillared front porch and beautifully arched windows enhance the stucco exterior.

Features:

- Ceiling Height: 8 ft.

- Kitchen: Cooking will be a pleasure in this bright and spacious kitchen. There is ample counter space for food preparation, in addition to a center island. The kitchen is flooded with light from sliding glass doors that provide access to the outdoors.

- Family Room: Nothing warms you on a cold winter day quite like the radiant heat from the cozy wood-burning fireplace/stove you will find in this family gathering room.

- Front Porch: Step directly out of the living room onto this spacious front porch. Relax in a porch rocker, and enjoy a summer breeze with your favorite book or just rock and watch the sun set.

- Bedrooms: Three family bedrooms share a full bathroom complete with dual vanities and laundry facilities.

Images provided by designer/architect.

Copyright by designer/architect.

SMARTtip

Electrical Safety in the Kitchen

Sometimes the special needs of the disabled may seem to conflict with those of the very young. A case in point is accessible switch placement, which is lower on a wall. The NKBA recommends locating outlets and switches inside the front of an adult-accessible tilt-down drawer to conceal them from children. Alternatively, an outlet strip can be kept out of a child's reach and at a convenient adult location while lessening the reach to outlets and switches installed in the backsplash.

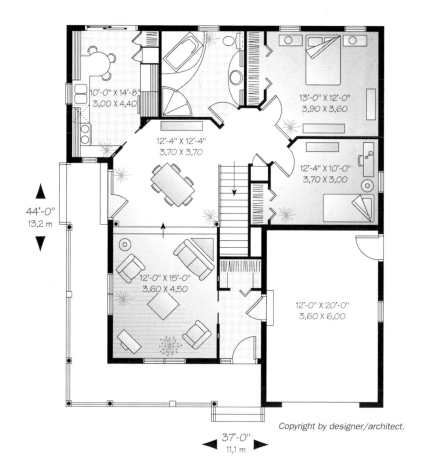

Plan #181021

Dimensions: 37' W x 44' D

Levels: 1

Square Footage: 1,124

Bedrooms: 2

Bathrooms: 1

Foundation: Basement

Materials List Available: Yes

Price Category: B

Images provided by designer/architect.

This cozy country cottage is enhanced by lattice trim details over the porch and garage.

Features:

- Ceiling Height: 8 ft.

- Living Room: This living room gets extra architectural interest from a sunken floor. The room, located directly to the left of the entry hall, has plenty of space for entertaining.

- Dining Room: This dining room is located in center of the home. It's adjacent to the kitchen to make it easy to serve meals.

- Kitchen: This bright and efficient kitchen is a real pleasure in which to work. It includes a pantry and double sinks. There's a breakfast bar that will see plenty of informal meals for families on the go.

- Covered Porch: This is the perfect place to which to retire after dinner on a warm summer evening.

- Bedrooms: Each of the two bedrooms has its own closet. They share a full bathroom.

Copyright by designer/architect.

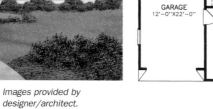

Plan #341022

Dimensions: 58'4" W x 31'10" D

Levels: 1

Square Footage: 1,281

Bedrooms: 3

Bathrooms: 2

Foundation: Crawl space, slab, or basement

Materials List Available: Yes

Price Category: B

Images provided by designer/architect.

Copyright by designer/architect.

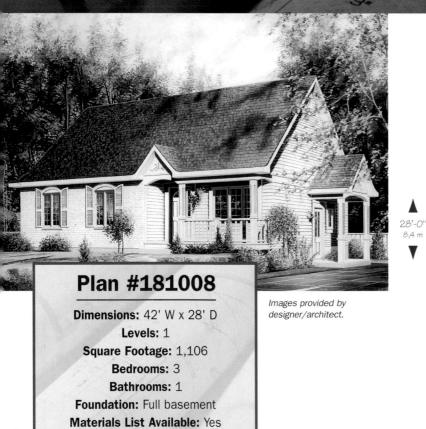

Plan #181008

Dimensions: 42' W x 28' D

Levels: 1

Square Footage: 1,106

Bedrooms: 3

Bathrooms: 1

Foundation: Full basement

Materials List Available: Yes

Price Category: B

Images provided by designer/architect.

Copyright by designer/architect.

Plan #201027

Dimensions: 58'10" W x 46'10" D

Levels: 1

Square Footage: 1,494

Bedrooms: 3

Bathrooms: 2

Foundation: Crawl space, slab, or basement

Materials List Available: Yes

Price Category: B

Images provided by designer/architect.

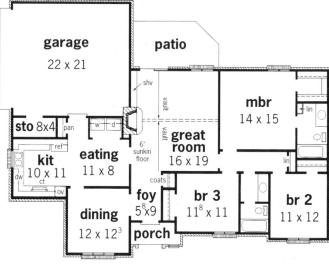

Copyright by designer/architect.

Plan #201006

Dimensions: 69'10" W x 25'10" D

Levels: 1

Square Footage: 1,172

Bedrooms: 3

Bathrooms: 2

Foundation: Crawl space, slab, or basement

Materials List Available: Yes

Price Category: B

Images provided by designer/architect.

SMARTtip

Bathroom Fans

Especially in large bathrooms, more than one fan is recommended for efficient venting. Of course, first check with your local building department about codes that may stipulate where to install bathrooms fans. If possible, include a fan in the toilet area, one near the shower, and one over the bathtub.

Copyright by designer/architect.

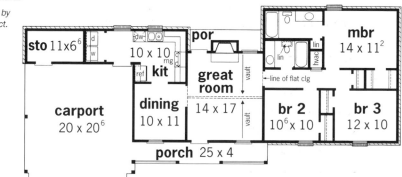

Plan #281011

Dimensions: 50' W x 54' D

Levels: 1

Square Footage: 1,314

Bedrooms: 3

Bathrooms: 2

Foundation: Basement

Materials List Available: Yes

Price Category: B

Images provided by designer/architect.

This attractive ranch home takes advantage of views at both the front and rear.

Features:

- Ceiling Height: 8 ft.

- Porch: This large, inviting porch welcomes your guests and provides shade for the big living-room window on hot summer days.

- Living Room: This large main living area has plenty of room for entertaining and family activities.

- Dining Room: This room can accommodate large dinner parties. It's located near the living room and the kitchen for convenient entertaining.

- Deck: Family and friends will enjoy stepping out on this large covered sun deck that is accessible from the living room, dining room, and kitchen.

- Master Suite: You'll enjoy retiring at the end of the day to this luxurious master suite, which features its own walk-in closet and bathroom.

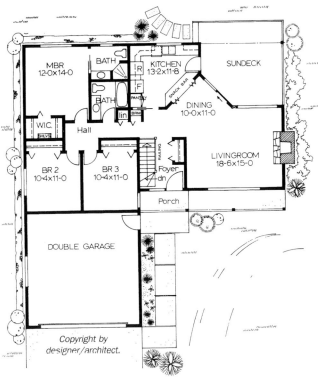

Copyright by designer/architect.

Rear Elevation

SMARTtip

Rag-Rolling Off

Paint Tip: Work with a partner. One person can roll on the glaze while the other lifts it off with the rag in a rhythmic pattern of even, steady strokes.

Plan #321002

Dimensions: 72' W x 28' D
Levels: 1
Square Footage: 1,400
Bedrooms: 3
Bathrooms: 2
Foundation: Basement, crawl space
Materials List Available: Yes
Price Category: B

If you're looking for a well-designed compact home with contemporary amenities, this could be the home of your dreams.

Features:

- Porch: Just the right size for some rockers and a swing, this porch could become your outdoor living area when the weather is fine.

- Living Room: A vaulted ceiling adds to the spacious feeling in this room, where friends and family are sure to gather.

- Kitchen: This space-saving design, in combination with the ample counter and cabinet space, makes cooking a pleasure.

- Utility Room: This large room is fitted with cabinets for extra storage space. You'll find storage space in the large garage, too.

- Master Bedroom: This room is somewhat secluded for privacy, making it an ideal place for some quiet time at the end of the day.

SMARTtip

Fabric Draping Ability

Test a fabric's draping ability by looking at a large piece in a fabric store. Gather at least two to three yards of material, holding one end in your hand. Check how it drapes. Does it fall into folds easily? Also look at the pattern when it is gathered. Does the design become lost in the folds? Ask a salesclerk or a friend to hold the fabric, and look at it from a few feet away.

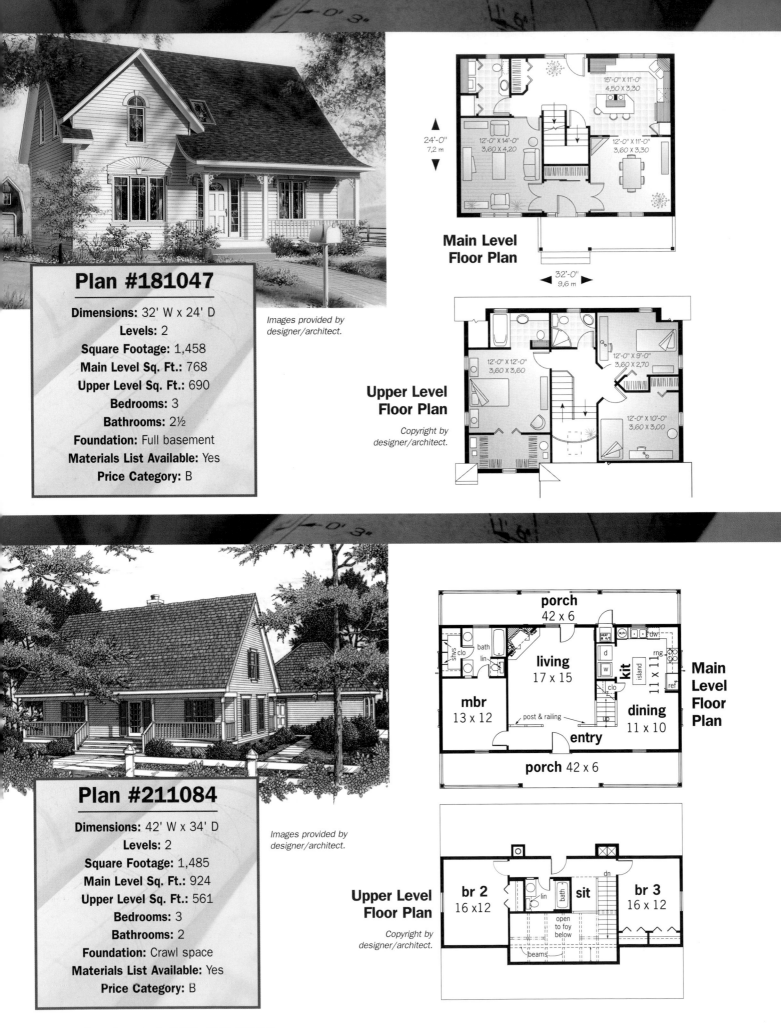

Plan #181047

Dimensions: 32' W x 24' D
Levels: 2
Square Footage: 1,458
Main Level Sq. Ft.: 768
Upper Level Sq. Ft.: 690
Bedrooms: 3
Bathrooms: 2½
Foundation: Full basement
Materials List Available: Yes
Price Category: B

Images provided by designer/architect.

Main Level Floor Plan

24'-0"
7,2 m

32'-0"
9,6 m

15'-0" X 11'-0"
4,50 X 3,30

12'-0" X 14'-0"
3,60 X 4,20

12'-0" X 11'-0"
3,60 X 3,30

Upper Level Floor Plan

Copyright by designer/architect.

12'-0" X 12'-0"
3,60 X 3,60

12'-0" X 9'-0"
3,60 X 2,70

12'-0" X 10'-0"
3,60 X 3,00

Plan #211084

Dimensions: 42' W x 34' D
Levels: 2
Square Footage: 1,485
Main Level Sq. Ft.: 924
Upper Level Sq. Ft.: 561
Bedrooms: 3
Bathrooms: 2
Foundation: Crawl space
Materials List Available: Yes
Price Category: B

Images provided by designer/architect.

Main Level Floor Plan

porch 42 x 6

shvs clo
bath lin
clo

living
17 x 15

HEAT A/C
d
w
clo
kit
island
11 x 11
rng
ref
dw

mbr
13 x 12

post & railing

dining
11 x 10

entry

porch 42 x 6

Upper Level Floor Plan

Copyright by designer/architect.

br 2
16 x12

lin
bath
sit

dn

br 3
16 x 12

open to foy below

beams

Plan #151150

Dimensions: 48" W x 54" D

Levels: 1

Square Footage: 1,193

Bedrooms: 3

Bathrooms: 2

Foundation: Crawl space, slab

Materials List Available: Yes

Price Category: B

Images provided by designer/architect.

Copyright by designer/architect.

Plan #151149

Dimensions: 47'5" W x 46'5" D

Levels: 1

Square Footage: 1,157

Bedrooms: 3

Bathrooms: 2

Foundation: Crawl space, slab

Materials List Available: Yes

Price Category: B

Images provided by designer/architect.

Copyright by designer/architect.

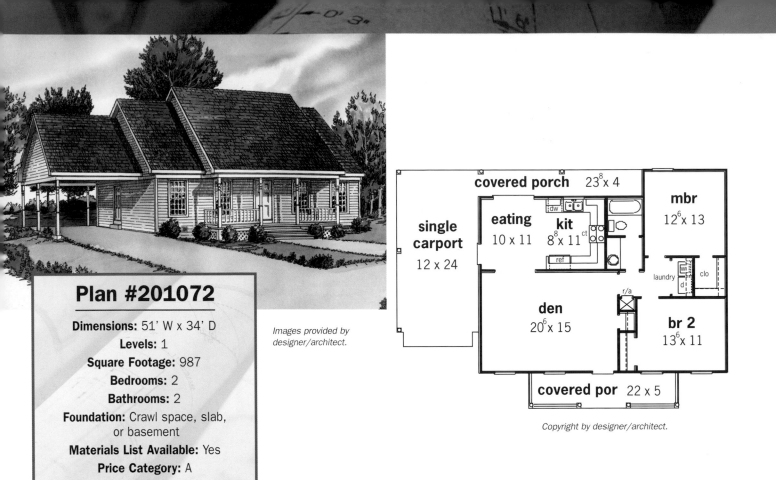

Plan #201072

Dimensions: 51' W x 34' D

Levels: 1

Square Footage: 987

Bedrooms: 2

Bathrooms: 2

Foundation: Crawl space, slab, or basement

Materials List Available: Yes

Price Category: A

Images provided by designer/architect.

Copyright by designer/architect.

Plan #201025

Dimensions: 62' W x 46' D

Levels: 1

Square Footage: 1,379

Bedrooms: 3

Bathrooms: 2

Foundation: Crawl space, slab, or basement

Materials List Available: Yes

Price Category: B

Images provided by designer/architect.

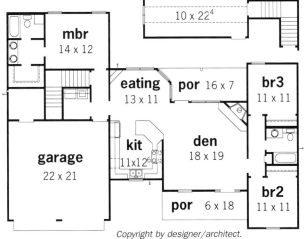

Copyright by designer/architect.

SMARTtip

Arrangement of Mantle Objects

On a fireplace mantle, group objects of different heights for visual interest—a straight line can be boring. Raise one or two pieces with a small pedestal or stand, and stagger the pieces from back to front. If you have three or more objects, make a triangle or overlapping triangles.

Plan #181153

Dimensions: 46' W x 34' D

Levels: 1

Square Footage: 1,478

Bedrooms: 3

Bathrooms: 1

Foundation: Full basement

Materials List Available: Yes

Price Category: B

Images provided by designer/architect.

Copyright by designer/architect.

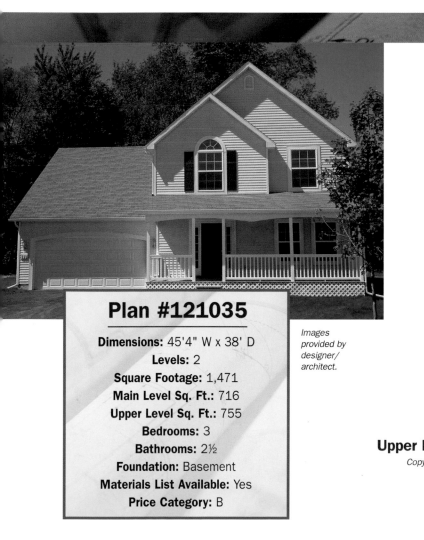

Plan #121035

Dimensions: 45'4" W x 38' D

Levels: 2

Square Footage: 1,471

Main Level Sq. Ft.: 716

Upper Level Sq. Ft.: 755

Bedrooms: 3

Bathrooms: 2½

Foundation: Basement

Materials List Available: Yes

Price Category: B

Images provided by designer/ architect.

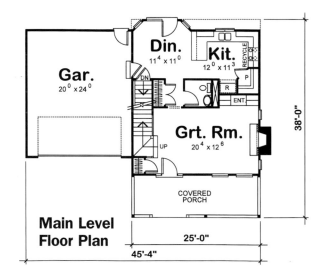

Main Level Floor Plan

Upper Level Floor Plan

Copyright by designer/architect.

Images provided by designer/architect.

Plan #341003

Dimensions: 60' W x 30' D

Levels: 1

Square Footage: 1,200

Bedrooms: 3

Bathrooms: 2

Foundation: Crawl space, slab, or basement

Materials List Available: Yes

Price Category: B

If you're looking for the ideal plan for a first home or an empty-nester, this romantic cottage will meet your needs with style.

Features:

- **Outdoor Living Space:** Use the porch at the front of the house and the deck at the back as extra living area in fine weather.

- **Living Room:** Open to both the dining area and the kitchen, this room also looks out to the deck and backyard.

- **Kitchen:** This well-planned area combines a step-saving layout with conveniently placed counter and storage space.

- **Laundry Closet:** Open the door to this centrally located closet to find a full washer and dryer.

- **Bedrooms:** Choose between the bedrooms with spacious walk-in closets for your room, and depending on need, use the others for children's rooms, a guestroom, or an office.

Copyright by designer/architect.

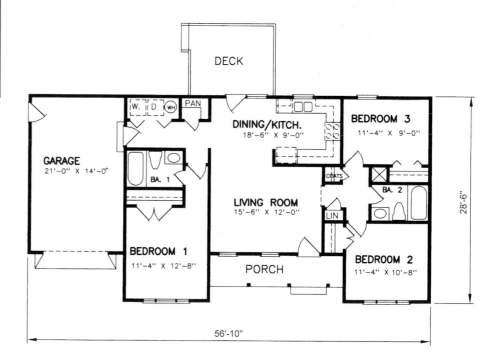

Plan #341004

Dimensions: 56'10" W x 28'6" D

Levels: 1

Square Footage: 1,101

Bedrooms: 3

Bathrooms: 2

Foundation: Crawl space, slab, or basement

Materials List Available: Yes

Price Category: B

Images provided by designer/architect.

You'll love the romantic feeling that the gables and front porch give to this well designed home, with its family-oriented layout.

Features:

- **Living Room:** The open design between this spacious room and the kitchen/dining area makes this home as ideal for family activities as it is for entertaining.

- **Outdoor Living Space:** French doors open to the back deck, where you're sure to host alfresco dinners or easy summer brunches.

- **Kitchen:** Designed for the cook's convenience, this kitchen features ample work area as well as excellent storage space in the nearby pantry.

- **Laundry Area:** Located behind closed doors to shut out the noise, this laundry closet is conveniently placed.

- **Master Suite:** With triple windows, a wide closet, and a private bath, this is a luxurious suite.

Copyright by designer/architect.

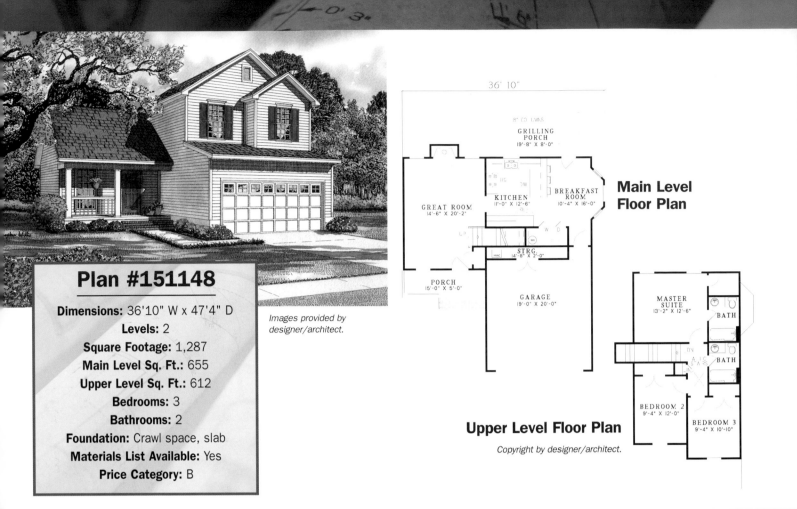

Main Level Floor Plan

GRILLING PORCH
19'-8" X 8'-0"

GREAT ROOM
14'-6" X 20'-2"

KITCHEN
11'-0" X 12'-6"

BREAKFAST ROOM
10'-4" X 16'-0"

STRG.
14'-8" X 2'-0"

PORCH
15'-0" X 5'-0"

GARAGE
19'-0" X 20'-0"

Upper Level Floor Plan

MASTER SUITE
13'-2" X 12'-6"

BATH

BATH

BEDROOM 2
9'-4" X 12'-0"

BEDROOM 3
9'-4" X 10'-10"

Images provided by designer/architect.

Copyright by designer/architect.

Plan #151148

Dimensions: 36'10" W x 47'4" D

Levels: 2

Square Footage: 1,287

Main Level Sq. Ft.: 655

Upper Level Sq. Ft.: 612

Bedrooms: 3

Bathrooms: 2

Foundation: Crawl space, slab

Materials List Available: Yes

Price Category: B

Main Level Floor Plan

62'-0"

COVERED PORCH
16'-10" X 8'-0"

GARAGE
11'-4" X 19'-4"

GRILLING PORCH
8'-0" X 11'-8"

KITCHEN
10'-7" X 10'-6"

OPTIONAL BASEMENT STAIRS

FOYER
6'-4" X 10'-8"

M. BATH

STACKED W/D

NOOK
10'-7" X 6'-3"

BALCONY LINE

MASTER SUITE
13'-10" X 11'-8"

GREAT RM.
16'-2" X 17'-8"
OPEN TO ABOVE

FRENCH DOORS

FRENCH DOORS

STONE FIREPLACE

FRENCH DOORS

FRENCH DOORS

DECK

39'-2"

Upper Level Floor Plan

LOFT
16'-2" X 14'-3"
VAULTED CEILING

BATH
10'-8" X 6'-4"

6'8" WALL

ATTIC STORAGE

BEDROOM 2
14'-2" X 11'-2"

SLOPED CEILING

8' LINE

BEAMS

OPEN TO BELOW

5' WALL

Images provided by designer/architect.

Copyright by designer/architect.

Plan #151156

Dimensions: 62' W x 39'2" D

Levels: 2

Square Footage: 1,408

Main Level Sq. Ft.: 917

Upper Level Sq. Ft.: 491

Bedrooms: 2

Bathrooms: 2

Foundation: Crawl space, slab

Materials List Available: Yes

Price Category: B

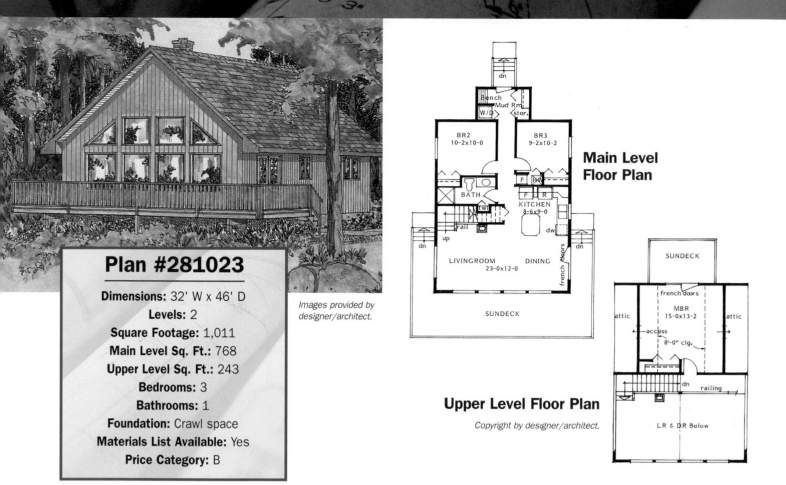

Plan #281023

Dimensions: 32' W x 46' D

Levels: 2

Square Footage: 1,011

Main Level Sq. Ft.: 768

Upper Level Sq. Ft.: 243

Bedrooms: 3

Bathrooms: 1

Foundation: Crawl space

Materials List Available: Yes

Price Category: B

Images provided by designer/architect.

Main Level Floor Plan

Upper Level Floor Plan

Copyright by designer/architect.

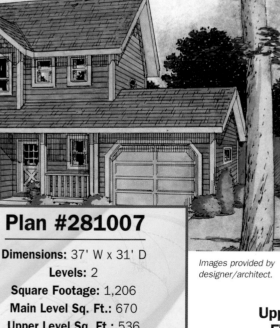

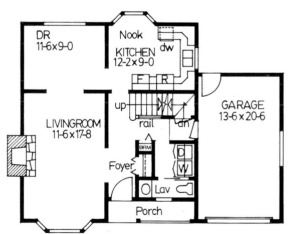

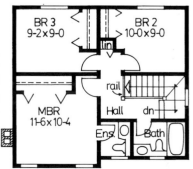

Plan #281007

Dimensions: 37' W x 31' D

Levels: 2

Square Footage: 1,206

Main Level Sq. Ft.: 670

Upper Level Sq. Ft.: 536

Bedrooms: 3

Bathrooms: 1 full, 2 half

Foundation: Full basement

Materials List Available: Yes

Price Category: B

Images provided by designer/architect.

Main Level Floor Plan

Upper Level Floor Plan

Copyright by designer/architect.

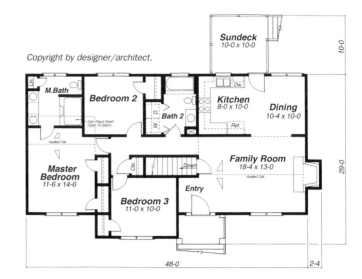

Sundeck
10-0 x 10-0

10-0

M.Bath

Bedroom 2

Opt·Plant Shelf
Open To Bdrm.

Vaulted Cel.

W. D.

Bath 2

Kitchen
8-0 x 10-0

Ref.

Dining
10-4 x 10-0

Family Room
18-4 x 13-0

Vaulted Cel.

Master
Bedroom
11-6 x 14-6

Clts

Down

Bedroom 3
11-0 x 10-0

Entry

29-0

48-0

2-4

Plan #141001

Dimensions: 48' W x 29' D

Levels: 1

Square Footage: 1,208

Bedrooms: 3

Bathrooms: 2

Foundation: Basement

Materials List Available: Yes

Price Category: B

Images provided by designer/architect.

SMARTtip

Hydro-seeding

An alternative to traditional seeding is hydro-seeding. In this process, a slurry of grass seed, wood fibers, and fertilizer is spray-applied in one step. Hydro-seeding is relatively inexpensive. Compared with seeding by hand, hydro-seeding is also very fast.

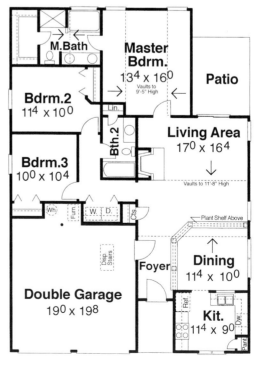

M.Bath

Master
Bdrm.
13⁴ x 16⁰

Patio

Bdrm.2
11⁴ x 10⁰

Vaults to
9'-5" High

Lin.

Bth.2

Living Area
17⁰ x 16⁴

Bdrm.3
10⁰ x 10⁴

Vaults to 11'-8" High

Wh

Furn.

W. D.

Clts

Plant Shelf Above

Disp.
Stairs

Foyer

Dining
11⁴ x 10⁰

Double Garage
19⁰ x 19⁸

Ref.

Kit.
11⁴ x 9⁰

Dw.

Paint.

Plan #141002

Dimensions: 48' W x 29' D

Levels: 1

Square Footage: 1,365

Bedrooms: 3

Bathrooms: 2

Foundation: Slab, basement

Materials List Available: No

Price Category: B

Images provided by designer/architect.

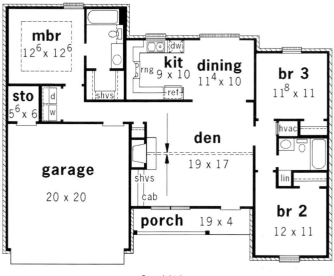

Plan #201016

Dimensions: 51'10" W x 40'4" D

Levels: 1

Square Footage: 1,293

Bedrooms: 3

Bathrooms: 2

Foundation: Crawl space, slab, or basement

Materials List Available: Yes

Price Category: B

Images provided by designer/architect.

Copyright by designer/architect.

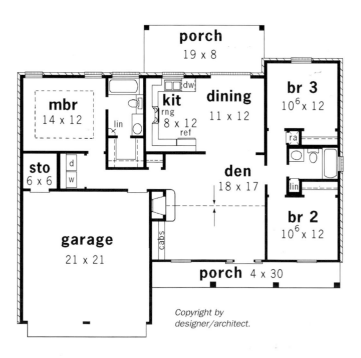

Plan #201018

Dimensions: 51'10" W x 47' D

Levels: 1

Square Footage: 1,294

Bedrooms: 3

Bathrooms: 2

Foundation: Crawl space, slab, or basement

Materials List Available: Yes

Price Category: B

Images provided by designer/architect.

Copyright by designer/architect.

Plan #341009

Dimensions: 44'5" W x 39'4" D

Levels: 1

Square Footage: 1,280

Bedrooms: 3

Bathrooms: 2

Foundation: Crawl space, slab, or basement

Materials List Available: Yes

Price Category: B

Images provided by designer/architect.

If you admire the exterior features of this home — the L-shaped front porch, nested gables, and transom lights — you'll love its interior.

Features:

- **Ceiling Height:** Ceilings are 9-ft. high to enhance this home's spacious feeling.

- **Living Room:** A fireplace creates a cozy feeling in this open, spacious room.

- **Dining Room:** Decorative columns grace the transition between this room and the living room.

- **Kitchen:** This open kitchen features a serving bar, a large pantry, and access to the back deck.

- **Laundry:** The washer and dryer are housed in a large utility closet to minimize noise.

- **Master Suite:** A designer window, vaulted ceiling, and walk-in closet make the bedroom luxurious, and the garden tub and shower make the private bath a true retreat.

DECK
10'-0"X10'-0"

Copyright by
designer/architect.

RANGE
SINK
DW
REF
PANTRY
ELEVATED BAR

KITCHEN/DINING
20'-3" X 11'-2"

DECORATIVE COLUMNS

BEDROOM 3
10'-0"X11'-2"

CLOSET

CLOSET

COATS

BEDROOM 2
10'-1"X11'-2"

BATH 2

UTILITIES
DRY WASH WH
LINENS

VENTLESS GAS LOGS

FAMILY ROOM
16'-7" X 13'-0"

GARDEN TUB & SHWR

BATH 1

CLOSET

PORCH

BEDROOM 1
15'-2" X 12'-3"

VAULTED CEILING

39'-4"

44'-5"

Plan #341013

Dimensions: 44' W x 34' D

Levels: 1

Square Footage: 1,363

Bedrooms: 3

Bathrooms: 2

Foundation: Crawl space, slab, or basement

Materials List Available: Yes

Price Category: B

Images provided by designer/architect.

The luxurious amenities in this compact, well designed home are sure to delight everyone in the family.

Features:

- Ceiling Height: 9-ft. ceilings add to the spacious feeling created by the open design.

- Family Room: A vaulted ceiling and large window area add elegance to this comfortable room, which will be the heart of this home.

- Dining Area: Adjoining the kitchen, this room features a large bayed area as well as French doors that open onto the back deck.

- Kitchen: This step-saving design will make cooking a joy for everyone in the family.

- Utility Room: Near the kitchen, this room includes cabinets and shelves for extra storage space.

- Master Suite: A triple window, tray ceiling, walk-in closet, and luxurious bath make this area a treat.

Copyright by designer/architect.

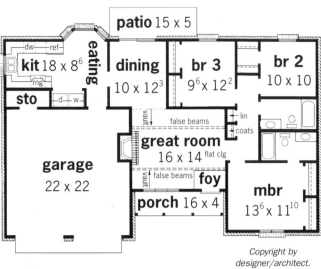

patio 15 x 5

kit 18 x 8⁶ eating dining 10 x 12³ br 3 9⁶ x 12² br 2 10 x 10

sto

vault false beams lin coats

great room 16 x 14 flat clg

garage 22 x 22

vault false beams foy

porch 16 x 4 mbr 13⁶ x 11¹⁰

Images provided by designer/architect.

Copyright by designer/architect.

Plan #201002

Dimensions: 54'10" W x 33'10" D

Levels: 1

Square Footage: 1,191

Bedrooms: 3

Bathrooms: 2

Foundation: Crawl space, slab, or basement

Materials List Available: Yes

Price Category: B

SMARTtip

Kitchen Color

The type of light in a room will affect how a color looks. Place large swatches of the colors you are thinking about using throughout your kitchen to see how they react to morning, afternoon, evening, and artificial light.

patio 22 x 8

mbr 12 x 14

kit 12² x 14

br 2 12 x 11⁶ eating foy 10 x 7⁶ dining 12² x 10 garage 21⁶ x 22

great room 16 x 16 porch trash sto 11⁶ x 4

Images provided by designer/architect.

Copyright by designer/architect.

Plan #201003

Dimensions: 55'10" W x 45'4" D

Levels: 1

Square Footage: 1,144

Bedrooms: 2

Bathrooms: 1

Foundation: Crawl space, slab, or basement

Materials List Available: Yes

Price Category: B

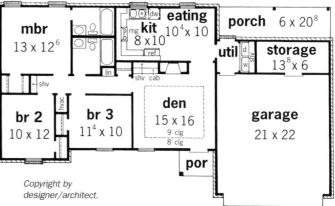

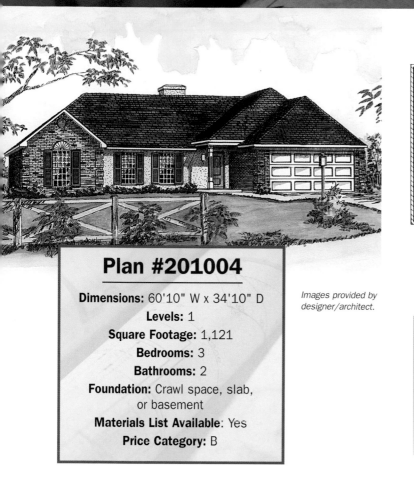

Plan #201004

Dimensions: 60'10" W x 34'10" D

Levels: 1

Square Footage: 1,121

Bedrooms: 3

Bathrooms: 2

Foundation: Crawl space, slab, or basement

Materials List Available: Yes

Price Category: B

Images provided by designer/architect.

Copyright by designer/architect.

SMARTtip

Color Basics

Use color effectively to enhance the perception of the space itself. Make a large room feel cozy with warm colors, which tend to advance. Conversely, open up a small room with cool colors or neutrals, which tend to recede.

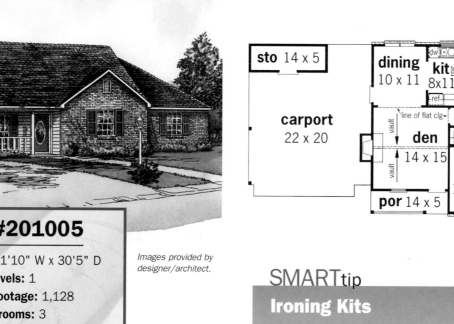

Plan #201005

Dimensions: 61'10" W x 30'5" D

Levels: 1

Square Footage: 1,128

Bedrooms: 3

Bathrooms: 2

Foundation: Crawl space, slab, or basement

Materials List Available: Yes

Price Category: B

Images provided by designer/architect.

Copyright by designer/architect.

SMARTtip

Ironing Kits

Plan for a built-in ironing board near the laundry area. Ironing board kits come in cabinets that are surface mounted to the wall or fit between studs. Most include a built-in electrical outlet.

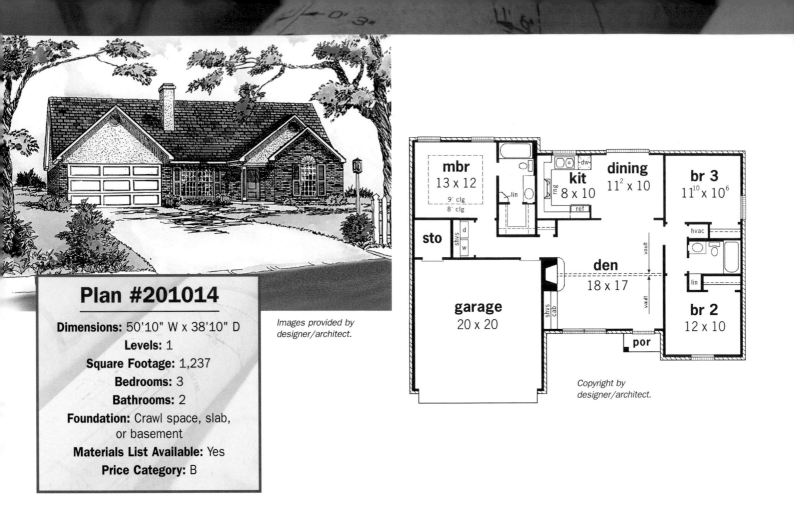

Plan #201014

Dimensions: 50'10" W x 38'10" D

Levels: 1

Square Footage: 1,237

Bedrooms: 3

Bathrooms: 2

Foundation: Crawl space, slab, or basement

Materials List Available: Yes

Price Category: B

Images provided by designer/architect.

Copyright by designer/architect.

Plan #201017

Dimensions: 64'10" W x 38'10" D

Levels: 1

Square Footage: 1,265

Bedrooms: 3

Bathrooms: 2

Foundation: Crawl space, slab, or basement

Materials List Available: Yes

Price Category: B

Images provided by designer/architect.

SMARTtip

Kitchen Underlayment

Check with the manufacturer when selecting an underlayment material. Two that most manufacturers reject:

- Particleboard because it swells greatly when wet. If you have particleboard on the floor now, remove it or cover it with underlayment-grade plywood.

- Hardboard because some tile manufacturers do not consider it a suitable underlayment for their products.

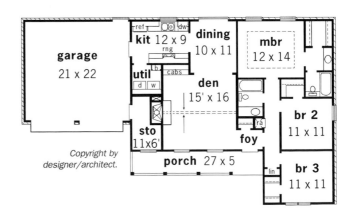

Copyright by designer/architect.

Plan #151131

Dimensions: 28' W x 77' D
Levels: 1
Square Footage: 1,446
Bedrooms: 3
Bathrooms: 2
Foundation: Crawl space, slab
Materials List Available: Yes
Price Category: B

The 10-in. columns on the lovely front porch make this traditional and gracious home seem a part of the old South.

Features:

- **Great Room:** A 10-ft. boxed ceiling gives presence to this spacious room, and an angled corner fireplace lets you create a cozy nook where everyone will gather in chilly weather.

- **Kitchen:** The snack bar and large adjoining breakfast room encourage friends and family to gather here at all times of day. All the household cooks will appreciate the thoughtful layout that makes cooking a delight.

- **Master Suite:** A 10-ft. ceiling emphasizes the luxury you'll find in both the bedroom and private bath, with its two vanities, spacious walk-in closets, and whirlpool tub.

- **Additional Bedrooms:** A deluxe full bath separates bedrooms 2 and 3, and both rooms feature generous closet space.

Images provided by designer/architect.

Copyright by designer/architect.

SMARTtip

Creating Depth with Wall Frames

Wall frames create an illusion of depth and density because 1) they are three-dimensional and 2) they divide the wall area into smaller, denser segments. The three-dimensional quality of wall frames is fundamentally different from that of the alternative treatment: raised panels. Despite the name, raised panels actually produce a concave-like, or receding, effect whereas wall frames are more convex, protruding outward. In terms of sculpture, concave units create negative space while convex units create positive space. Raised panels, therefore, deliver a uniform sense of volume, mass, and density, while wall frames create a higher level of tension and dramatic interest.

Country Style

Country as a decorating term can be defined only loosely—and that's fine with most Country-decorating enthusiasts. They're drawn to a style that offers the comfort of the familiar and traditional yet allows plenty of scope for the highly individual imagination.

Country rooms are easygoing and seldom confined to a specific historical period. They hark back to a time when people lived closer to the land and in tune with nature, when life was harder but less frenetic than it is today.

In earlier times, objects were made for a specific purpose—homeowners who needed a chair or a shelf or a basket either asked a local artisan to produce one or made it themselves. Conversely, today's manufacturers determine society's "needs" and produce identical goods in mass quantities. While this industrial age tempts with copious material products, Country decorating encourages paring down to fewer but more-treasured things.

Despite appreciating modern technology and conveniences, people may need to hold on to simpler pleasures. It's natural to romanticize the past, and amid the accelerating social changes of the nineteenth century, the United States' 1876 centennial celebration prompted a nostalgic "Colonial Revival" in decorating. In the Jazz Age of the 1920s, Tudor and Georgian houses filled the booming new suburbs. Closer to recent times, following the 1976 bicentennial and the tumult of the preceding decade, America rediscovered its heritage of painted furniture, rag rugs, tole ware, and quilts.

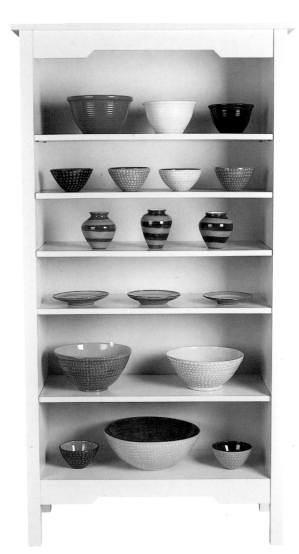

"Country" can have many interpretations, from American cottage, left, to international with a French twist, right. Feel free to mix Country's various looks to create a personal style that's all your own.

Today's Country Style

Putting aside the ebb-and-flow of fashion, peope keep returning to Country decorating because it restores their surroundings to a human scale and celebrates the charm in everyday things. The Country room's decorative flourishes incline toward rustic baskets, pottery jugs, whittled and carved woods, colorful needlework, or casual displays of collections gathered over the years. It's rich with objects that show the work of hands or reflect personal stories. And to add a touch of spice, there are accessories and collectibles that sum up Country spirit, especially when they are displayed to advantage.

You can't live in any time but the present, however, and Country decorating is not about dreamy nostalgia. It's about creating rooms that are practical, fun, and personal—rooms that you can enjoy today but that lend a little old-fashioned charm to the daily routine. Country decorating also adds a distinction and a considerably welcoming mood to almost any type of architecture. All it takes is an imaginative spirit and your ability to trust your own personal likes and tastes. After all, Country decorating cannot be defined by any one personality but by diversity.

Is it Just "Old Stuff?"

You've probably already developed some answers to this question. Country style certainly draws on history and a sense of connection with those who came before. It emphasizes the homegrown and the handmade. In this view, a room is never "done"—it evolves over time. Our ancestors didn't discard things as new styles came along, but turned items to new uses. Often, homey objects are beloved because they show such ingenuity. When you freely mix objects from different eras, your rooms have a relaxed, eclectic, and high-spirited look.

There's nothing highfalutin about Country decorating. It's as casual as this comfortable denim-covered sofa, right.

Traditionally, the appearance of a Country room is simply a working background for a busy life. Beauty is often a byproduct of the textures and colors of honest necessities—the weathered wood of a much-scrubbed table, the soft wool of a lap robe, and the rough stone of a fireplace surround. Yet our ancestors didn't hesitate to embellish the necessities. Where a plain piece would serve just as well, they'd weave a bright pattern into a basket, carve the handles of wooden ware, stencil a floor, or decorate the furniture with freehand painting.

Country's Many Facets

This look inclines toward America's Country traditions from the seventeenth to the early twentieth century. But American Country is an especially broad river, fed by

Keep it natural with fresh or dried-flower arrangements, above.

The patina of age and distressed finishes add character to a country interior, right.

many meandering streams. In your decorating reveries, you may feel drawn toward one of those tributaries. The varied approaches to Country decorating do not fall into strict categories. They do, however, borrow from many cultures.

International Appeal

Folk traditions around the world share many basic elements—the rugged woods, the natural colors, the satisfying solidity of stone, clay, and plaster, and the natural fibers. The details provide local flavor. Here's a survey of some of Country's many popular international interpretations.

English Country Style. Even as the American colonies rebelled against British rule, they still followed Britain's decorative lead. English Country offers two disparate inspirations: the grand manor and the humble cottage.

To suggest the country manor house in your own decorating efforts, imagine an aristocratic household, over generations, filling the large rooms of a family estate with heirlooms and the occasional skillfully crafted new piece. Grand, lushly draped windows should complement the substantial furniture and overstuffed upholstery, which, depending on the season, could sport worn leather or casual linen slipcovers. And carved furnishings of fine oak and mahogany might include some slightly worn pieces retired from "city dwellings."

In an English Country house, the fabrics tend toward fine, if somewhat aged, chintzes, wools, and linens rather than sophisticated satins and velvets. The clutter should appear comfortable and personal, with family portraits, books, photos, souvenirs, and maybe an Oriental rug or two. Tiled fireplaces or papered walls can add another layer of pattern to a room.

The humbler English Cottage look is charmingly cluttered, although with more rustic touches. There may be rough-finished plaster walls with sturdy exposed beams or a planked chair rail. The woods tend toward "deal," the British term for fir or pine, which was often painted and sometimes stenciled in centuries past. Stone, tile, or wood are typically underfoot, and homespun gingham and stripes often frame small windows. Useful baskets, throws, rugs, and candles may commonly double as decorative accents.

Look for documentary-inspired motifs when selecting wallcovering, below.

Simple classic beadboard that's been painted looks fresh on furniture, opposite.

Swedish Country Style. In the late eighteenth century, King Gustav III of Sweden and the Swedish aristocracy embraced the formal neoclassicism of France and England. This enthusiasm filtered down to Sweden's provinces, which, in turn, created symmetrical rooms designed around a palette of buttercream yellow, gentle blue, and dove gray. To re-create the look, think of bleached floors, gilded mirrors, and large bare or lightly dressed windows (originally intended to maximize Sweden's sunlight). Light woods—birch and alder for formal rooms and pine and beech for humbler spaces—often feature carving.

These so-called Gustavian touches blend with the earthier Swedish traditional handcrafts of painted furniture, stenciled and faux-marbled architectural trim, and striped rag rugs and runners tinted with natural dyes. Kitchens, which originally provided a special focus, can be brightened with yellow ware pottery and copper pots or pudding molds.

French Country Style. To suggest French Country ambiance, recall the warm climate of the southern Provence region and the brilliant sunshine that entranced nineteenth-century British travelers. Here the classic farmhouse, like dwellings in many hot regions, fends off the midday heat with massive stone and clay walls that may wear washes of gold, rosy pink, or cool blue-violet tints. Local terra-cotta tile floors, with fancy hand-painted glazed tiles, brighten the interior.

Mediterranean trade, which introduced exotic fabrics from Asia, spurred France's textile industry. You can evoke a French Provincial mood by using bright cottons in small-scale prints, especially those with designs in saturated blues, yellows, and reds that glow in the sunlight.

An antique Irish pine hutch, left, is a beautiful display and storage piece for a collection of vintage glass and pottery.

In keeping with France's love of good food, the kitchen boasts bright pottery and copperwares. Influenced by the aristocracy's ornate furniture, farmhouse chairs and tables feature gentle curves and simple carvings. You could emphasize a few solid pieces, such as an armoire filled with table linens and china. Use open shelves in place of wall cabinets with doors.

Original Provençal kitchens had large limestone hearths. If a fireplace is not in your plans, you could introduce limestone by installing it on the floor or countertops. As an alternative, use rustic clay tiles, which have a warm earthy feeling. For the appearance of a hearth, design a cooking alcove to house the range or the cooktop. Accent it with colorful tiles or brick. Create a focal point at the cooking area with a handsome copper range hood. Hang a rack for copper pots and saucepans. Suspend baskets, too.

Carry the copper over to the sink; one with a hammered finish is particularly striking. Because this metal may need some extra care, you might reserve the copper finish for a bar sink, and choose a large porcelain exposed-apron style sink for heavy everyday use.

Italian Country Style. Like Provence, rural Italy is scattered with villas and farmhouses boasting large, breeze-swept rooms of thick masonry that open onto wide courtyards and shadowy verandas. To create an Italian flavor, paint plastered walls with soft, faded colors such as earthy tints of red and yellow ochre, and use russet terra-cotta tile or quarried stone for the floors. Try fabrics that are rich but simple, with stripes or woven textures. Install shutters on windows to imitate Italian Country's similar window attire.

In Tuscany, the abundant wood supply encouraged elegantly carved furniture finished with buffed wax, a soft color-wash, or bold hand-painted flourishes. Furniture here tends to be arranged symmetrically, against the walls, with a formal spareness. Bright hand-painted tiles and pottery recall the region's colorful ambiance.

Painted pieces, like the cabinet, left, and the pencil-post bed, right, borrow details from eighteenth- and nineteenth-century design and yet look perfectly at home in today's traditional Country house.

Compatible Styles and Influences

In general, the architecture of a house is often the jumping off point for the interior design, whatever the style. Unless you are a purist, you can mix other styles with most Country decors. Some styles are more compatible than others. For example, in a Craftsman-style bungalow, wallpaper with a little sprigged print may be too fussy and off-key, while a draker, bold floral—though not strictly of the period—may appear perfectly in tune. In the same way, "homespun" will be too rustic for a classic Federal house, yet a rich wood will look appropriate while retaining a Country appeal.

Similarly, a sleek ranch house lends itself to retro-cottage freshness more than a Craftsman aura. These architectural cues, taken as suggestions, can be a fertile source of Country decorating inspiration.

If you like an eclectic approach to pulling together a look for your Country home, consider one of the following styles, which can blend nicely.

Shaker. Shaker craftsmen reduced the era's familiar Country furniture—the slat-back chair, the rocker, the candle stand—to graceful, sturdy essentials. The quest for plain and practical surroundings, free of distracting ornament, created a fertile source of design inspiration and furniture of beautiful austerity.

Shaker rooms are spare. The usually whitewashed walls can be set off by simple chair rails, built-in cabinetry, and often an upper peg rail where chairs or baskets can be hung out of the way. Chair seats are often webbed with red or blue fabric tape, while woodwork can be painted in rich blues, grays, and greens. Today, many manufacturers offer Shaker-inspired furniture and accessories.

Victorian. The high-spirited nineteenth century offered a grab bag of design ideals. Victorian decorating summons images of high-style rooms lavish with rich colors, a variety of exotic revival styles of furniture, abundant ornament, and pattern-on-pattern fabric and wallcovering. Original Victorian interiors were dark, and heavy draperies diluted the light over convoluted button-tufted fringed upholstery. Today's formal rendition of the look is lighter and less cluttered than the over-the-top original.

Victorian Country can also be a relaxed cottage or farmhouse style with airy window treatments, gingerbread trim, and wicker furniture.

Storage amenities, whether built-in like these bookcases, right, or freestanding like this seat chest, below, can be decorative as well as practical. Look for details that harken to authentic period pieces.

Arts and Crafts. Arts and Crafts glorifies hand craftsmanship and natural materials. Furniture pieces demand a rich wood background with paneling, squared pillars, and heavily framed doorways. Other accoutrements may include a stone fireplace, hand-molded tile, hammered-copper trimmings, stained glass, and fabrics and wallcoverings with stylized floral and geometric patterns.

Western Styles. Picture the rugged ranch houses of the American West with their rough wood walls, plank floors, pinched-tin chests, and wide windows dressed in gingham and calico. Or evoke the region's Spanish heritage with smooth adobe walls and carved furniture draped in woven wools of natural white or vivid blues and Cochineal Red. A literal interpretation of the style would also include vivid Native American textiles and other craft pieces.

Retro Country. Vintage 1930s and '40s kitchen linens in primary-color prints of flowers, teacups, and puppies are at home with the era's bright pottery and streamlined housewares. The furniture, slightly pared down or covered in contrasting veneers, stops short of the urban Art Deco look.

A Country Furniture Favorite

You can't finish up Country Style without mentioning one of its enduring symbols. The rocking chair's origins are misty, but by the 1700s it was an American favorite. Early versions were standard chairs with the addition of rockers. But the notion soon engendered a variety of friendly styles. A slat-back, or ladder-back, rocker was popular from the 1700s to early 1800s when the Shakers perfected it. Victorian rockers were curvier and intricate. Arts and Crafts rockers were massive and straightlined. Today's gliders have roots in a nineteenth-century design.

An heirloom Swedish sofa, left, was passed down through several generations. Along with other old and some new pieces, it complements a Country home.

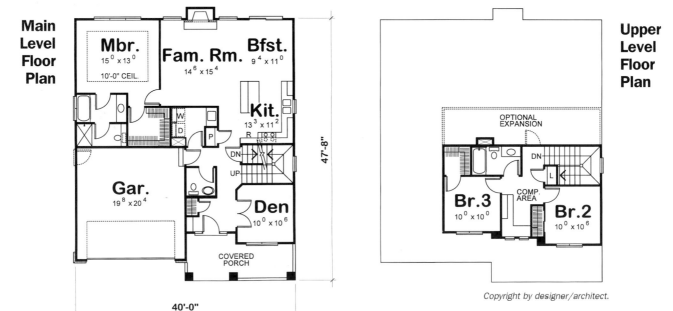

Plan #121099

Dimensions: 40' W x 47'8" D

Levels: 2

Square Footage: 1,699

Main Level Sq. Ft.: 1,268

Upper Level Sq. Ft.: 431

Bedrooms: 3

Bathrooms: 2½

Foundation: Basement

Materials List Available: Yes

Price Category: C

Images provided by designer/architect.

You'll love the open, spacious design of the living areas in this home, as well as the privacy you'll find in the bedrooms.

Features:

- Den: French doors just off the entry lead to this private den, which could easily serve as a home-office area.

- Living Area: At the rear of the home, you'll find this open living area. Decorate to emphasize the flow from one spot to another or to create a secluded nook or two.

- Kitchen: An island with space for a snack bar and a pantry combine to add convenience to this well-designed kitchen area.

- Master Suite: A boxed ceiling and triple window give this private area an elegant feeling, and the bath has a whirlpool tub, shower, and vanity.

- Upper Level: A computer area here is centrally located, and bedroom 3 features a walk-in closet.

Main Level Floor Plan

Mbr.
15⁰ x 13⁰
10'-0" CEIL.

Fam. Rm.
14⁶ x 15⁴

Bfst.
9⁴ x 11⁰

Kit.
13³ x 11²

Gar.
19⁸ x 20⁴

Den
10⁰ x 10⁶

COVERED PORCH

40'-0"

47'-8"

Upper Level Floor Plan

OPTIONAL EXPANSION

Br.3
10⁰ x 10⁰

COMP. AREA

Br.2
10⁰ x 10⁶

Copyright by designer/architect.

Plan #141012

Dimensions: 44'4" W x 38' D

Levels: 2

Square Footage: 1,870

Main Level Sq. Ft.: 1,159

Upper Level Sq. Ft.: 711

Bedrooms: 3

Bathrooms: 2½

Foundation: Basement

Materials List Available: Yes

Price Category: D

Images provided by designer/architect.

Country charm comes to mind with this classic 1½ story design.

Features:

- Ceiling Height: 8 ft.

- Porch: This full shed porch with dormers creates a look few can resist.

- Living/Dining: This open living/dining area invites you to come in and sit a spell.

- Kitchen: This kitchen allows the host to see their guests from the sink through the opening in the angled walls.

- Breakfast Area: The cathedral ceiling in this breakfast area creates a sunroom effect at the rear of the house.

- Master Suite: This spacious master suite has all the amenities, including a double bowl vanity, corner tub, walk in closet, and 5-ft. shower.

- Bedrooms: Two large bedrooms upstairs share a hall bath.

- Balcony: This upstairs balcony is lit by the center dormer, creating a cozy study alcove.

Copyright by designer/architect.

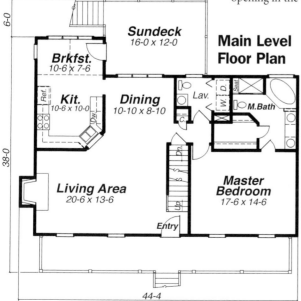

Main Level Floor Plan

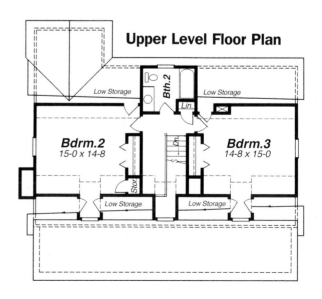

Upper Level Floor Plan

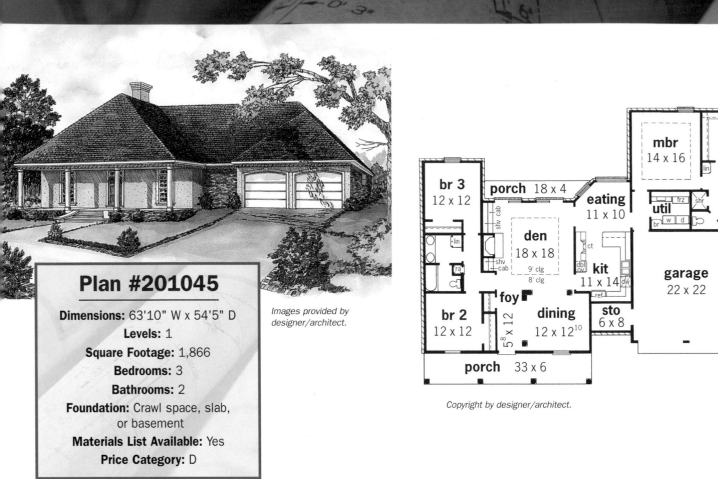

Plan #201045

Dimensions: 63'10" W x 54'5" D

Levels: 1

Square Footage: 1,866

Bedrooms: 3

Bathrooms: 2

Foundation: Crawl space, slab, or basement

Materials List Available: Yes

Price Category: D

Images provided by designer/architect.

Copyright by designer/architect.

br 3
12 x 12

porch 18 x 4

eating
11 x 10

mbr
14 x 16

util

den
18 x 18
9' clg
8' clg

kit
11 x 14

garage
22 x 22

foy

br 2
12 x 12

5⁸ x 12

dining
12 x 12¹⁰

sto
6 x 8

porch 33 x 6

Plan #211046

Dimensions: 62' W x 68' D

Levels: 1

Square Footage: 1,936

Bedrooms: 3

Bathrooms: 2

Foundation: Crawl space

Materials List Available: Yes

Price Category: D

Images provided by designer/architect.

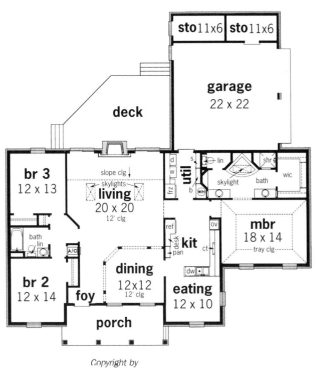

sto 11x6   sto 11x6

garage
22 x 22

deck

br 3
12 x 13

living
20 x 20
12' clg

util

skylight   bath   wic

mbr
18 x 14
tray clg

br 2
12 x 14

bath

kit

dining
12 x 12
12' clg

eating
12 x 10

foy

porch

Copyright by designer/architect.

Images provided by designer/architect.

Copyright by designer/architect.

Plan #101006

Dimensions: 63' W x 58' D

Levels: 1

Square Footage: 1,982

Bedrooms: 3

Bathrooms: 2½

Foundation: Slab, crawl space, or basement

Materials List Available: No

Price Category: D

Plan #201056

Dimensions: 70'10" W x 50'10" D

Levels: 1

Square Footage: 1,956

Bedrooms: 3

Bathrooms: 2

Foundation: Crawl space, slab, or basement

Materials List Available: Yes

Price Category: D

Images provided by designer/architect.

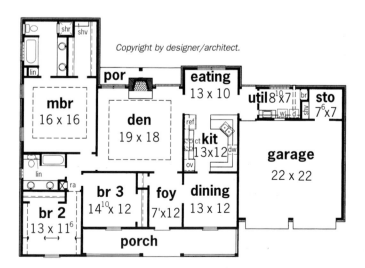

Copyright by designer/architect.

Plan #131035

Dimensions: 65'4" W x 45'10" D
Levels: 1
Square Footage: 1,892
Bedrooms: 3
Bathrooms: 2½
Foundation: Basement, crawl space, or slab
Materials List Available: Yes
Price Category: E

Images provided by designer/architect.

Families who love a mixture of traditional — a big front porch, simple roofline, and bay windows—and contemporary—an open floor plan—will love this charming home.

Features:

- Great Room: Central to this home, the open living and entertaining areas allow the family to gather effortlessly and create the perfect spot for entertaining.

- Dining Room: Volume ceilings both here and in the great room further enhance the spaciousness the open floor plan creates.

- Master Suite: Positioned on the opposite end of the other two bedrooms in the split-bedroom plan, this master suite gives an unusual amount of privacy and quiet in a home of this size.

- Bonus Room: Located over the attached garage, this bonus room gives you a place to finish for a study or a separate game room.

Rear Elevation

Copyright by designer/architect.

Bonus Area

Plan #101016

Dimensions: 31'2" W x 42' D

Levels: 2

Square Footage: 1,985

Main Level Sq. Ft.: 1,009

Upper Level Sq. Ft.: 976

Bedrooms: 3

Bathrooms: 2½

Foundation: Slab, crawl space, or basement

Materials List Available: No

Price Category: D

Images provided by designer/architect.

This delightful Victorian-style home has a compact footprint that is perfect for narrow lots.

Features:

• Ceiling Height: 9 ft. unless otherwise noted.

• Family Room: From the entry you'll step into this inviting family room. Family and friends alike will be drawn to the room's warming fireplace. A set of French doors leads out to a porch.

• Dining Room: Pass through another set of French doors from the family room into this elegant dining room.

• Deck: Yet another set of French doors from the living room lead to this enormous deck.

• Kitchen: Food preparation will be a pleasure, thanks to the 3-ft. x 5-ft. island that you'll find in this bright and airy open kitchen.

• Breakfast Area: This bayed breakfast area has a fourth set of French doors that lcads to the deck.

• Master Suite: This master bedroom has a 9-ft.-6-in. tray ceiling and a 7-ft. x 11-ft. walk-in closet.

Main Level Floor Plan

DECK
30'-6" x 11'-7"

BRKFST

KITCHEN
15'-0" x 17'-0"

DINING
14'-8" x 12'-8"

UP

ENTRY
7'-11" x 15'-6"

FAMILY
18'-8" x 16'-0"

PORCH
30'-6" x 7'-7"

42'-0"

 31'-2"

Upper Level Floor Plan

TRAY CEILING

MASTER BDRM
16'-4" x 15'-0"

D   W

DN

BEDROOM 2
12'-0" x 12'-8"

BEDROOM 3
12'-8" x 12'-0"

WINDOW SEAT

Copyright by designer/architect.

Plan #321010

Dimensions: 59' W x 37'8" D
Levels: 1
Square Footage: 1,787
Bedrooms: 3
Bathrooms: 2
Foundation: Basement
Materials List Available: Yes
Price Category: C

Images provided by designer/architect.

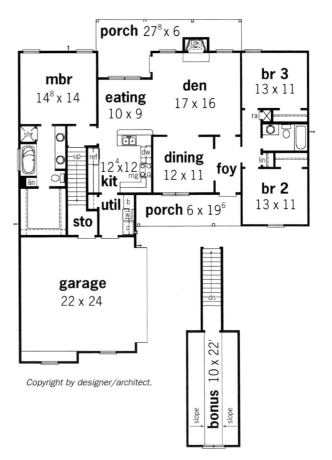

Copyright by designer/architect.

SMARTtip

Country Décor in Your Bathroom

Collections are often part of a country decor, even in the bathroom. All you need is three or more of anything that have size, shape, or color in common. You can mass them on walls, on shelves, on the windowsills, or even along the edge of the tub.

Plan #201073

Dimensions: 55' W x 65' D
Levels: 1
Square Footage: 1,610
Bedrooms: 3
Bathrooms: 2
Foundation: Crawl space, slab, or basement
Materials List Available: Yes
Price Category: C

Images provided by designer/architect.

Copyright by designer/architect.

Plan #201038

Dimensions: 71'10" W x 51'5" D

Levels: 1

Square Footage: 1,789

Bedrooms: 3

Bathrooms: 2

Foundation: Crawl space, slab, or basement

Materials List Available: Yes

Price Category: C

Images provided by designer/architect.

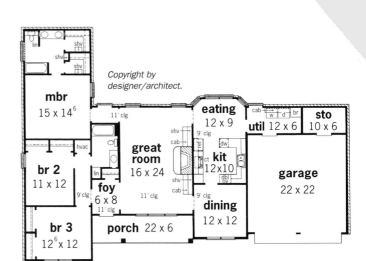

Copyright by designer/architect.

Plan #161007

Dimensions: 66'4" W x 43'10" D

Levels: 1

Square Footage: 1,611

Bedrooms: 3

Bathrooms: 2

Foundation: Basement

Materials List Available: Yes

Price Category: C

Images provided by designer/architect.

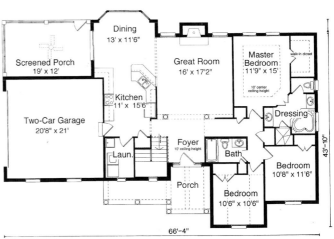

Copyright by designer/architect.

Rear Elevation

Plan #121014

Dimensions: 52' W x 47'4" D
Levels: 2
Square Footage: 1,869
Main Level Sq. Ft.: 1,421
Upper Level Sq. Ft.: 448
Bedrooms: 3
Bathrooms: 2½
Foundation: Basement
Materials List Available: Yes
Price Category: D

Images provided by designer/architect.

This compact home is packed with all the amenities you'll need for a gracious lifestyle.

Features:

• Ceiling Height: 8 ft. except as noted.

• Great Room: A soaring ceiling and six tall transom-topped windows make this a light and airy spot for entertaining.

• Formal Dining Room: This elegant room is ideal for entertaining dinner guests.

• Breakfast Area: This sunny area shares a see-through fireplace with the great room. It's the perfect place to start the day.

• Master Suite: Here are all the features you expect to find in large luxury homes. Wake up to tall, sloped ceilings, and enjoy the corner whirlpool, separate shower, and vanity. A large walk-in closet provides plenty of wardrobe storage.

• Attached Garage: The garage provides two bays of parking plus plenty of storage space.

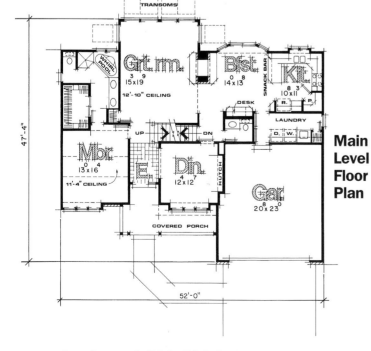

Main Level Floor Plan

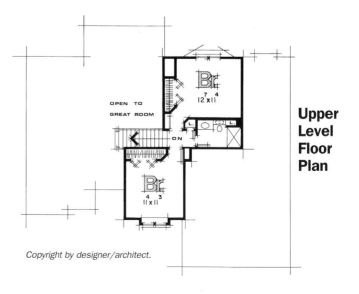

Upper Level Floor Plan

Copyright by designer/architect.

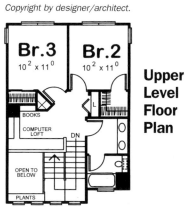

Plan #121040

Dimensions: 50' W x 48' D

Levels: 2

Square Footage: 1,818

Main Level Sq. Ft.: 1,302

Upper Level Sq. Ft.: 516

Bedrooms: 3

Bathrooms: 2½

Foundation: Basement

Materials List Available: Yes

Price Category: D

Images provided by designer/architect.

Offering plenty of architectural style, this home is designed with the busy modern lifestyle in mind.

Features:

- Ceiling Height: 8 ft. unless otherwise noted.

- Great Room: This is sure to be the central gathering place of the home with its volume ceiling, abundance of windows, and its handsome fireplace.

- Kitchen: This convenient and attractive kitchen offers a center island. It includes a snack bar that will get lots of use for impromptu family meals.

- Breakfast Area: Joined to the kitchen by the snack bar, this breakfast area will invite you to linger over morning coffee. It includes a pantry and access to the backyard.

Copyright by designer/architect.

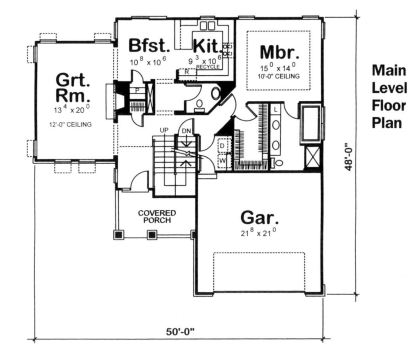

Main Level Floor Plan

Upper Level Floor Plan

- Master Bedroom: This private retreat offers the convenience of a walk-in closet and the luxury of its own whirlpool bath and shower.

- Computer Loft: Designed with the family computer in mind, this loft overlooks a two-story entry.

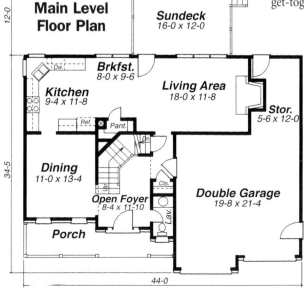

Plan #141009

Dimensions: 44' W x 34' D

Levels: 2

Square Footage: 1,683

Main Level Sq. Ft.: 797

Upper Level Sq. Ft.: 886

Bedrooms: 3

Bathrooms: 2½

Foundation: Basement, crawl space or slab

Materials List Available: No

Price Category: C

Images provided by designer/architect.

A full front porch combined with brick, wood siding, and metal roofing create a visually interesting facade.

Features:

- Ceiling Height: 8 ft. unless otherwise noted.

- Foyer: Guests will be greeted with a sense of spaciousness in this two-story entrance, with its dramatic angled staircase.

- Living Area: This large area is designed to accommodate formal gatherings as well as more intimate family get-togethers.

- Kitchen: You'll love the corner window above the sink. It's perfect for an indoor kitchen herb garden.

- Breakfast Area: Just off the kitchen, this breakfast area is the perfect spot for informal family dining. There's a private bathroom just off this area.

- Master Bath: This luxurious bath boasts a garden tub, his and her vanities, and a commode closet, features usually associated with larger homes.

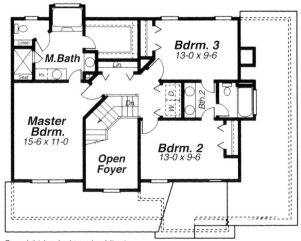

Copyright by designer/architect.

Plan #141010

Dimensions: 43'4" W x 37' D

Levels: 2

Square Footage: 1,765

Main Level Sq. Ft.: 1,210

Upper Level Sq. Ft.: 555

Bedrooms: 3

Bathrooms: 2½

Foundation: Basement

Materials List Available: No

Price Category: C

A Palladian window in a stone gable adds a new twist to a classical cottage design.

Features:

- Ceiling Height: 8 ft. unless otherwise noted.

- Living Area: Dormers open into this handsome living area, which is designed to accommodate gatherings of any size.

- Master Suite: This beautiful master bedroom opens off the foyer. It features a modified cathedral ceiling that makes the front Palladian window a focal point inside as well as out. The master bath offers a dramatic cathedral ceiling over the tub and vanity.

- Balcony: U-shaped stairs lead to this elegant balcony, which overlooks the foyer while providing access to two additional bedrooms.

- Garage: This garage is tucked under the house to improve the appearance from the street. It offers two bays for plenty of parking and storage space.

Images provided by designer/architect.

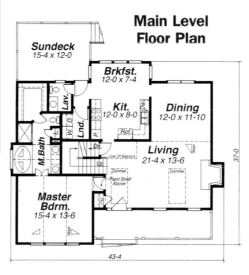

Copyright by designer/architect.

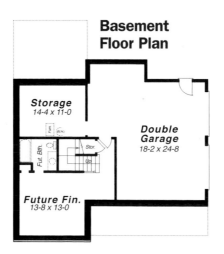

SMARTtip

Stone Tables

Marble- and stone-topped tables with plants are perfect for use in light-filled rooms. Warmed by the sun during the day, the tabletops catch leaf droppings and can stand up to the splatters of watering cans and plant sprayers.

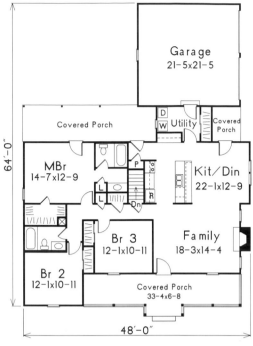

Plan #321015

Dimensions: 48' W x 64' D

Levels: 1

Square Footage: 1,501

Bedrooms: 3

Bathrooms: 2

Foundation: Basement

Materials List Available: Yes

Price Category: C

Images provided by designer/architect.

Copyright by designer/architect.

Plan #161005

Dimensions: 60' W x 48'10" D

Levels: 1

Square Footage: 1,593

Bedrooms: 3

Bathrooms: 2

Foundation: Basement

Materials List Available: Yes

Price Category: C

Images provided by designer/architect.

Rear Elevation

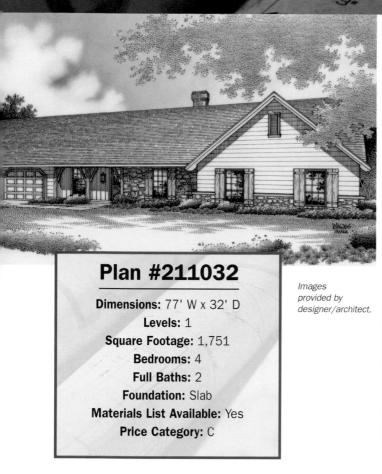

Plan #211032

Dimensions: 77' W x 32' D

Levels: 1

Square Footage: 1,751

Bedrooms: 4

Full Baths: 2

Foundation: Slab

Materials List Available: Yes

Price Category: C

Images provided by designer/architect.

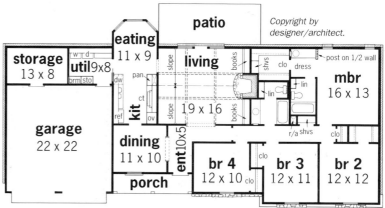
Copyright by designer/architect.

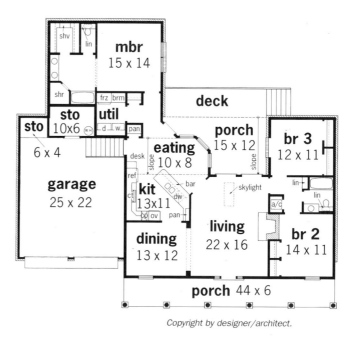

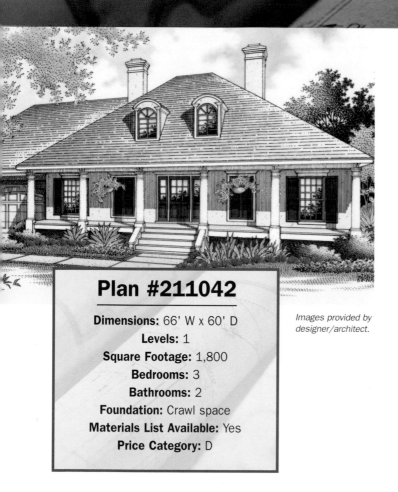

Plan #211042

Dimensions: 66' W x 60' D

Levels: 1

Square Footage: 1,800

Bedrooms: 3

Bathrooms: 2

Foundation: Crawl space

Materials List Available: Yes

Price Category: D

Images provided by designer/architect.

Copyright by designer/architect.

Plan #121044

Dimensions: 40' W x 55'8" D

Levels: 2

Square Footage: 1,923

Main Level Sq. Ft.: 1,351

Upper Level Sq. Ft.: 572

Bedrooms: 3

Bathrooms: 3

Foundation: Basement

Materials List Available: Yes

Price Category: D

Images provided by designer/architect.

The layout of this gracious home is designed with the contemporary family in mind.

Features:

- Ceiling Height: 8 ft. unless otherwise noted.

- Foyer: This elegant entry is graced with an open stairway that enhances the sense of spaciousness.

- Kitchen: Located just beyond the entry, this convenient kitchen features a center island that doubles as a snack bar.

- Breakfast Area: A sloped ceiling unites this area with the family room. Here you will find a planning desk for compiling menus and shopping lists.

- Master Bedroom: This bedroom has a distinctively contemporary appeal, with its cathedral ceiling and triple window.

- Computer Loft: Designed to house a computer, this loft overlooks the family room.

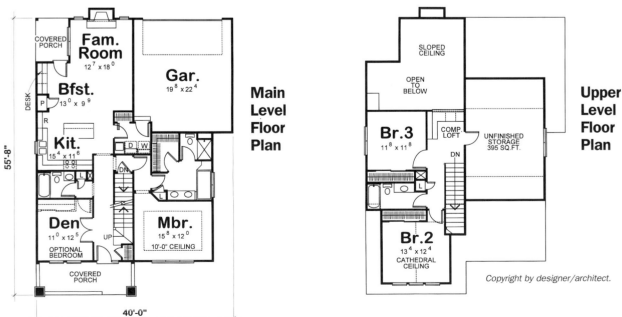

Main Level Floor Plan

COVERED PORCH

Fam. Room 12⁷ x 18⁰

Gar. 19⁸ x 22⁴

Bfst. 13⁰ x 9⁹

DESK

Kit. 15⁴ x 11⁶

Den 11⁰ x 12⁵ OPTIONAL BEDROOM

Mbr. 15⁸ x 12⁰ 10'-0" CEILING

COVERED PORCH

55'-8"

40'-0"

Upper Level Floor Plan

SLOPED CEILING

OPEN TO BELOW

Br.3 11⁸ x 11⁸

COMP. LOFT

UNFINISHED STORAGE 395 SQ.FT.

DN

Br.2 13⁴ x 12⁴ CATHEDRAL CEILING

Copyright by designer/architect.

Plan #121010

Dimensions: 50' W x 62' D
Levels: 1
Square Footage: 1,902
Bedrooms: 2
Bathrooms: 2
Foundation: Basement
Materials List Available: Yes
Price Category: D

This home is replete with architectural details that provide a convenient and gracious lifestyle.

Features:

- Ceiling Height: 8 ft.

- Great Room: The entry enjoys a long view into this room. Family and friends will be drawn to the warmth of its handsome fireplace flanked by windows.

- Breakfast Area: You'll pass through cased openings from the great room into the cozy breakfast area that will lure the whole family to linger over informal meals.

- Kitchen: Another cased opening leads from the breakfast area into the well-designed kitchen with its convenient island.

- Master Bedroom: To the right of the great room special ceiling details highlight the master bedroom where a cased opening and columns lead to a private sitting area.

- Den/Library: Whether you are listening to music or relaxing with a book, this special room will always enhance your lifestyle.

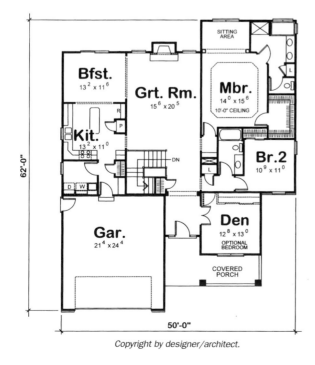

Copyright by designer/architect.

SMARTtip

Accentuating Your Fireplace with Faux Effects

Experiment with faux effects to add an aged look or a specific style to a fireplace mantel and surround. Craft stores sell inexpensive kits with directions for adding the appearance of antiqued or paneled wood or plaster, rusticated stone, marble, terra cotta, and other effects that make any style achievable.

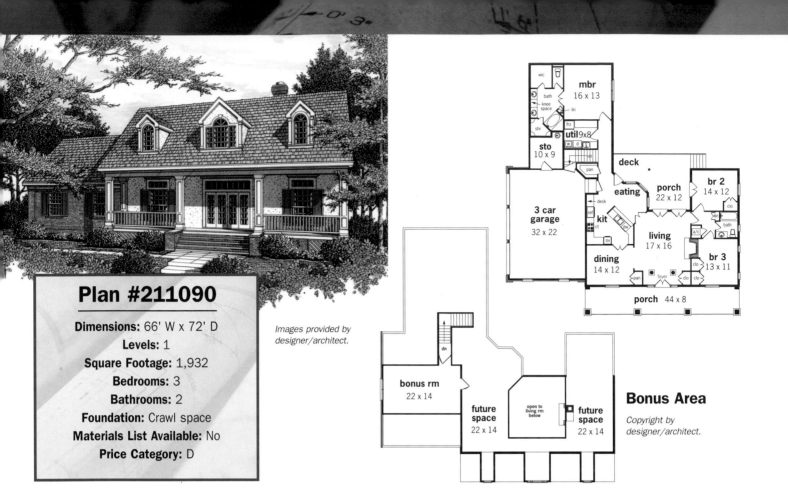

Plan #211090

Dimensions: 66' W x 72' D
Levels: 1
Square Footage: 1,932
Bedrooms: 3
Bathrooms: 2
Foundation: Crawl space
Materials List Available: No
Price Category: D

Images provided by designer/architect.

Bonus Area

Copyright by designer/architect.

Plan #211036

Dimensions: 80' W x 40' D
Levels: 1
Square Footage: 1,800
Bedrooms: 3
Bathrooms: 2
Foundation: Slab
Materials List Available: Yes
Price Category: D

Images provided by designer/architect.

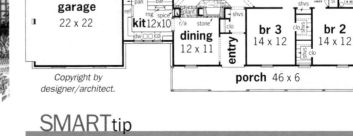

Copyright by designer/architect.

SMARTtip

Dimmer Switches

You can dim lights just slightly to extend lamp life and save energy, and there will be very little perceptible change in light level. For instance, dimming the light to 50 percent will be perceived as though the light were only dimmed to 70 percent. Therefore, there is no dramatic dilation or constriction of the eye due to light level change.

Plan #111013

Dimensions: 33' W x 59' D

Levels: 1

Square Footage: 1,606

Bedrooms: 3

Bathrooms: 2

Foundation: Slab

Materials List Available: No

Price Category: C

Porch

Stor.

Master Bedroom
13'x 15'2"

Breakfast

Bedroom
12'x 10'4"

Living
13'8"x 17'

Bedroom
12'x 11'6"

Porch

Plan #141037

Dimensions: 40'4" W x 44' D

Levels: 2

Square Footage: 1,735

Main Level Sq. Ft.: 1,045

Upper Level Sq. Ft.: 690

Bedrooms: 3

Bathrooms: 2½

Foundation: Basement with drive under garage

Materials List Available: No

Price Category: C

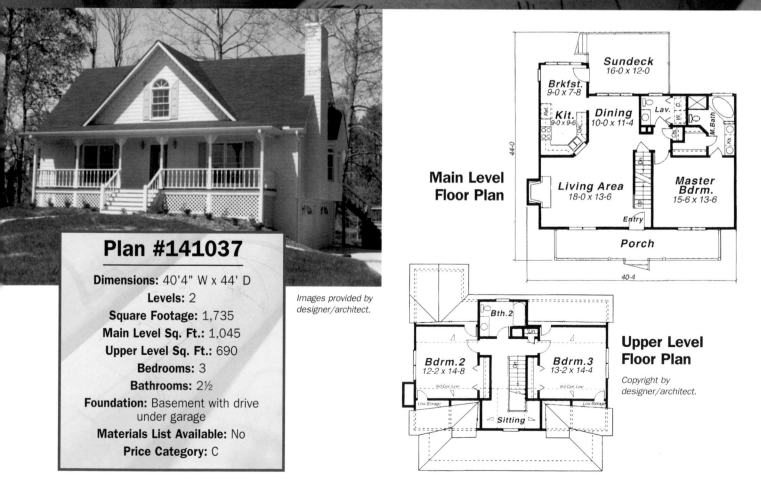

Sundeck
16-0 x 12-0

Brkfst.
9-0 x 7-8

Kit.
9-0 x 9-6

Dining
10-0 x 11-4

Lav.

M.Bath

Main Level Floor Plan

Living Area
18-0 x 13-6

Master Bdrm.
15-6 x 13-6

Entry

Porch

40-4

44-0

Upper Level Floor Plan

Bth.2

Bdrm.2
12-2 x 14-8

Bdrm.3
13-2 x 14-4

Sitting

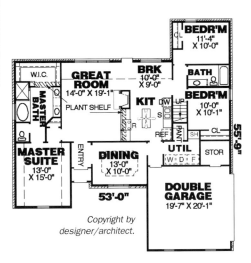

Plan #241005

Dimensions: 53' W x 55'9" D
Levels: 1
Square Footage: 1,670
Bedrooms: 3
Bathrooms: 2
Foundation: Slab
Materials List Available: No
Price Category: C

This charming starter home, in split-bedroom format, combines big-house features in a compact design.

Features:

- Great Room: With easy access to the formal dining room, kitchen, and breakfast area, this great room features a cozy fireplace.

- Kitchen: This big kitchen, with easy access to a walk-in pantry, features an island for added work space and a lovely plant shelf that separates it from the great room.

- Master Suite: Separated for privacy, this master suite offers a roomy bath with whirlpool tub, dual vanities, a separate shower, and a large walk-in closet.

- Additional Rooms: Additional rooms include a laundry/utility room—with space for a washer, dryer, and freezer—a large area above the garage, well-suited for a media or game room, and two secondary bedrooms.

Copyright by designer/architect.

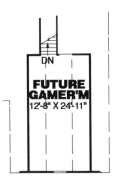

SMARTtip

Window Scarf

The best way to wrap a window scarf around a pole is as follows:

- Lay out the material on a large, clean surface. Gather the fabric at the top of each jabot, and use elastic to hold it together.

- Swing one jabot into place over the pole and, starting from there, wind the swag portion as many times as you need around the pole until you reach the elastic at the second jabot, which should have landed at the opposite pole end.

- Readjust wraps along the pole. Generally, wrapped swags just touch or slightly overlap.

- For a dramatic effect, stuff the wrapped swags with tissue paper or thin foam, depending on the translucence and weight of fabric.

- Release elastics at tops of jabots.

Plan #101014

Dimensions: 52' W x 28' D
Levels: 2
Square Footage: 1,598
Main Level Sq. Ft.: 812
Upper Level Sq. Ft.: 786
Bedrooms: 3
Bathrooms: 2½
Foundation: Slab, crawl space
Materials List Available: No
Price Category: C

This lovely Victorian home has a perfect balance of ornamental features and modern amenities.

Features:

• Ceiling Height: 8 ft. unless otherwise noted.

• Foyer: An impressive beveled glass-front door invites you into this roomy foyer.

• Kitchen: This bright and open kitchen offers an abundance of counter space to make cooking a pleasure.

• Breakfast Room: You'll enjoy plenty of informal family meals in this sunny and open spot next to the kitchen.

• Family Room: The whole family will be attracted to this handsome room. A full-width bay window adds to the Victorian charm.

• Master Suite: This dramatic suite features a multi-faceted vaulted ceiling and his and her closets and vanities. A separate shower and 6-ft. garden tub complete the lavish appointments.

Main Level Floor Plan

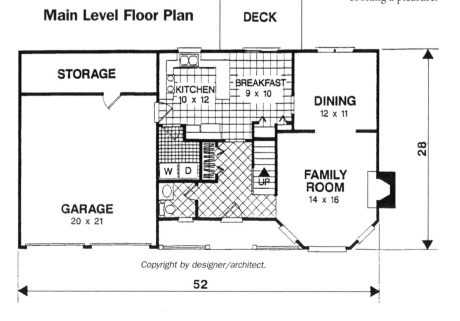

Upper Level Floor Plan

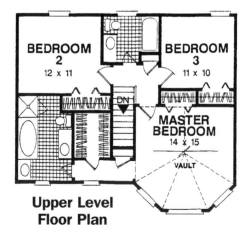

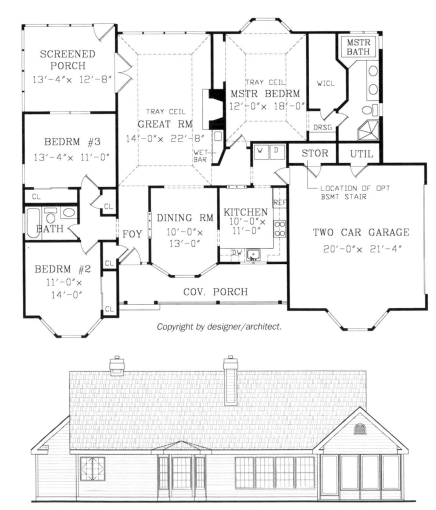

Plan #131007

Dimensions: 59'10" W x 47'8" D
Levels: 1
Square Footage: 1,595
Bedrooms: 3
Bathrooms: 2
Foundation: Crawl space, slab, basement, or walkout
Materials List Available: Yes
Price Category: D

Images provided by designer/architect.

Imagine living in this home, with its traditional country comfort and individual brand of charm.

Features:

- Exterior elements: The mixture of a front porch with a cameo front door, decorative posts, bay windows, and dormers will delight you.

- Great Room: A tray ceiling gives distinction to this large room, and a wet bar eases entertaining.

- Screened Porch: At dusk and dawn, this porch is sure to be your favorite outdoor spot.

- Kitchen: Eat any meal in this large kitchen for a touch of homey charm.

- Dining Room: Perfect for hosting a formal dinner, this bayed dining room can increase your enjoyment of simple family meals.

- Master Bedroom: For the sake of privacy, this room is somewhat secluded. Decorate to emphasize the elegant tray ceiling.

Copyright by designer/architect.

Rear Elevation

Alternate Front View

Foyer / Dining Room

Great Room

Add the Extras

Simple or plain, it's the little conveniences and miscellaneous touches that push the dining experience to perfection. Here are some extra things to think about.

- You can never have too many serving trays when you entertain outside. For carrying food or drinks from the kitchen or the grill, trays are indispensable.

- A serving cart on wheels makes a perfect movable outdoor bar and provides an additional serving surface. Look for one at yard sales or buy one new.

- Chances are you won't have a sideboard, but a few small tables to hold excess items are great substitutes for one. They're also easier to position in the different places where you need them.

- For cooler weather or even a summer's evening with a bit of nip in the air, nothing beats an outdoor fireplace for comfort. You could build one into the house, but various types of stand alone units are sold in home centers. To add a Southwest ambiance, consider a chiminea, a clay fireplace. Try burning some piñon pine, and you'll feel as if you're in Santa Fe. Be sure to follow manufacturers' instructions when using these fireplaces. You might also have to store them during the winter.

- Pots of fragrant plants—lavender, scented geraniums, flowering tobacco, or jasmine—provide a sensual aroma. Flowers such as roses climbing up an arbor or trellis are beautiful, evoke a romantic feeling, and lend a delicate scent to the atmosphere as well.

Nothing adds romance and intrigue to an evening soiree as candlelight does. Include just a few candles for an intimate dinner. Use more for a larger gathering, placing one or more on each table. Scatter luminaries around the yard. As the beautiful evening dusk begins, light candles, a few at a time, so your eyes can adjust to the dimming light. Not only do the candles illuminate the night in a magical way but they can also keep bugs at bay.

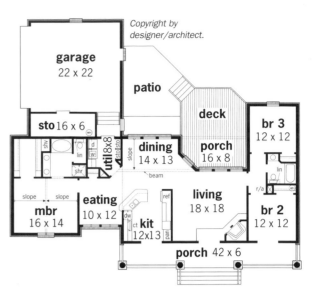

Copyright by designer/architect.

garage
22 x 22

patio

sto 16 x 6

deck

br 3
12 x 12

dining
14 x 13

porch
16 x 8

living
18 x 18

br 2
12 x 12

mbr
16 x 14

eating
10 x 12

kit
12x13

porch 42 x 6

Plan #211029

Images provided by designer/architect.

Dimensions: 68' W x 60' D

Levels: 1

Square Footage: 1,672

Bedrooms: 3

Bathrooms: 2

Foundation: Crawl space

Materials List Available: Yes

Price Category: C

SMARTtip
Ponds

If a pond or small body of water already exists on your property, arrange your garden elements to take advantage of it. Build a bridge over it to connect it to other areas of the garden. If there's a dock already in place, make use of it for an instant midday picnic for one.

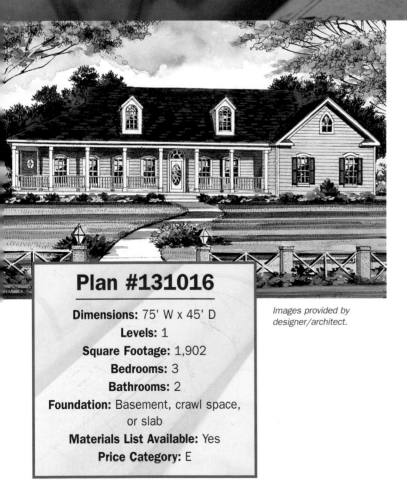

BEDRM 2
11'-0"x11'-0"
9' CEILING

GREAT ROOM
21'-0"x14'-0"
9' CEILING

KITCH/BRKFST
18'-6"x13'-0"
9' CEILING

MASTER BEDRM
12'-6"x17'-6"
10'-0"
STEPPED CLG

BATH

BEDRM 3
11'-0"x11'-0"
9' CEILING

LIVING
13'-0"x14'-8"
10' STEPPED CLG

DINING
11'-0"x12'-0"
9' CEILING

FOYER

UTIL

LAUN

STORAGE

LOCATION OF OPTIONAL BASEMENT STAIR

GARAGE
20'-0"x26'-4"

STORAGE

PORCH

Copyright by designer/architect.

Plan #131016

Images provided by designer/architect.

Dimensions: 75' W x 45' D

Levels: 1

Square Footage: 1,902

Bedrooms: 3

Bathrooms: 2

Foundation: Basement, crawl space, or slab

Materials List Available: Yes

Price Category: E

Great Room

Plan #171008

Dimensions: 72' W x 40' D
Levels: 1
Square Footage: 1,652
Bedrooms: 3
Bathrooms: 2
Foundation: Slab, crawl space
Materials List Available: Yes
Price Category: C

Images provided by designer/architect.

Copyright by designer/architect.

SMARTtip

Lighting for Decorative Shadows

Use lighting to create decorative shadows. For interesting, undefined shadows, set lights at ground level aiming upward in front of a shrub or tree that is close to a wall. For silhouetting, place lights directly behind a plant or garden statue that is near a wall. In both cases, using a wide beam will increase the effect.

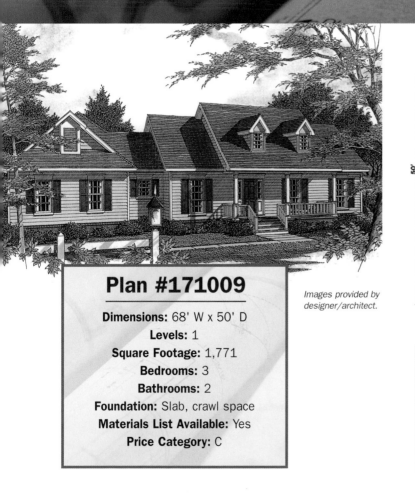

Plan #171009

Dimensions: 68' W x 50' D
Levels: 1
Square Footage: 1,771
Bedrooms: 3
Bathrooms: 2
Foundation: Slab, crawl space
Materials List Available: Yes
Price Category: C

Images provided by designer/architect.

Copyright by designer/architect.

SMARTtip

Deck Awnings

Awnings come in bright colors. As light filters through, it will cast a hue to anything under the deck. Warm colors, such as red or pink, will create a rosy glow; cool colors, such blues or greens, will enhance the shade.

Plan #191023

Dimensions: 56' W x 42' D
Levels: 1
Square Footage: 1,785
Bedrooms: 3
Bathrooms: 2
Foundation: Basement
Materials List Available: No
Price Category: C

Two large porches and a spacious family room make this lovely home ideal for a busy family with an active social life.

Features:

- Ceiling Height: 9-ft. ceilings add to the airy feeling inside this cheery home.

- Great Room: Highlights here include a built-in entertainment center and French doors with overhead transoms that open onto the rear covered porch.

- Dining Room: An arched opening to this room emphasizes its lovely dimensions.

- Kitchen: This well-planned kitchen includes a central island with downdraft range, a snack bar, and lots of counter and cabinet space.

- Breakfast Area: You'll find the family using this convenient and sunny room at all times of day.

- Master Suite: With its walk-in closet and deluxe bath, this suite will live up to your fondest dreams.

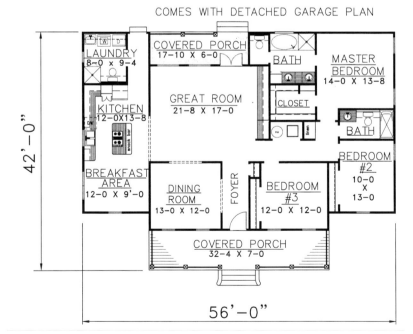

COMES WITH DETACHED GARAGE PLAN

Copyright by designer/architect.

Plan #191003

Dimensions: 56' W x 42' D

Levels: 1

Square Footage: 1,785

Bedrooms: 3

Bathrooms: 3

Foundation: Crawl space, slab, or basement

Materials List Available: No

Price Category: C

Images provided by designer/architect.

Enjoy the amenities you'll find in this gracious home, with its traditional Southern appearance.

Features:

- **Great Room:** This expansive room is so versatile that everyone will gather here. A built-in entertainment area with desk makes a great lounging spot, and the French doors topped by transoms open onto the lovely rear porch.

- **Dining Room:** An arched entry to this room helps to create the open feeling in this home.

- **Kitchen:** Another arched entryway leads to this fabulous kitchen, which has been designed with the cook's comfort in mind. It features a downdraft range, many cabinets, a snack bar, and a sunny breakfast area, where the family is sure to gather.

- **Laundry:** A sink, shower, toilet area, and cabinets galore give total convenience in this room.

- **Master Suite:** Enjoy the walk-in closet and bath with toilet room, whirlpool tub, and shower.

56'-0" Width

Copyright by designer/architect.

42'-0" Depth including porch

LAUNDRY 8-0 X 9-4

COVERED PORCH 17-10 X 6-0

BATH

MASTER BEDROOM 14-0 X 13-8

GREAT ROOM 21-8 X 17-0

CLOSET

KITCHEN 12-0X13-8

snack bar

BATH

linen

BREAKFAST AREA 12-0 X 9-0

DINING ROOM 13-0 X 12-0

BEDROOM #3 12-0 X 12-0

BEDROOM #2 10-0 X 13-0

COVERED PORCH 32-4 X 7-0

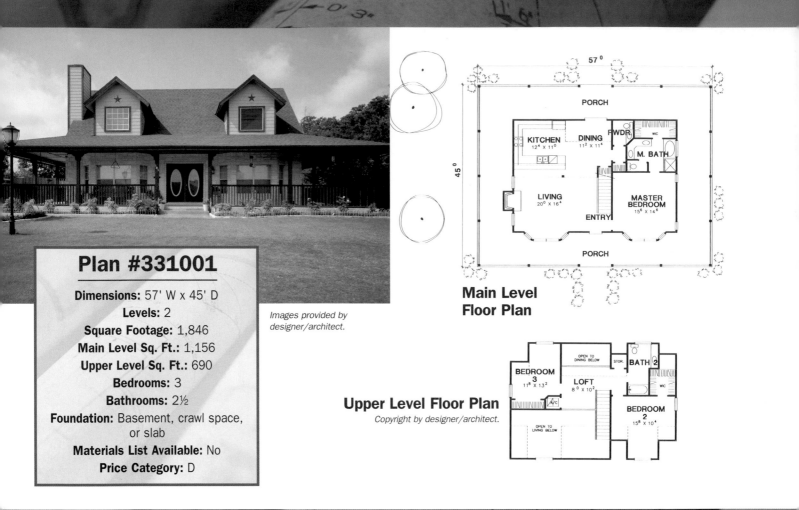

Plan #331001

Dimensions: 57' W x 45' D

Levels: 2

Square Footage: 1,846

Main Level Sq. Ft.: 1,156

Upper Level Sq. Ft.: 690

Bedrooms: 3

Bathrooms: 2½

Foundation: Basement, crawl space, or slab

Materials List Available: No

Price Category: D

Images provided by designer/architect.

Main Level Floor Plan

Upper Level Floor Plan

Copyright by designer/architect.

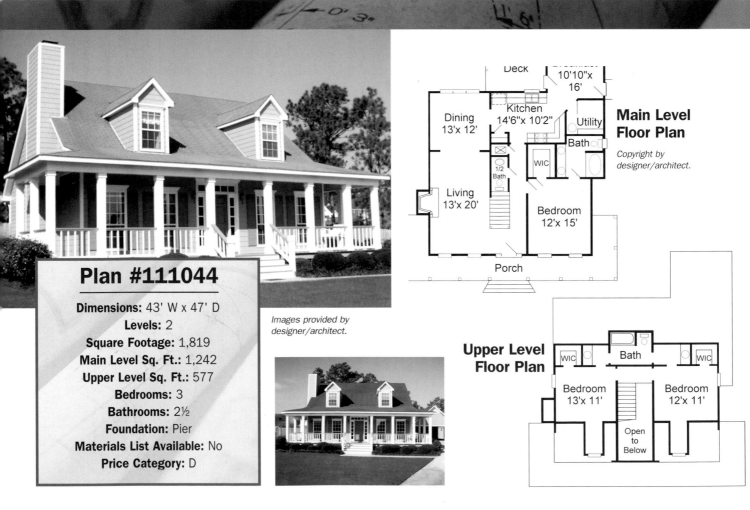

Plan #111044

Dimensions: 43' W x 47' D

Levels: 2

Square Footage: 1,819

Main Level Sq. Ft.: 1,242

Upper Level Sq. Ft.: 577

Bedrooms: 3

Bathrooms: 2½

Foundation: Pier

Materials List Available: No

Price Category: D

Images provided by designer/architect.

Main Level Floor Plan

Copyright by designer/architect.

Upper Level Floor Plan

Plan #271097

Dimensions: 60' W x 42' D

Levels: 2

Square Footage: 1,645

Main Level Sq. Ft.: 1,136

Upper Level Sq. Ft.: 509

Bedrooms: 3

Bathrooms: 2

Foundation: Basement

Materials List Available: No

Price Category: C

Images provided by designer/architect.

Main Level Floor Plan

Upper Level Floor Plan

Copyright by designer/architect.

Plan #141025

Dimensions: 52' W x 36' D

Levels: 2

Square Footage: 1,721

Main Level Sq. Ft.: 902

Upper Level Sq. Ft.: 819

Bedrooms: 4

Bathrooms: 2½

Foundation: Basement

Materials List Available: Yes

Price Category: C

Images provided by designer/architect.

Main Level Floor Plan

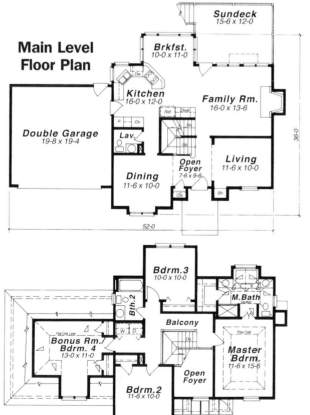

Upper Level Floor Plan

Copyright by designer/architect.

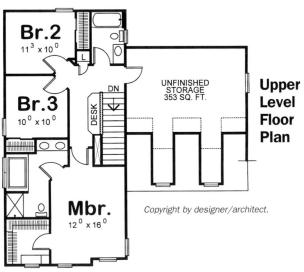

Plan #121045

Dimensions: 40' W x 48' D

Levels: 2

Square Footage: 1,575

Main Level Sq. Ft.: 787

Upper Level Sq. Ft.: 788

Bedrooms: 3

Bathrooms: 2½

Foundation: Basement

Materials List Available: Yes

Price Category: C

Images provided by designer/architect.

This home is carefully laid out to provide the convenience demanded by busy family life.

Features:

• Ceiling Height: 8 ft.

• Family Room: This charming family room, with its fireplace and built-in cabinetry, will become the central gathering place for family and friends.

• Kitchen: This kitchen offers a central island that makes food preparation more convenient and doubles

as a snack bar for a quick bite on the run. The breakfast area features a pantry and planning desk.

• Computer Loft: The second-floor landing includes this loft designed to accommodate the family computer.

• Room to Grow: Also on the second-floor landing you will find a large unfinished area waiting to accommodate the growing family.

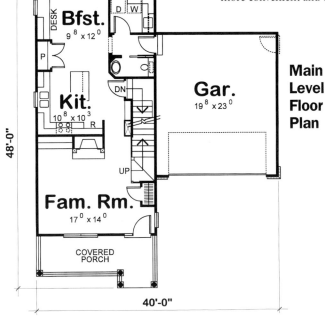

Main Level Floor Plan

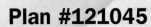

Upper Level Floor Plan

Copyright by designer/architect.

Plan #281015

Dimensions: 32' W x 48' D

Levels: 2

Square Footage: 1,660

Main Level Sq. Ft.: 964

Upper Level Sq. Ft.: 696

Bedrooms: 4

Bathrooms: 2½

Foundation: Basement

Materials List Available: Yes

Price Category: C

You'll love the gracious features and amenities in this charming home, which is meant for a narrow lot.

Features:

- **Foyer:** This two-story foyer opens into the spacious living room.

- **Living Room:** The large bay window in this room makes a perfect setting for quiet times alone or entertaining guests.

- **Dining Room:** The open flow between this room and the living room adds to the airy feeling.

- **Family Room:** With a handsome fireplace and a door to the rear patio, this room will be the heart of your home.

- **Kitchen:** The U-shaped layout, pantry, and greenhouse window make this room a joy.

- **Master Suite:** The bay window, large walk-in closet, and private bath make this second-floor room a true retreat.

Images provided by designer/architect.

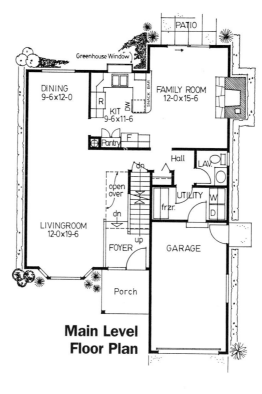

Main Level Floor Plan

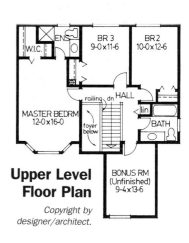

Upper Level Floor Plan

Copyright by designer/architect.

Left Side Elevation

Right Side Elevation

Rear Elevation

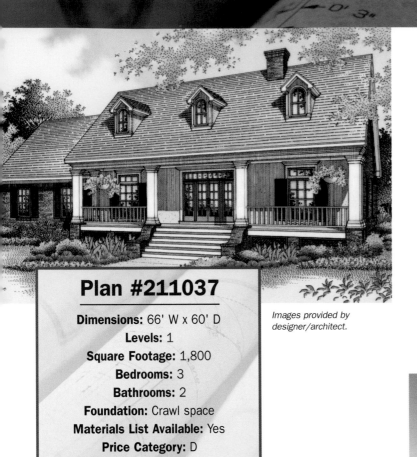

Plan #211037

Dimensions: 66' W x 60' D
Levels: 1
Square Footage: 1,800
Bedrooms: 3
Bathrooms: 2
Foundation: Crawl space
Materials List Available: Yes
Price Category: D

Images provided by designer/architect.

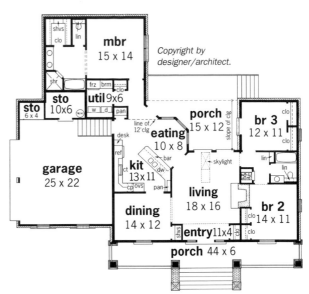

Copyright by designer/architect.

SMARTtip

Reflected Light in the Bathroom

The addition of a large mirror can bring reflected light into a small bathroom, adding the illusion of space without the expense of renovation.

SMARTtip

Brackets in Window Treatments

Although it is rarely noticed, a bracket plays an important role in supporting rods and poles. If a treatment rubs against a window frame, an extension bracket solves the problem. It projects from the wall at an adjustable length, providing enough clearance. A hold-down bracket anchors a cellular shade or a blind to the bottom of a door, preventing the treatment from moving when the door is opened or closed.

Plan #211030

Dimensions: 75' W x 37' D
Levels: 1
Square Footage: 1,600
Bedrooms: 3
Bathrooms: 2
Foundation: Slab
Materials List Available: Yes
Price Category: C

Images provided by designer/architect.

Copyright by designer/architect.

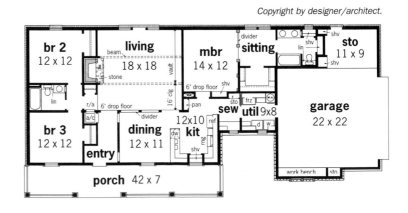

Plan #131011

Dimensions: 75'2" W x 60'9" D

Levels: 1

Square Footage: 1,897

Bedrooms: 4

Bathrooms: 2

Foundation: Basement, crawl space, or slab

Materials List Available: Yes

Price Category: E

Images provided by designer/architect.

Copyright by designer/architect.

Plan #201086

Dimensions: 68'6" W x 46' D

Levels: 1

Square Footage: 1,573

Bedrooms: 3

Bathrooms: 2

Foundation: Crawl space, slab, or basement

Materials List Available: Yes

Price Category: C

Images provided by designer/architect.

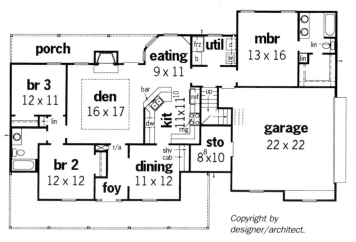

Copyright by designer/architect.

Plan #211038

Dimensions: 72' W x 42' D

Levels: 1

Square Footage: 1,898

Bedrooms: 3

Bathrooms: 2

Foundation: Slab

Materials List Available: Yes

Price Category: D

A railed front porch, a charming cupola, and stylish shutters add classic flair to this home.

Features:

- Ceiling Height: 8 ft. unless otherwise noted.

- Family Room: The welcoming entry flows into this attractive family gathering area. The room features a handsome fireplace and a 14-ft. vaulted ceiling with exposed beams. French doors lead to a backyard patio.

- Formal Dining Room: This elegant room adjoins the living room. You'll usher your guests through a half-wall with decorative spindles.

- Kitchen: Food preparation will be a pleasure working at the wraparound counter.

- Eating Nook: Modern life includes lots of quick, informal meals, and this is the spot to enjoy them. The nook includes a laundry closet, so you can change loads while cooking.

- Master Suite: This private retreat boasts a private bath with a separate dressing area and a roomy walk-in closet.

Images provided by designer/architect.

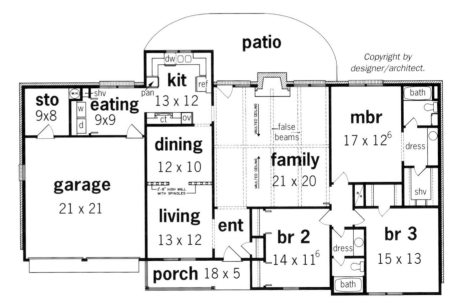

Copyright by designer/architect.

SMARTtip

Efficient Kitchen Appliances

Appliances that carry the **Energy Star** label — a program of the Department of Energy — are significantly more energy efficient than most other appliances. Dishwashers, for example, must be 25 percent more energy efficient than models that meet minimum federal energy requirements. Energy Star refrigerators must be 10 percent more efficient than the newest standards.

Plan #211089

Dimensions: 56' W x 61' D

Levels: 2

Square Footage: 1,956

Main Level Sq. Ft.: 1,320

Upper Level Sq. Ft.: 636

Bedrooms: 3 or 4

Bathrooms: 4

Foundation: Slab, crawl space

Materials List Available: Yes

Price Category: D

This home's 2 x 6 framing allows for super insulation—an energy saver in hot or cold areas.

Features:

- Ceiling Height: 8 ft.

- Family Room: Here is the perfect comfortable space for everyday family activities. Warm yourself by the handsome fireplace. Pluck a book off the built-in bookshelf, and settle in for a quiet read.

- Master Suite: This master suite enjoys its own private area, making it the perfect retreat after a long, busy day. Luxuriate in the master bath, complete with a garden tub.

- Front Porch: This large front porch adds an inviting feel to the entrance. It's sized to accommodate old-fashioned rocking chairs or porch swings.

Images provided by designer/architect.

SMARTtip

The Cottage Look in Your Kitchen

For authenticity, the overall look has to appear slightly worn, but not shabby. You can accomplish this by distressing wood surfaces, such as a tabletop, or adding a crackle finish to woodwork. Another idea is to use a natural dye on table linens or cotton fabric window treatments. Compared with synthetics, these dyes seem slightly faded and will lend a comfortable lived-in feeling to your cottage-style kitchen.

Main Level Floor Plan

Copyright by designer/architect.

Upper Level Floor Plan

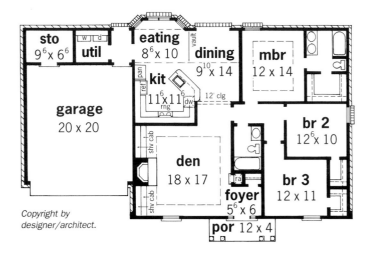

Plan #201031

Dimensions: 60'10" W x 41'5" D

Levels: 1

Square Footage: 1,531

Bedrooms: 3

Bathrooms: 2

Foundation: Crawl space, slab, or basement

Materials List Available: Yes

Price Category: C

SMARTtip

Dimmer Switches

You can dim lights just slightly to extend lamp life and save energy, and there will be very little perceptible change in light level. For instance, dimming the light to 50 percent will be perceived as though the light were only dimmed to 70 percent, so there is no dramatic dilation or constriction of the eye due to light level change.

Plan #341030

Dimensions: 52' W x 40' D

Levels: 1

Square Footage: 1,660

Bedrooms: 3

Bathrooms: 2

Foundation: Crawl space, slab, or basement

Materials List Available: Yes

Price Category: C

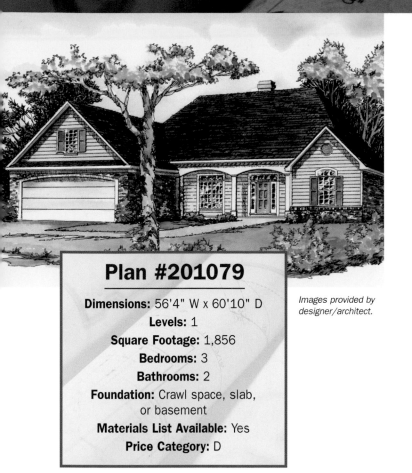

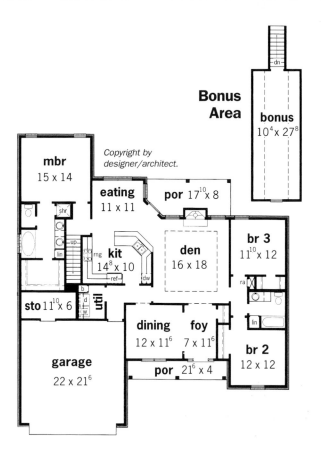

Plan #201079

Dimensions: 56'4" W x 60'10" D

Levels: 1

Square Footage: 1,856

Bedrooms: 3

Bathrooms: 2

Foundation: Crawl space, slab, or basement

Materials List Available: Yes

Price Category: D

Images provided by designer/architect.

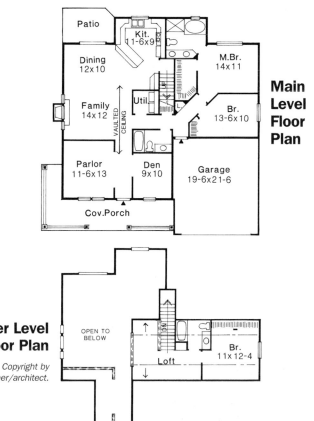

Plan #231035

Dimensions: 50' W x 50' D

Levels: 2

Square Footage: 1,954

Main Level Sq. Ft.: 1,508

Upper Level Sq. Ft.: 446

Bedrooms: 3

Bathrooms: 3

Foundation: Crawl space, slab

Materials List Available: No

Price Category: D

Images provided by designer/architect.

Plan #281016

Dimensions: 46' W x 44' D

Levels: 2

Square Footage: 1,945

Main Level Sq. Ft.: 1,211

Upper Level Sq. Ft.: 734

Bedrooms: 3

Bathrooms: 3

Foundation: Combination basement/slab

Materials List Available: Yes

Price Category: D

Images provided by designer/architect.

The fabulous window shapes on this Tudor-style home give just a hint of the beautiful interior design.

Features:

- **Living Room:** A vaulted ceiling in this raised room adds to its spectacular good looks.

- **Dining Room:** Between the lovely bay window and the convenient door to the covered sundeck, this room is an entertainer's delight.

- **Family Room:** A sunken floor, cozy fireplace, and door to the patio make this room special.

- **Study:** Just off the family room, this quiet spot can be a true retreat away from the crowd.

- **Kitchen:** The family cooks will be delighted by the ample counter and storage space here.

- **Master Suite:** A large walk-in closet, huge picture window, and private bath add luxurious touches to this second-floor retreat.

Main Level Floor Plan

Upper Level Floor Plan

Copyright by designer/architect.

Rear Elevation

Left Side Elevation

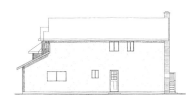

Right Side Elevation

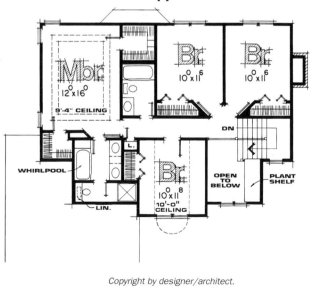

Plan #121064

Dimensions: 44' W x 40' D
Levels: 2
Square Footage: 1,846
Main Level Sq. Ft.: 919
Upper Level Sq. Ft.: 927
Bedrooms: 4
Bathrooms: 2½
Foundation: Basement
Materials List Available: Yes
Price Category: D

Images provided by designer/architect.

You'll love the features and design in this compact but amenity-filled home.

Features:

- **Entry:** A balcony overlooks this two-story entry, where a plant shelf tops the coat closet.
- **Great Room:** A trio of tall windows points up the large dimensions of this room, which is sure to be the hub of your home. Arrange the

furniture to create a cozy space around the fireplace, or leave it open to the room.

- **Kitchen:** You'll love to work in this well-designed kitchen area.
- **Master Suite:** On the second floor, this master suite features a tiered ceiling and two walk-in closets. In the bath, you'll find a double vanity, whirlpool tub, and separate shower.

Main Level Floor Plan

Upper Level Floor Plan

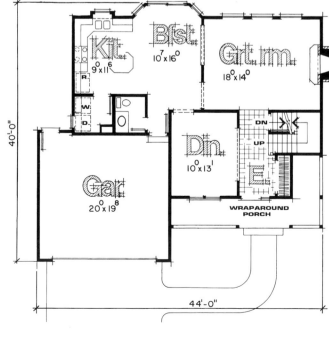

Copyright by designer/architect.

Plan #181074

Dimensions: 42' W x 40' D

Levels: 2

Square Footage: 1,760

Main Level Sq. Ft.: 880

Upper Level Sq. Ft.: 880

Bedrooms: 3

Full Baths: 2½

Foundation: Full basement

Materials List Available: Yes

Price Category: C

Images provided by designer/architect.

Main Level Floor Plan

Upper Level Floor Plan

Copyright by designer/architect.

Plan #181157

Dimensions: 45' 6" W x 29' D

Levels: 2

Square Footage: 1,795

Main Level Sq. Ft.: 890

Upper Level Sq. Ft.: 905

Bedrooms: 3

Bathrooms: 2½

Foundation: Full basement

Materials List Available: Yes

Price Category: C

Images provided by designer/architect.

Main Level Floor Plan

Upper Level Floor Plan

Copyright by designer/architect.

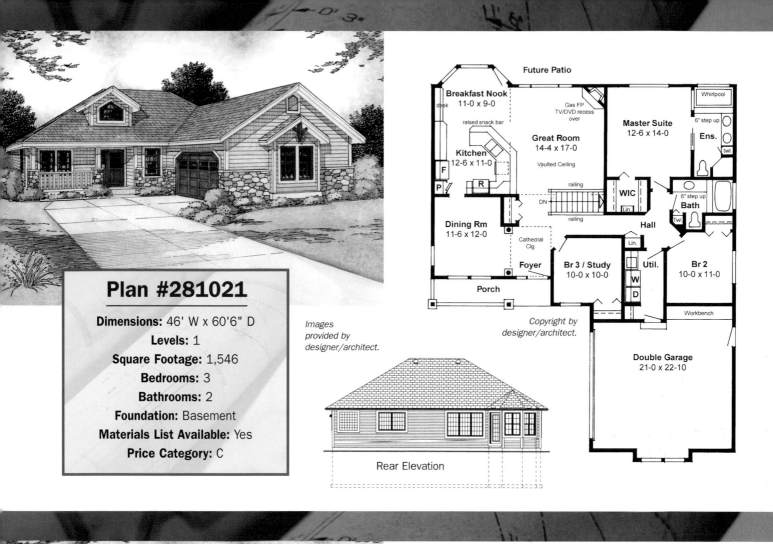

Future Patio

Breakfast Nook
11-0 x 9-0
desk

Whirlpool

Master Suite
12-6 x 14-0

6" step up

Gas FP
TV/DVD recess over

Ens.

twl.

Great Room
14-4 x 17-0

raised snack bar

Kitchen
12-6 x 11-0

Vaulted Ceiling

F

railing

DN

railing

WIC

Lin

6" step up

Bath

Twl.

P

R

Dining Rm
11-6 x 12-0

Hall

Lin.

Cathedral Clg.

Foyer

Br 3 / Study
10-0 x 10-0

Util.

W
D

Br 2
10-0 x 11-0

Porch

Workbench

Double Garage
21-0 x 22-10

Copyright by designer/architect.

Plan #281021

Dimensions: 46' W x 60'6" D

Levels: 1

Square Footage: 1,546

Bedrooms: 3

Bathrooms: 2

Foundation: Basement

Materials List Available: Yes

Price Category: C

Images provided by designer/architect.

Rear Elevation

Covered Deck

Whirlpool

Master Suite
16-0 x 12-0

French Doors

Ens

Dining
10-0 x 14-4

Kitchen
10-8 x 14-0

lin

WIC

raised snack bar

F

Br 2
10-0 x 10-0

P

Bath

3-sided Gas FP

1/2 wall

DN

railing

lin

Great Room
18-0 x 17-6

Hall

niche

Util.

Br 3
10-0 x 10-0

Foyer

W
D

French Doors

Gazebo

Porch

Double Garage
19-4 x 21-8

Copyright by designer/architect.

Plan #281022

Dimensions: 48' W x 58' D

Levels: 1

Square Footage: 1,506

Bedrooms: 3

Bathrooms: 2

Foundation: Basement

Materials List Available: Yes

Price Category: C

Images provided by designer/architect.

Rear Elevation

Kid's Rooms

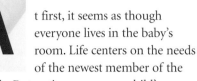t first, it seems as though everyone lives in the baby's room. Life centers on the needs of the newest member of the family. But as time goes on, a child's room becomes a place apart from the other family spaces. It takes on the parents' wishes for the child and the child's own character. That's why decorating the room can be fun. For the parents of very young children, the project is a chance to re-create some of their own childhood fantasies. As children grow and begin to develop preferences, Mom, Dad, and the kids can make decisions about furniture, colors, patterns, and themes together. Whatever the case, don't order the new carpeting or run off to the paint store yet. For the best result, one that pleases parents and child alike, it pays to plan. Whether the decorating scheme will be classic or totally unique and new, the goal is to create a balanced room that is both stimulating and soothing. To do it right, know ahead of time how much work will be entailed and what you will have to spend on the project. While you're doing your planning, remember that this is the one room in the house that is strictly your child's. He will do a lot of things in there besides sleeping: playing, alone or with friends; listening to music; reading; studying; and keeping up with hobbies. Try to accommodate all of these functions while making the room an attractive and comfortable haven that suits your child's individuality. That way you won't have to redecorate for years to come.

A young child's room is for sleeping and playing. Let his or her favorite game or story inspire a decorating motif.

Evaluating the Space

Start by developing a plan of action, which will begin with taking a critical look at the size and shape of the space, and trying various ways, on paper, for furnishing it. Follow the easy steps that are on pages 112 and 113 to help with the process. After you've made your analysis, you'll be able to organize a list of objectives—things you want to achieve

with the design—and decide whom you want to do the painting or building of the cabinets, for example. (If you prefer to do all of the work yourself, make sure that you have the time and any required skills and tools.)

It's always smart to put together a realistic materials budget for a project ahead of time so that you don't get caught short midway through the project. If you're all

thumbs when it comes to hammering out figures, get professional advice.

More than anything else, you can rely on your own personal taste and intuition, and that of your child's, to design the room because there are no hard and fast rules for decorating. But it always helps to keep in mind the basic principles of scale, proportion, line, balance, harmony, and rhythm when examining space—and all

A pretty bed canopy, left, is almost every young girl's dream. Here, dotted sheer fabric sweeps from inside a ceiling-mounted coronet to each of the bed poles where it is twisted before falling dramatically to the floor.

Sponged-on blocks of color is an easy way to decorate an unfinished toy box, opposite top left. For a textured wall, opposite top right, apply glaze and, while it's still wet, use a bunched up rag to pull off some of the color.

Pull a combing tool through wet glaze to add a pattern to painted furniture and accessories, opposite bottom left and right. Use decoupage medium to apply theme motifs, like these animals that have been cut out of wallpaper or fabric.

of the ways to fill it up. This is what professional designers do to create interiors that are both pleasing to the eye and practical for living. A brief consultation can be surprisingly affordable and may even save you money in the end.

It's an excellent idea to put your thoughts on paper. So, with a notepad and pencil in hand, take a look at the room at various times of the day. Is it small or large? Is it oddly shaped? Are the furnishings you are considering the proper scale for the space? Will they be easy to arrange in the room? How many doors and windows are there? Are they conveniently placed? Is the room too dark or too bright at certain times of the day? Are there enough closets and other types of storage space? If the physical space isn't perfect, now is the time to look for ways to compensate for or correct problems.

Taking Stock

Next, look at the surfaces in the room. Do the walls simply painting or wallpaper, or will you be adding a chair rail or border? Kids can be pretty tough on floors and carpeting. Take stock of any existing furniture. Is it adequate for your child's needs? What condition is it in? Minor damage to the finish, missing knobs, drawers that stick or need re-gluing are easy repair jobs. Don't forget to get input from the person who occupies the room, too. Your youngster may already have favorite colors or special needs that should be addressed.

Make notes on what can be used for now and what needs to be modified or made age-appropriate.

Here's how to look at the space critically and organize your thoughts into action.

Step One: Measure up. Take the overall dimensions of the room using a steel measuring tape; include the size of all of the openings (doors and windows). If there are any fixed features, such as a built-in desk or bookcases, measure and record their sizes, too.

Measure the existing furniture. With just a few adjustments to the layout, you may save yourself the expense of buying something new. If you're planning shelf storage for large toys, a TV, stereo, and computer equipment, measure them.

Make a freehand sketch of the space and the furnishings, and list the measurements you've taken in the margin. Don't forget to note the electrical switches and outlets, cable and phone jacks, radiators, heat registers, air ducts, and light fixtures.

Plan on enough floor space for furniture clearances around kids' play areas.

Step Two: Draw a floor plan to scale. You'll find this invaluable as a reference when you're shopping for furniture or arranging the layout of the room because like and how much space a piece of furniture will occupy ahead of time. When you're making notes, use shorthand; for 3 feet and 2 inches write 3' 2" and so on.

Work on ¼-inch graph paper. Each square will represent one foot. For example, if a wall measures 15 feet, the line you draw to indicate that wall will use 15 squares. Use a ruler or straightedge to make your lines; then record your measurements.

To try out different furniture arrangements, first draw and cut out furniture

Draw a floor plan to scale, above. On paper, try out different furniture arrangements, and then take the drawing with you when you shop.

Make a sample board, below. The sample board will show you at a glance how your choices for wallpaper, fabric and paint will look together. Use it to coordinate the various decorating elements. Add and subtract swatches and samples. You can experiment with different looks.

templates, using the same ¼-inch scale. Each one is drawn to scale based on average dimensions, but you'll have to adjust the scale to your furniture's true size. If you plan to buy new pieces, ask the salesperson to give you the manufacturer's spec sheets, which will include dimensions. Never guess about size.

Step Three: Create a focal point.

When you're playing with the room's layout and furniture arrangement, start by placing the largest piece first; that's typically the bed—the room's focal point. The focal point is the one element that grabs your attention when first you walk into the room. Even if it's a simple twin-size bed, where you locate it and how you dress it makes an impact on the overall look of the room.

Clearances. Whenever possible, plan enough space around the furniture to use it comfortably. For example, if there will be under-bed storage, such as roll-out drawers, make sure there's enough room on the side of the bed to pull the drawers out. Although you're limited by the actual size of the room, professionals recommend the following minimum allowances, whenever possible:

- 22 inches of space around the bed
- 36 inches of space between the bed and any door that opens into the room
- 18 inches between two beds that are placed side by side to accommodate a small night table and a pathway

- 3 feet of space in front of a closet for dressing and sorting items of clothing
- 40 inches of space into the room to open dresser drawers
- 10 to 20 inches of space to sit comfortably in a chair at a desk, plus 12 to 16 more inches to pull back the chair and rise from it
- a distance that is three times the size of the TV screen for optimum viewing

Take note of the location of vents, heating or air-conditioning units, phone jacks, and electrical switches and outlets. Maintain a distance of 6 inches between baseboard heating and air-conditioning units and furniture. Don't block or obstruct outlets or switches.

Traffic Patterns. Make them as convenient as possible for you and your children. For example, in a nursery, locate the changing table closest to the door and the crib farther into the room.

Traffic patterns are especially important in shared rooms. Allow clearances for one child to pass another child without disruption when someone is seated at a desk or play area. Strategic storage in the play area will be used more often than something that's inconvenient. If your kids play in the middle of the floor, a rolling cart that can be pushed against the wall when not in use can make picking up toys easier.

A teenager's room, right, reflects her maturing taste.

Make room for a computer and home-work, below.

Adaptability. Floor plans that detail present and future needs can help when you're making decisions about furniture. If you're planning to stay in the same house, consider how the room you design now can be adapted later as your child grows older and requires more furniture and storage.

Shared Spaces

Common areas and equally important private ones are necessary to preserve the peace in a room shared by two children. Size isn't as important as organized function paired with an understanding of the two unique personalities and needs of the two kids who will use the room.

When those two children are very young, a shared play area can totally dominate the space. That means you'll have to find a way to partially block off the sleeping area so that one child can rest quietly while the other plays, if necessary. Doubled storage space for toys helps to promote shared responsibility. Each child should be expected to care for his own things.

School-age kids require separate quiet places for reading, studying, and hobby pursuits. Take into account the different study habits and interests of siblings when you're planning these places. As a child differentiates herself and develops her own

A small chaise, above, provides a place for reading or for entertaining friends.

interests, her needs for reserved space, where she is totally in control, becomes more important for maturing with a healthy sense of self. Both children benefit from having clearly defined areas where the other child cannot play or use things without asking her roommate first.

The problems are somewhat more difficult when children who are separated by several years share space. Younger children don't understand property rights as yet. In these situations, walls or half-walls make sharing a room easier.

Plan #281018

Dimensions: 50' W x 52'6" D
Levels: 1
Square Footage: 1,565
Bedrooms: 3
Bathrooms: 2
Foundation: Basement
Materials List Available: Yes
Price Category: C

You'll love the arched window that announces the grace of this home to the rest of the world.

Images provided by designer/architect.

Features:

- **Living Room:** Scissor trusses on the ceiling and a superb window design make this room elegant.

- **Dining Room:** Open to the living room, this dining room features an expansive window area and contains a convenient, inset china closet.

- **Family Room:** A gas fireplace in the corner and a doorway to the patio make this room the heart of the house.

- **Breakfast Room:** The bay window here makes it a lovely spot at any time of day.

- **Kitchen:** A raised snack bar shared with both the family and breakfast rooms adds a nice touch to this well-planned, attractive kitchen.

- **Master Suite:** A bay window, walk-in closet, and private bath add up to luxurious comfort in this suite.

Rear Elevation

Left Side Elevation

Right Side Elevation

Copyright by designer/architect.

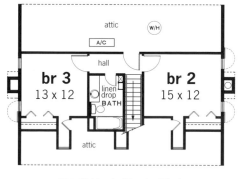

Plan #211070

Dimensions: 46' W x 68' D
Levels: 2
Square Footage: 1,700
Main Level Sq. Ft.: 1,160
Upper Level Sq. Ft.: 540
Bedrooms: 3
Bathrooms: 2½
Foundation: Crawl space, optional slab, or basement
Materials List Available: Yes
Price Category: C

You'll be charmed by the three roof dormers and the full-width covered porch on this traditional home.

Images provided by designer/architect.

Features:

- **Living Room:** With 9-ft. ceilings throughout the living room, dining room, and kitchen merge to maximize usable space and create a spacious, airy feeling in this home. You'll find a fireplace here and three pairs of French doors.

- **Dining Room:** Walk through this room to the rear covered porch beyond that connects the house to the garage.

- **Kitchen:** Designed for convenience, this kitchen features a wet bar that is centrally located so that it can easily serve both the living and dining rooms.

- **Master Suite:** A sloped ceiling with a skylight and French doors leading to the front porch make this area luxurious. The bath includes a raised marble tub, dual-sink vanity, and walk-in closet.

Main Level Floor Plan

carport 22 x 22

ATTIC STAIRS

porch 14 x 10

sto 8x6

kit 13x9

dining 13 x 9

bar
pan

living 21 x 15

utl
w d
clo

mbr 13 x 13

ent

porch

Upper Level Floor Plan

attic
W/H
A/C
hall

br 3 13 x 12

linen drop
BATH

br 2 15 x 12

attic

Copyright by designer/architect.

Images provided by designer/architect.

Copyright by designer/architect.

Plan #311017

Dimensions: 72' W x 55'2" D

Levels: 1

Square Footage: 1,974

Bedrooms: 3

Bathrooms: 2½

Foundation: Slab or crawl space or basement

Materials List Available: Yes

Price Category: D

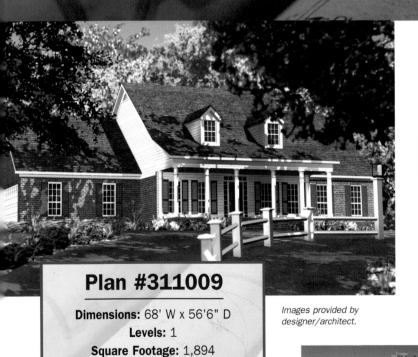

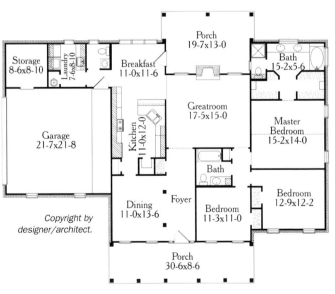

Copyright by designer/architect.

Images provided by designer/architect.

Plan #311009

Dimensions: 68' W x 56'6" D

Levels: 1

Square Footage: 1,894

Bedrooms: 3

Bathrooms: 2½

Foundation: Basement, crawl space, or slab

Materials List Available: Yes

Price Category: D

Basement Stair Option

Laun. 7-6x5-5

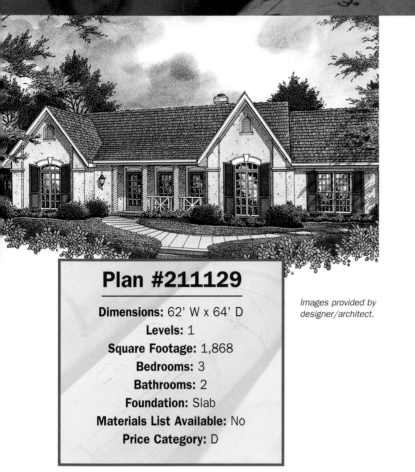

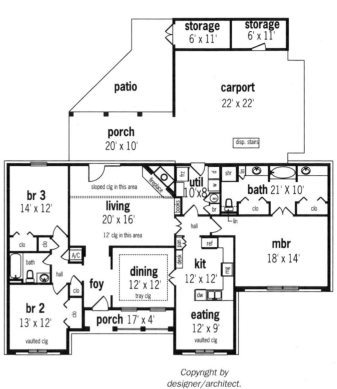

Plan #211129

Dimensions: 62' W x 64' D

Levels: 1

Square Footage: 1,868

Bedrooms: 3

Bathrooms: 2

Foundation: Slab

Materials List Available: No

Price Category: D

Images provided by designer/architect.

Copyright by designer/architect.

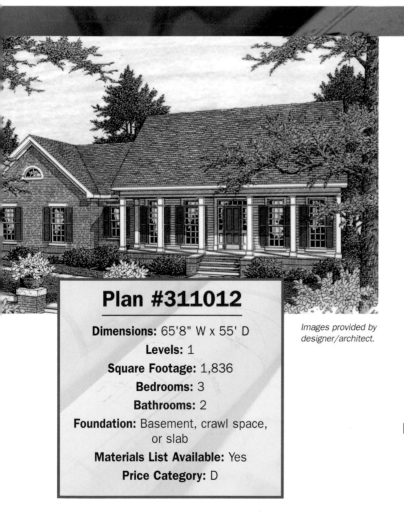

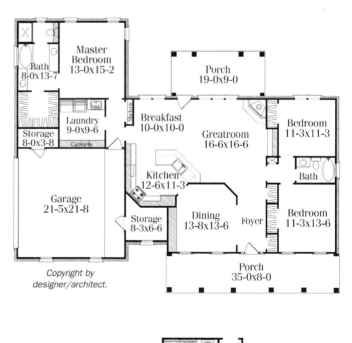

Plan #311012

Dimensions: 65'8" W x 55' D

Levels: 1

Square Footage: 1,836

Bedrooms: 3

Bathrooms: 2

Foundation: Basement, crawl space, or slab

Materials List Available: Yes

Price Category: D

Images provided by designer/architect.

Copyright by designer/architect.

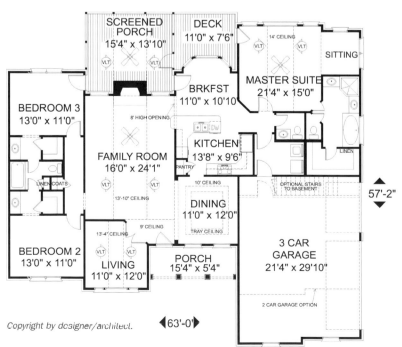

Plan #101005

Dimensions: 63' W x 57'2" D

Levels: 1

Square Footage: 1,992

Bedrooms: 3

Bathrooms: 2½

Foundation: Slab, crawl space, or basement

Materials List Available: Yes

Price Category: D

Images provided by designer/architect.

Rear View

This midsized ranch is accented with Palladian windows and inviting front porch.

Features:

- Ceiling Height: 9 ft. unless otherwise noted.

- Special Ceilings: Tray or vaulted ceilings adorn the living room, family room, dining room, and master suite.

- Kitchen: This bright and airy kitchen is designed to be a pleasure in which to work. It shares a big bay window with the contiguous breakfast room.

- Breakfast Room: The light streaming in from the bay window makes this the perfect place to linger with coffee and the Sunday paper.

- Master Suite: This exceptional suite has a sitting area and direct access to the deck, as well as a sitting area, full-featured bath, and spacious walk-in closet.

- Secondary Bedrooms: The other bedrooms each measure about 13 ft. x 11 ft. They have walk-in closets and share a "Jack-and-Jill" bath.

Copyright by designer/architect.

Plan #131044

Dimensions: 57'6" W x 42'4" D
Levels: 1
Square Footage: 1,994
Bedrooms: 3
Bathrooms: 2
Foundation: Basement, crawl space, or slab
Materials List Available: Yes
Price Category: E

Images provided by designer/architect.

Under a covered porch, Victorian-detailed bay windows grace each side of the brick-faced facade at the center of this ranch-style home, giving it a formal air.

Features:

• Ceiling Height: 10-ft. ceilings grace the central living area and the master bedroom of this home.

• Entry: Round top windows make this area and the flanking rooms bright and cheery.

• Great Room: A fireplace and built-ins that are visible from anywhere in this large room make it a natural gathering place for friends and family.

• Optional Office: Use the room just off the central hall as a home office, fourth bedroom, or study.

• Master Suite: You'll love the bay window, tray ceiling, two walk-in closets, and private bath.

• Bonus Space: Finish this large area in the attic for extra living space, or use it for storage.

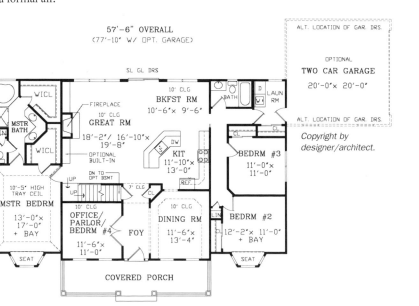

Copyright by designer/architect.

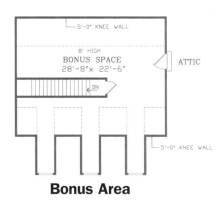

Rear Elevation

Bonus Area

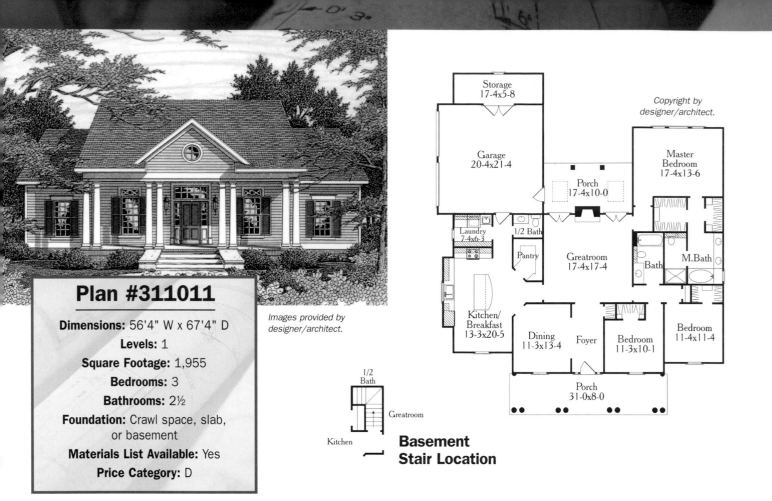

Plan #311011

Dimensions: 56'4" W x 67'4" D

Levels: 1

Square Footage: 1,955

Bedrooms: 3

Bathrooms: 2½

Foundation: Crawl space, slab, or basement

Materials List Available: Yes

Price Category: D

Images provided by designer/architect.

Basement Stair Location

Plan #171007

Dimensions: 62' W x 44' D

Levels: 2

Square Footage: 1,650

Main Level Sq. Ft.: 1,097

Upper Level Sq. Ft.: 553

Bedrooms: 3

Bathrooms: 2

Foundation: Slab, crawl space

Materials List Available: Yes

Price Category: C

Images provided by designer/architect.

Main Level Floor Plan

Upper Level Floor Plan

Copyright by designer/architect.

Plan #151145

Dimensions: 42' W x 67'4" D

Levels: 1

Square Footage: 1,774

Bedrooms: 2

Bathrooms: 2

Foundation: Crawl space, slab

Materials List Available: Yes

Price Category: C

Images provided by designer/architect.

Copyright by designer/architect.

Optional Bonus Area

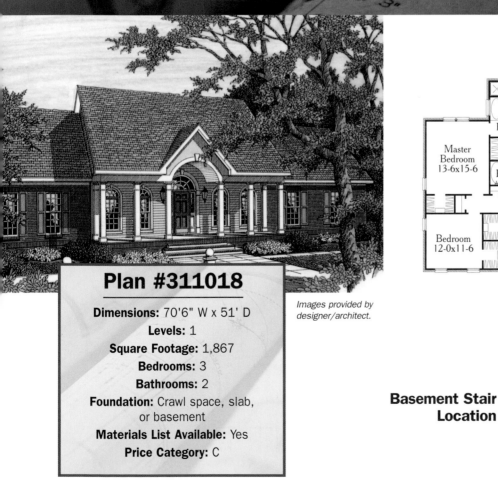

Plan #311018

Dimensions: 70'6" W x 51' D

Levels: 1

Square Footage: 1,867

Bedrooms: 3

Bathrooms: 2

Foundation: Crawl space, slab, or basement

Materials List Available: Yes

Price Category: C

Images provided by designer/architect.

Copyright by designer/architect.

Basement Stair Location

Images provided by designer/architect.

Plan #131024

Dimensions: 36' W by 54'4" D
Levels: 2
Square Footage: 1,635
Main Level Sq. Ft.: 880
Upper Level Sq. Ft.: 755
Bedrooms: 3
Bathrooms: 2½
Foundation: Basement, crawl space, or slab
Materials List Available: Yes
Price Category: D

You'll love the combination of early-American detailing on the outside and the contemporary, open layout of the interior.

Features:

• Ceiling Height: 8 ft.

• Front Porch: Use this wraparound front porch as an extra room when the weather's fine.

• Living Room: Separated only by columns, the open arrangement of the living and dining rooms enhances the spacious feeling in this home.

• Family Room/Kitchen: This combination family room/country kitchen includes a large work island and snack bar for convenience.

• Master Suite: A tray ceiling creates a contemporary look in the spacious master bedroom, and three closets make it practical. A compartmented full bath completes the suite.

• Bedrooms: Two additional bedrooms share a second full bath.

• Attic: Finish the attic space that's over the garage for even more living space.

Main Level Floor Plan

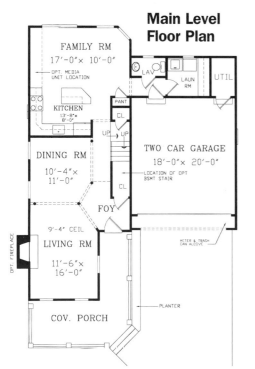

Upper Level Floor Plan

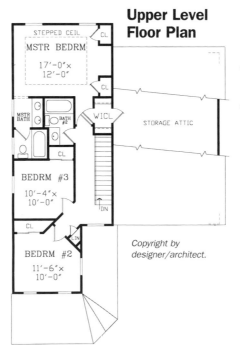

Copyright by designer/architect.

Rear Elevation

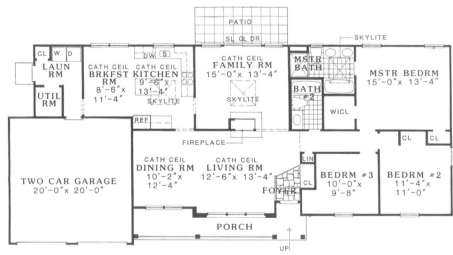

Plan #131001

Dimensions: 72'4" W x 32'4" D
Levels: 1
Square Footage: 1,615
Bedrooms: 3
Bathrooms: 2
Foundation: Basement, crawl space, or slab
Materials List Available: Yes
Price Category: D

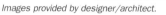

Images provided by designer/architect.

Copyright by designer/architect.

Cathedral ceilings and illuminating skylights add drama and beauty to this practical ranch house.

Features:

Ceiling Height: 8 ft.

- **Front Porch:** Watch the rain in comfort from the covered front porch.

- **Foyer:** The stone-tiled foyer flows into the living areas.

- **Living Room:** Oriented towards the front of the house, the living room opens to the dining room and shares a lovely three-sided fireplace with the family room.

- **Family Room:** Conveniently located to share the fireplace with the living room, this room is bright and cheery thanks to its skylights as well as the sliding glass doors that open onto the rear patio.

- **Kitchen:** An island makes this sunny room both efficient and attractive.

- **Breakfast Nook:** Located just off the kitchen, this area can serve double-duty as a spot for kitchen visitors to sit.

- **Dining Room:** The open design between the dining and living rooms adds to the spacious feeling that the cathedral ceiling creates in this area.

- **Laundry Room:** This area opens from the kitchen for convenience.

- **Master Suite:** A walk-in closet makes this room practical, but the master bathroom with a skylight, dual-sink vanity, soaking tub, and separate shower makes it luxurious.

- **Bedrooms:** The two additional bedrooms share a bathroom.

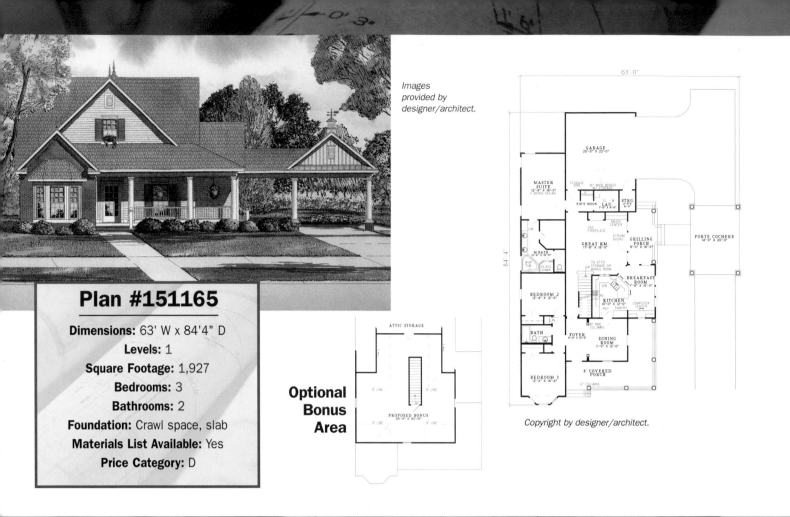

Images provided by designer/architect.

Plan #151165

Dimensions: 63' W x 84'4" D

Levels: 1

Square Footage: 1,927

Bedrooms: 3

Bathrooms: 2

Foundation: Crawl space, slab

Materials List Available: Yes

Price Category: D

Optional Bonus Area

Copyright by designer/architect.

Plan #151160

Dimensions: 65'4" W x 86'8" D

Levels: 1

Square Footage: 1,845

Bedrooms: 3

Bathrooms: 2

Foundation: Crawl space, slab

Materials List Available: Yes

Price Category: D

Images provided by designer/architect.

Optional Bonus Area

Copyright by designer/architect.

Plan #151164

Dimensions: 62'4" W x 83'6" D

Levels: 1

Square Footage: 1,848

Bedrooms: 3

Bathrooms: 2

Foundation: Crawl space, slab

Materials List Available: Yes

Price Category: D

Images provided by designer/architect.

Copyright by designer/architect.

Plan #151163

Dimensions: 63' W x 90' D

Levels: 1

Square Footage: 1,832

Bedrooms: 3

Bathrooms: 2

Foundation: Crawl space, slab

Materials List Available: Yes

Price Category: D

Images provided by designer/architect.

Optional Bonus Area

Copyright by designer/architect.

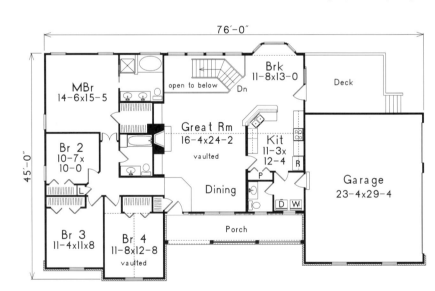

Plan #321006

Dimensions: 76' W x 45' D

Levels: 1, optional lower

Square Footage: 1,977

**Optional Basement Level
Sq. Ft.:** 1,416

Bedrooms: 4

Bathrooms: 2½

Foundation: Basement

Materials List Available: Yes

Price Category: D

Images provided by designer/architect.

This design is ideal if you're looking for a home with space to finish as your family and your budget grow.

Features:

- **Great Room:** A vaulted ceiling in this room sets an elegant tone that the gorgeous atrium windows pick up and amplify.

- **Atrium:** Elegance marks the staircase here that leads to the optional lower level.

- **Kitchen:** Both experienced cooks and beginners will appreciate the care that went into the design of this step-saving kitchen, with its ample counter space and generous cabinets.

- **Master Suite:** Enjoy the luxuries you'll find in this suite, and revel in the quiet that the bedroom can provide.

- **Lower Level:** Finish the 1,416 sq. ft. here to create a family room, two bedrooms, two bathrooms, and a study.

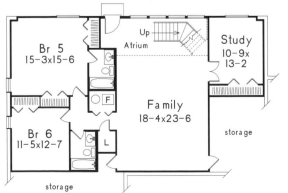

Optional Basement Level Floor Plan

Copyright by designer/architect.

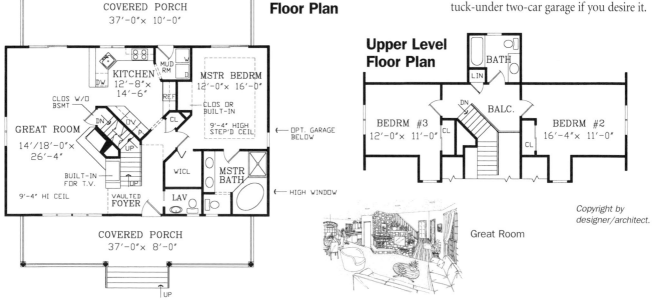

Plan #131041

Dimensions: 42' W x 45' D

Levels: 2

Square Footage: 1,679

Main Level Sq. Ft.: 1,134

Upper Level Sq. Ft.: 545

Bedrooms: 3

Bathrooms: 2½

Foundation: Crawl space, slab, or basement

Materials List Available: Yes

Price Category: D

This rustic-looking two-story cottage includes contemporary amenities for your total comfort.

Features:

- Great Room: With a 9-ft.-4-in.-high ceiling, this large room makes everyone feel at home. A fireplace with raised hearth and built-in niche for a TV will encourage the whole family to gather here on cool evenings, and sliding glass doors leading to the rear covered porch make it an ideal entertaining area in mild weather.

- Kitchen: When people aren't in the great room, you're likely to find them here, because the convenient serving bar welcomes casual dining, and this room also opens to the p porch.

- Master Suite: Relax at the end of the day in this room, with its 9-ft.-4-in.-high ceiling and walk-in closet, or luxuriate in the private bath with whirlpool tub and dual-sink vanity.

- Optional Basement: This area can include a tuck-under two-car garage if you desire it.

Main Level Floor Plan

COVERED PORCH 37'-0" x 10'-0"

UP

KITCHEN 12'-8" x 14'-6"

MUD RM

MSTR BEDRM 12'-0" x 16'-0"

CLOS W/O BSMT

CLOS OR BUILT-IN

9'-4" HIGH STEP'D CEIL

OPT. GARAGE BELOW

GREAT ROOM 14'/18'-0" x 26'-4"

DN

OV

CL

UP

BUILT-IN FOR T.V.

WICL

MSTR BATH

9'-4" HI CEIL

VAULTED FOYER

LAV

HIGH WINDOW

COVERED PORCH 37'-0" x 8'-0"

UP

Upper Level Floor Plan

BATH

LIN

DN

BALC.

BEDRM #3 12'-0" x 11'-0"

CL

BEDRM #2 16'-4" x 11'-0"

CL

UP

Copyright by designer/architect.

Great Room

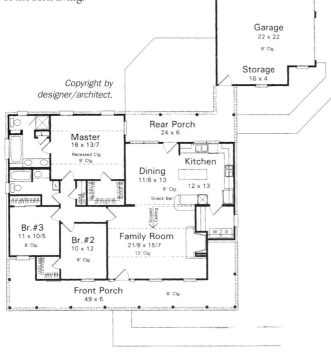

Plan #251004

Dimensions: 50'9" W x 42'1" D
Levels: 1
Square Footage: 1,500
Bedrooms: 3
Bathrooms: 2
Foundation: Crawl space, slab
Materials List Available: Yes
Price Category: C

Images provided by designer/architect.

Combine the old-fashioned appeal of a country farmhouse with all the comforts of modern living.

Features:

- Ceiling Height: 9 ft.
- Foyer: When guests enter this inviting foyer, they will be greeted by a view of the lovely family room.
- Family Room: Usher family and friends into this welcoming family room, where they can warm up in front of the fireplace. The room's 12-ft. ceiling enhances its sense of spaciousness.

- Kitchen: Gather around and keep the cook company at the snack bar in this roomy kitchen. There's still plenty of counter space for food preparation, thanks to the kitchen island.
- Master Bedroom: This elegant master bedroom features a large walk-in closet and a 9-ft. recessed ceiling.
- Master Bath. This master bath includes a double vanity, a tub, and a walk-in shower.
- Garage: This attached garage provides plenty of extra storage space, as well as parking for two cars.

Copyright by designer/architect.

SMARTtip

Shaker Style in Your Bathroom

This warm, likable style fits in perfectly with a country home because of its old-fashioned values. But it blends in well with contemporary interiors, too, because of its clean lines and plain geometric shapes. In fact, adding a few Shaker elements can warm up the sometimes cold look of a thoroughly modern room.

Images provided by designer/architect.

Plan #251005

Dimensions: 50' W x 44'2" D
Levels: 1
Square Footage: 1,631
Bedrooms: 3
Bathrooms: 2
Foundation: Basement
Materials List Available: Yes
Price Category: C

This elegant home features hip roof lines that will add appeal in any neighborhood.

Features:

- Ceiling Height: 9 ft.
- Front Porch: The porch stretches across the entire front of the home, offering plenty of space to sit and enjoy evening breezes.
- Family Room: This family room features a handsome fireplace and has plenty of room for all kinds of family activities.
- Dining Room: This dining room has plenty of room for dinner parties. After dinner, guests can step through French doors onto the rear deck.
- Kitchen: This kitchen is a pleasure in which to work. It features an angled snack bar with plenty of room for informal family meals.
- Master Bedroom: You'll enjoy retiring at day's end to this master bedroom, with its large walk-in closet.
- Master Bath. This master bath features a double vanity, a deluxe tub, and a walk-in shower.

SMARTtip

Victorian Style

Victorian, today, is a very romantic look. To underscore this, add the scent of lavender or some other dried flower to the room or use potpourri, which you can keep in a bowl on the vanity. Hang a fragrant pomander on a hook, display lavender soaps on a wall shelf, or tuck sachets between towels on a shelf. For an authentic touch, display a Victorian favorite, the spider plant.

Copyright by designer/architect.

Plan #151161

Dimensions: 63' W x 76' D

Levels: 1

Square Footage: 1,915

Bedrooms: 3

Bathrooms: 2

Foundation: Crawl space, slab

Materials List Available: Yes

Price Category: D

Images provided by designer/architect.

Copyright by designer/architect.

Plan #281020

Dimensions: 60' W x 48' D

Levels: 1

Square Footage: 1,734

Bedrooms: 3

Bathrooms: 2½

Foundation: Basement

Materials List Available: Yes

Price Category: C

Images provided by designer/architect.

Copyright by designer/architect.

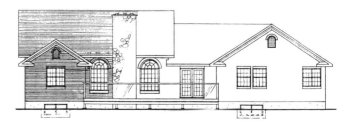

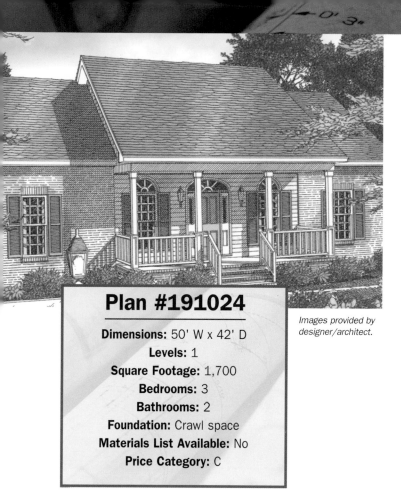

Plan #191024

Dimensions: 50' W x 42' D

Levels: 1

Square Footage: 1,700

Bedrooms: 3

Bathrooms: 2

Foundation: Crawl space

Materials List Available: No

Price Category: C

Images provided by designer/architect.

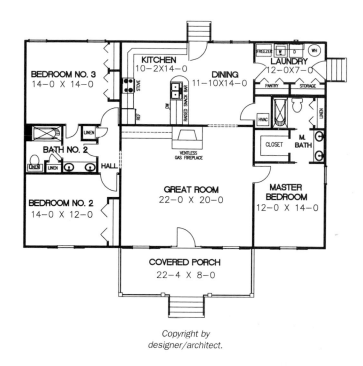

BEDROOM NO. 3
14-0 X 14-0

KITCHEN
10-2X14-0

DINING
11-10X14-0

LAUNDRY
12-0X7-0

FREEZER | W | D | WH

PANTRY | STORAGE

STOVE

RAISED SNACK BAR

DW

REF

HVAC

LINEN

CLOSET

M. BATH

LINEN

BATH NO. 2

LINEN | LINEN

HALL

VENTLESS GAS FIREPLACE

GREAT ROOM
22-0 X 20-0

MASTER BEDROOM
12-0 X 14-0

BEDROOM NO. 2
14-0 X 12-0

COVERED PORCH
22-4 X 8-0

Copyright by designer/architect.

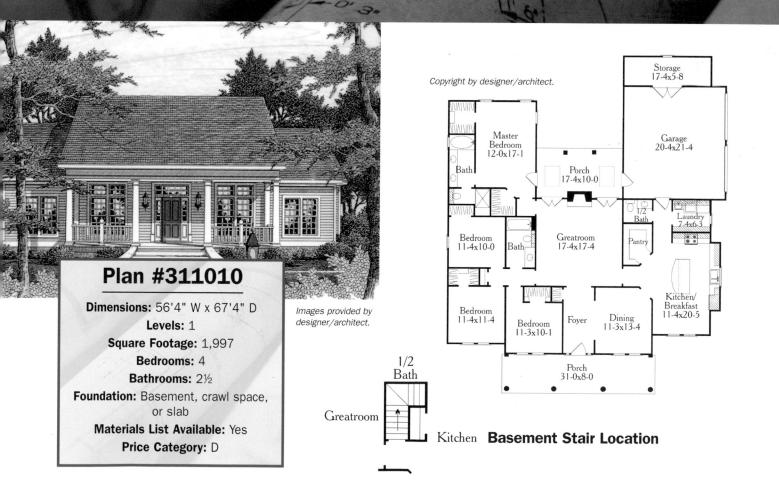

Plan #311010

Dimensions: 56'4" W x 67'4" D

Levels: 1

Square Footage: 1,997

Bedrooms: 4

Bathrooms: 2½

Foundation: Basement, crawl space, or slab

Materials List Available: Yes

Price Category: D

Images provided by designer/architect.

Copyright by designer/architect.

Storage
17-4x5-8

Master Bedroom
12-0x17-1

Garage
20-4x21-4

Bath

Porch
17-4x10-0

Bedroom
11-4x10-0

Bath

Greatroom
17-4x17-4

1/2 Bath

Laundry
7-4x6-3

Pantry

Kitchen/Breakfast
11-4x20-5

Bedroom
11-4x11-4

Bedroom
11-3x10-1

Foyer

Dining
11-3x13-4

Porch
31-0x8-0

1/2 Bath

Greatroom

Kitchen

Basement Stair Location

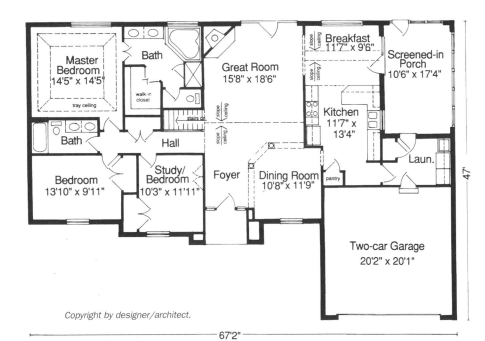

Plan #161001

Dimensions: 67'2" W x 47' D

Levels: 1

Square Footage: 1,782

Bedrooms: 3

Bathrooms: 2

Foundation: Basement

Materials List Available: Yes

Price Category: C

Images provided by designer/architect.

An all-brick exterior displays the solid strength that characterizes this gracious home.

Features:

- **Gathering Area:** A feeling of spaciousness permeates this gathering area, created by the foyer, great room, and dining room. Multiple windows provide natural light that dances along a sloped ceiling, spilling onto decorative columns and a fireplace.

- **Breakfast Area:** A continuation of the sloped ceiling leads to this breakfast area, where French doors open to a screened porch.

- **Kitchen:** An abundance of cabinets and counter space are the hallmarks of this large kitchen, with its easy access to a spacious laundry room and storage area.

- **Master Suite:** A tray ceiling and spacious walk-in closet in the master bedroom, along with a whirlpool tub and double-bowl vanity in the bathroom, enable you to pamper yourself.

Copyright by designer/architect.

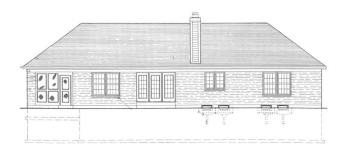

Rear Elevation

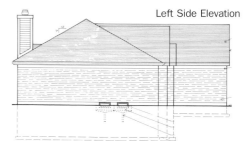

Left Side Elevation

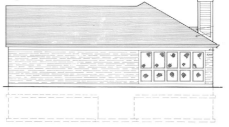

Right Side Elevation

Front View

Great Room / Foyer

Images provided by designer/architect.

Copyright by designer/architect.

Plan #311013

Dimensions: 66' W x 49'11" D

Levels: 1

Square Footage: 1,698

Bedrooms: 3

Bathrooms: 2

Foundation: Crawl space, slab, or basement

Materials List Available: Yes

Price Category: C

Basement Stair Location

Kitchen

Garage

Dining

Stor.

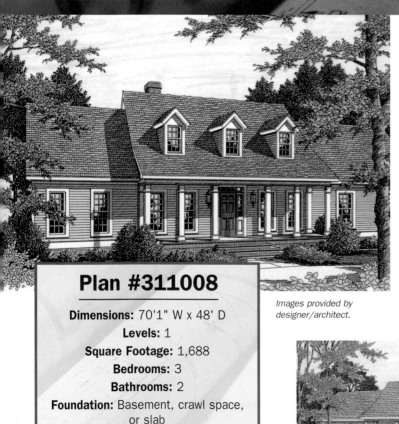

Plan #311008

Dimensions: 70'1" W x 48' D

Levels: 1

Square Footage: 1,688

Bedrooms: 3

Bathrooms: 2

Foundation: Basement, crawl space, or slab

Materials List Available: Yes

Price Category: C

Images provided by designer/architect.

Copyright by designer/architect.

Basement Stair Option

Laun. 8-6x5-6

Storage

Main Level Floor Plan

Copyright by designer/architect.

Family Dr
17-0 x 10-2

Gas FP

Great Room
14-0 x 16-6

Two-story high clg.

up

dw

Kitchen
13-4 x 11-0

F

P

br

Foyer

D

Laundry

Hall

dn

W

Pwdr Rm

Flex Room
(Dr, Study or Home Office)
11-0 x 14-10

Double Garage
21-0 x 20-6

Porch

Patio

Upper Level Floor Plan

Master Suite
16-6 x 14-0

Great Room Below

Ens

WIC

railing

Bath

dn

Study/Computer
14-0 x 9-6

Br 3
9-6 x 10-0

Br 2
10-0 x 9-6

Images provided by designer/architect.

Rear Elevation

Plan #281026

Dimensions: 40' W x 52' D

Levels: 2

Square Footage: 1,858

Main Level Sq. Ft.: 1,004

Upper Level Sq. Ft.: 854

Bedrooms: 3

Bathrooms: 2½

Foundation: Basement

Materials List Available: Yes

Price Category: D

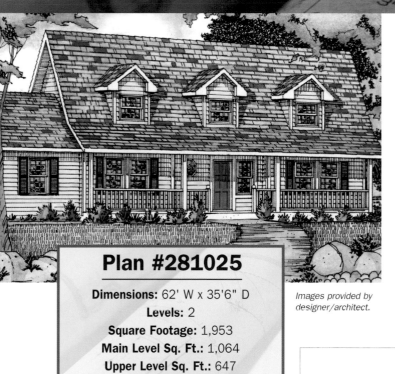

Main Level Floor Plan

Copyright by designer/architect.

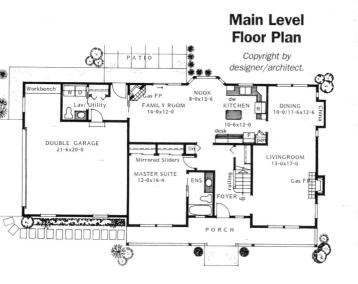

Workbench

W D

Gas FP

NOOK
8-0x13-6

dw

KITCHEN

Lav/Utility

FAMILY ROOM
14-0x12-0

10-6x12-0

DINING
10-0/11-6x12-6

China

DOUBLE GARAGE
21-6x20-0

desk

F

pan

Mirrored Sliders

lin

LIVINGROOM
13-0x17-0

MASTER SUITE
12-0x14-4

ENS

railing

FOYER

up

Gas FP

PORCH

PATIO

Upper Level Floor Plan

Attic Storage

lin

br

Hall

dn

BEDROOM #2
12-2x11-2

BATH

BEDROOM #3
13-0x11-2

twl

seat

seat

seat

Images provided by designer/architect.

Rear Elevation

Plan #281025

Dimensions: 62' W x 35'6" D

Levels: 2

Square Footage: 1,953

Main Level Sq. Ft.: 1,064

Upper Level Sq. Ft.: 647

Bedrooms: 3

Bathrooms: 2½

Foundation: Crawl space

Materials List Available: Yes

Price Category: D

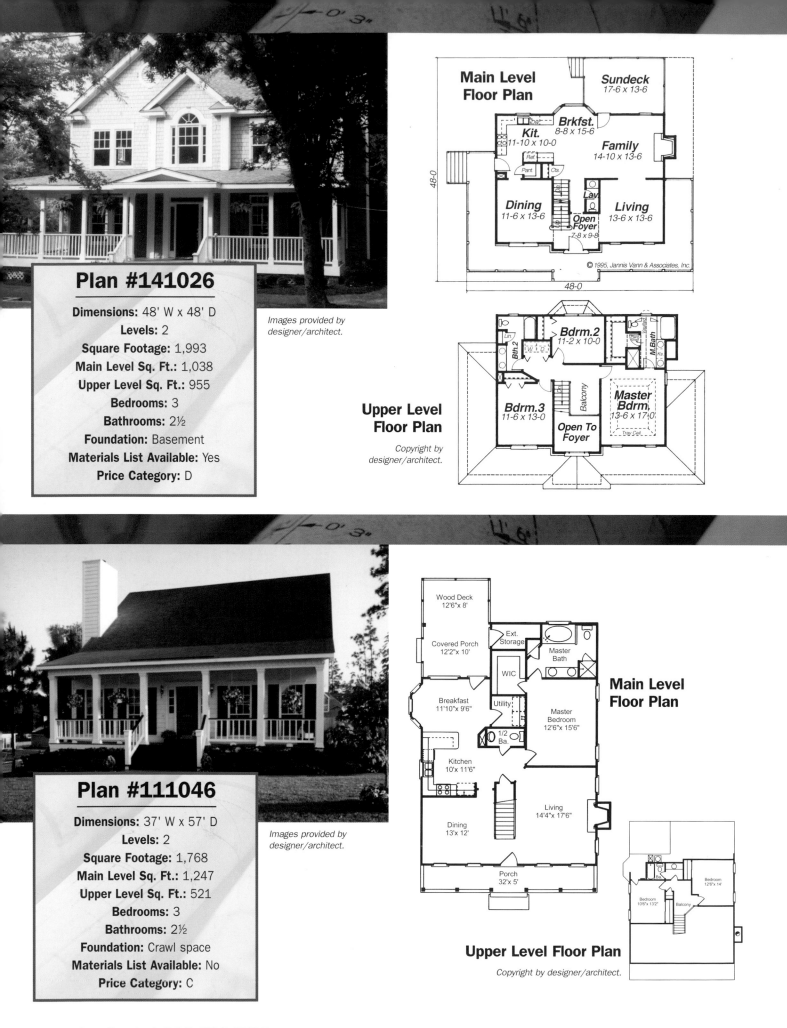

Main Level Floor Plan

Sundeck 17-6 x 13-6

Brkfst. 8-8 x 15-6

Kit. 11-10 x 10-0

Family 14-10 x 13-6

Dining 11-6 x 13-6

Living 13-6 x 13-6

Open Foyer 7-8 x 9-8

Lav

48-0

48-0

© 1995, Jannis Vann & Associates, Inc.

Upper Level Floor Plan

Bdrm.2 11-2 x 10-0

M.Bath

Bth.2

Bdrm.3 11-6 x 13-0

Balcony

Master Bdrm. 13-6 x 17-0

Open To Foyer

Copyright by designer/architect.

Plan #141026

Dimensions: 48' W x 48' D

Levels: 2

Square Footage: 1,993

Main Level Sq. Ft.: 1,038

Upper Level Sq. Ft.: 955

Bedrooms: 3

Bathrooms: 2½

Foundation: Basement

Materials List Available: Yes

Price Category: D

Images provided by designer/architect.

Wood Deck 12'6"x 8'

Covered Porch 12'2"x 10'

Ext. Storage

Master Bath

Breakfast 11'10"x 9'6"

WIC

Utility

Kitchen 10'x 11'6"

Master Bedroom 12'6"x 15'6"

1/2 Ba.

Dining 13'x 12'

Living 14'4"x 17'6"

Porch 32'x 5'

Main Level Floor Plan

Bedroom 12'6"x 14'

Bedroom 10'6"x 13'2"

Balcony

Upper Level Floor Plan

Copyright by designer/architect.

Plan #111046

Dimensions: 37' W x 57' D

Levels: 2

Square Footage: 1,768

Main Level Sq. Ft.: 1,247

Upper Level Sq. Ft.: 521

Bedrooms: 3

Bathrooms: 2½

Foundation: Crawl space

Materials List Available: No

Price Category: C

Images provided by designer/architect.

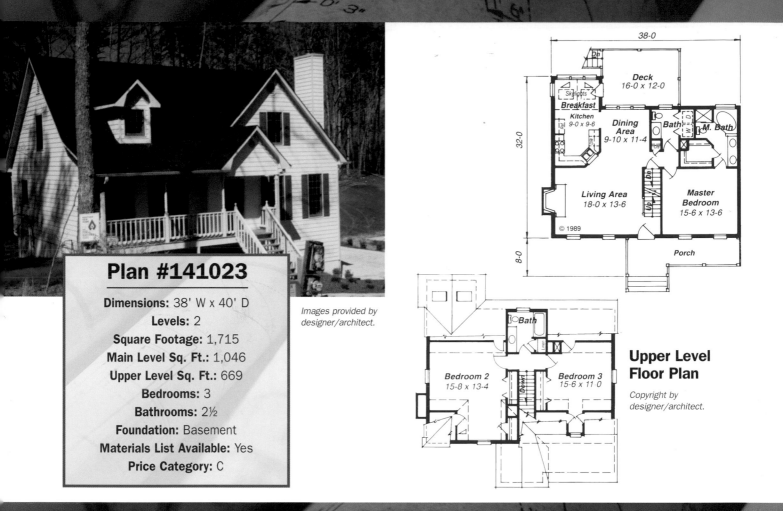

Plan #141023

Dimensions: 38' W x 40' D

Levels: 2

Square Footage: 1,715

Main Level Sq. Ft.: 1,046

Upper Level Sq. Ft.: 669

Bedrooms: 3

Bathrooms: 2½

Foundation: Basement

Materials List Available: Yes

Price Category: C

Images provided by designer/architect.

Upper Level Floor Plan

Copyright by designer/architect.

Plan #141024

Dimensions: 59' W x 46' D

Levels: 2

Square Footage: 1,732

Main Level Sq. Ft.: 1,128

Lower Level Sq. Ft.: 604

Bedrooms: 3

Bathrooms: 2½

Foundation: Basement

Materials List Available: Yes

Price Category: C

Images provided by designer/architect.

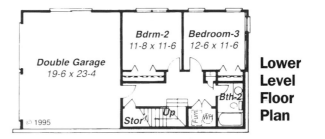

Lower Level Floor Plan

Copyright by designer/architect.

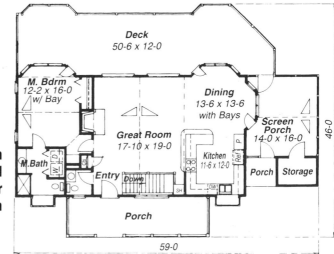

Main Level Floor Plan

Images provided by designer/architect.

Plan #251008

Dimensions: 44'4" W x 73'2" D

Levels: 2

Square Footage: 1,808

Main Level Sq. Ft.: 1,271

Upper Level Sq. Ft.: 537

Bedrooms: 3

Bathrooms: 2½

Foundation: Basement

Materials List Available: Yes

Price Category: D

An elegant front dormer adds distinction to this country home and brings light into the foyer.

Features:

• Ceiling Height: 9 ft. unless otherwise noted.

• Front Porch: A full-length front porch adds to the country charm and provides a relaxing place to sit.

• Foyer: This impressive foyer soars to two stories thanks to the front dormer.

• Dining Room: This dining room has ample space for entertaining. After dinner, guests can step out of the dining room directly onto the rear deck.

• Kitchen: This well-designed kitchen has a double sink. It features a snack bar with plenty of room for impromptu meals.

• Master Bedroom: This distinctive master bedroom features a large-walk-in closet.

• Master Bath: This master bath features walk-in closets in addition to a double vanity and a deluxe tub.

Copyright by designer/architect.

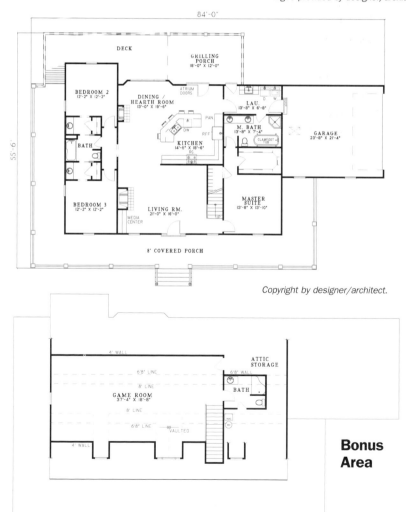

Images provided by designer/architect.

Plan #151089

Dimensions: 84' W x 55'6" D
Levels: 1
Square Footage: 1,921
Bedrooms: 3
Bathrooms: 3
Foundation: Crawl space, slab, or basement
Materials List Available: Yes
Price Category: D

If your family loves to combine indoor and outdoor living, this home's fabulous porches and deck space make it perfect.

Features:

- **Porches:** A huge wraparound front porch, sizable rear porch, and deck that joins them give you space for entertaining or simply lounging.

- **Living Room:** A fireplace and built-in media center could be the focal points in this large room.

- **Hearth Room:** Open to both the living room and kitchen, this hearth room also features a fireplace.

- **Kitchen:** This step-saving kitchen includes ample storage and work space, as well as an angled bar it shares with the hearth room. Atrium doors lead to the rear porch.

- **Bonus Upper Level:** A large game room and a full bath make this area a favorite with the children.

Copyright by designer/architect.

Bonus Area

Images provided by designer/architect.

Main Level Floor Plan

Upper Level Floor Plan

Copyright by designer/architect.

Plan #251007

Dimensions: 71' W x 42'6" D

Levels: 2

Square Footage: 1,597

Main Level Sq. Ft.: 982

Upper Level Sq. Ft.: 615

Bedrooms: 4

Bathrooms: 2½

Foundation: Basement

Materials List Available: Yes

Price Category: C

Images provided by designer/architect.

Main Level Floor Plan

Upper Level Floor Plan

Copyright by designer/architect.

Plan #251009

Dimensions: 57' W x 60' D

Levels: 2

Square Footage: 1,829

Main Level Sq. Ft.: 1,339

Upper Level Sq. Ft.: 490

Bedrooms: 4

Bathrooms: 2½

Foundation: Basement

Materials List Available: No

Price Category: D

Plan #201034

Dimensions: 66'10" W x 46'10" D

Levels: 1

Square Footage: 1,660

Bedrooms: 3

Bathrooms: 2

Foundation: Crawl space, slab, or basement

Materials List Available: Yes

Price Category: C

Images provided by designer/architect.

SMARTtip

Wall Frame Widths

Trim Tip: Depending on the room, widths of wall frames usually vary from wall to wall. This is okay as long as you keep variations as small as possible while trying to maintain dimensions close to the ideal 1:0.635 ratio of the Golden Rectangle. Doors and windows will dictate exceptions to the rule.

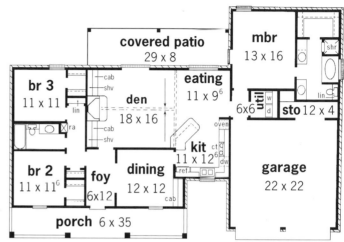

covered patio 29 x 8

mbr 13 x 16

br 3 11 x 11

den 18 x 16

eating 11 x 9⁶

util 6x6

sto 12 x 4

kit 11 x 12⁶

garage 22 x 22

br 2 11 x 11⁶

foy 6x12

dining 12 x 12

porch 6 x 35

Plan #201051

Dimensions: 58'10" W x 59'5" D

Levels: 1

Square Footage: 1,899

Bedrooms: 3

Bathrooms: 2

Foundation: Crawl space, slab, or basement

Materials List Available: Yes

Price Category: D

Images provided by designer/architect.

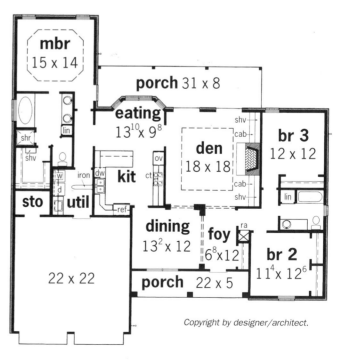

mbr 15 x 14

porch 31 x 8

eating 13¹⁰ x 9⁸

den 18 x 18

br 3 12 x 12

kit

sto

util

dining 13² x 12

foy 6⁸ x 12

br 2 11⁴ x 12⁶

22 x 22

porch 22 x 5

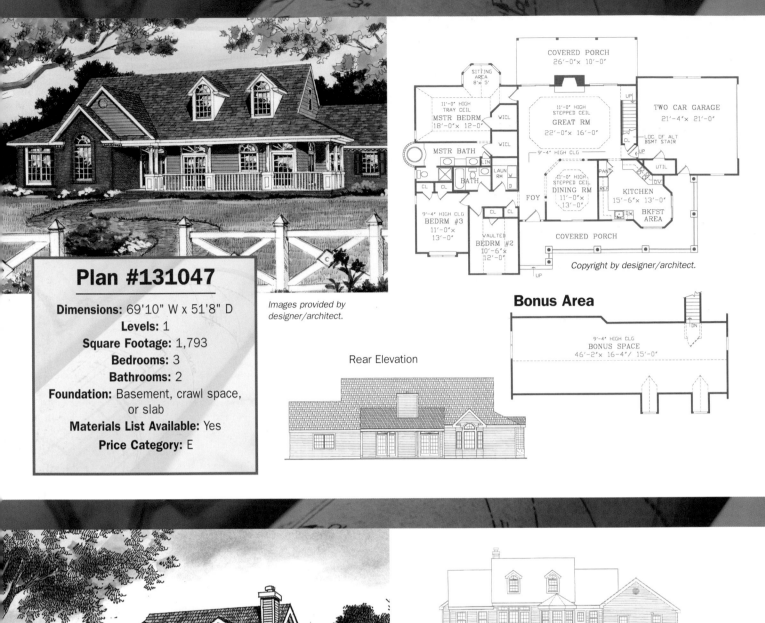

Plan #131047

Dimensions: 69'10" W x 51'8" D
Levels: 1
Square Footage: 1,793
Bedrooms: 3
Bathrooms: 2
Foundation: Basement, crawl space, or slab
Materials List Available: Yes
Price Category: E

Images provided by designer/architect.

Rear Elevation

Bonus Area

Copyright by designer/architect.

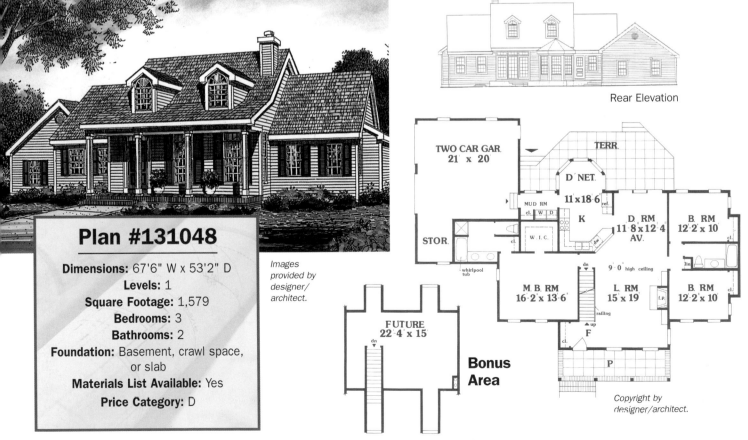

Plan #131048

Dimensions: 67'6" W x 53'2" D
Levels: 1
Square Footage: 1,579
Bedrooms: 3
Bathrooms: 2
Foundation: Basement, crawl space, or slab
Materials List Available: Yes
Price Category: D

Images provided by designer/architect.

Rear Elevation

Bonus Area

Copyright by designer/architect.

Plan #131002

Dimensions: 70'1" W x 60'7" D
Levels: 1
Square Footage: 1,709
Bedrooms: 3
Bathrooms: 2½
Foundation: Basement, crawl space, or slab
Materials List Available: Yes
Price Category: D

Images provided by designer/architect.

Copyright by designer/architect.

Rear View

You'll love the way this angled ranch brings out the best in a corner lot or on a slope.

Features:

Ceiling Height: 8 ft.

- Front Porch: Hang baskets of plants from the roof of this porch, which is just the right size for a couple of rockers and a side table.

- Dining Room: Well-placed windows flood this room with sunlight during the day and a built-in cabinet gives ample storage space for all your china, linens, and collectables.

- Foyer: Open to the great room, the foyer gives a lovely area to greet your visitors.

- Great Room: A built-in media center surrounds the fireplace where friends and family are sure to gather.

- Master Suite: You'll love the privacy of this somewhat isolated but easily accessed room. Decorate to show off the large bay window and tray ceiling, and enjoy the luxury of a compartmented bathroom.

Living Room

Plan #211069

Dimensions: 58' W x 42' D
Levels: 1½
Square Footage: 1,600
Main Level Sq. Ft.: 1,136
Upper Level Sq. Ft.: 464
Bedrooms: 3
Bathrooms: 2
Foundation: Crawl space
Materials List Available: Yes
Price Category: C

Images provided by designer/architect.

Enjoy the large front porch on this traditionally styled home when it's too sunny for the bugs, and use the screened back porch at dusk and dawn.

Features:

• Living Room: Call this the family room if you wish, but no matter what you call it, expect friends and family to gather here, especially when the fireplace gives welcome warmth.

• Kitchen: You'll love the practical layout that pleases everyone from gourmet chefs to beginning cooks.

• Master Suite: Positioned on the main floor to give it privacy, this suite has two entrances for convenience. You'll find a large walk-in closet here as well as a dressing room that includes a separate vanity and mirror makeup counter.

• Storage Space: The 462-sq.-ft. garage is roomy enough to hold two cars and still have space to store tools, out-of-season clothing, or whatever else that needs a dry, protected spot.

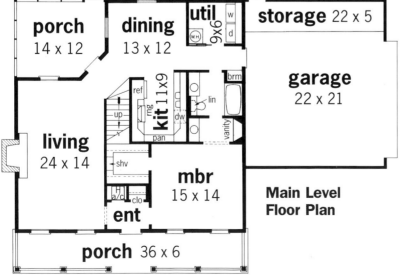

Main Level Floor Plan

Upper Level Floor Plan

Copyright by designer/architect.

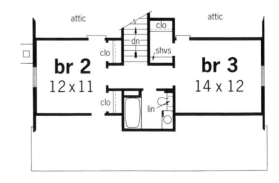

Plan #291001

Dimensions: 62'8" W x 38'4" D

Levels: 1

Square Footage: 1,550

Bedrooms: 3

Bathrooms: 2

Foundation: Basement

Materials List Available: No

Price Category: C

A handsome porch with Greek Revival details greets visitors to this Early-American style home.

Features:

- Ceiling Height: 8 ft. unless otherwise noted.

- Foyer: Upon entering this foyer you'll be struck by the space provided by the vaulted ceiling in the dining room, living room, and kitchen.

- Dining Room: This dining room is perfectly suited for formal dinner parties as well as less formal family meals.

- Decks: Two rear decks are conveniently accessible from the master bedroom, kitchen, and living room.

- Kitchen: You'll enjoy cooking in this well-designed kitchen, which features an eating area that is perfect for informal family meals.

- Master Bedroom: This master retreat is separated from the other bedrooms for additional privacy. It features an elegant vaulted ceiling and is graced with a dressing area, private bath, and walk-in closet.

Images provided by designer/architect.

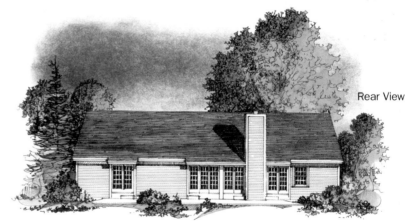

Rear View

Copyright by designer/architect.

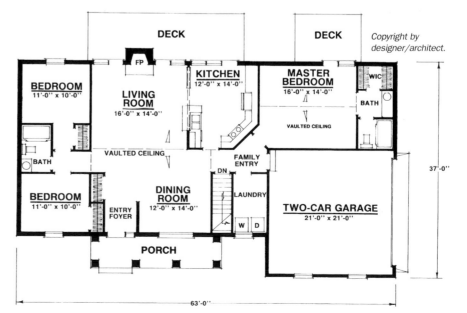

Images provided by designer/architect.

Plan #291002

Dimensions: 62'8" W x 38'4" D

Levels: 1

Square Footage: 1,550

Bedrooms: 3

Bathrooms: 2

Foundation: Basement

Materials List Available: No

Price Category: C

This comfortable Southwestern-style ranch house will fit perfectly into any setting.

Features:

- Ceiling Height: 8 ft. unless otherwise noted.

- Front Porch: This scalloped front porch offers plenty of room for enjoying a cool summer breeze.

- Foyer: Upon entering this impressive foyer you'll be greeted by a soaring space encompassing the living room and dining room.

- Living/Dining Area: This combined living room and dining room has a handsome fireplace as its focal point. When dinner is served, guests will flow casually into the dining area.

- Kitchen: Take your cooking up a notch in this terrific kitchen. It features a 42-in.-high counter that will do double-duty as a snack bar for family meals and a wet bar for entertaining.

- Master Suite: This master retreat is separated from the other bedrooms and features an elegant vaulted ceiling. The dressing area has a compartmentalized bath and a walk-in closet.

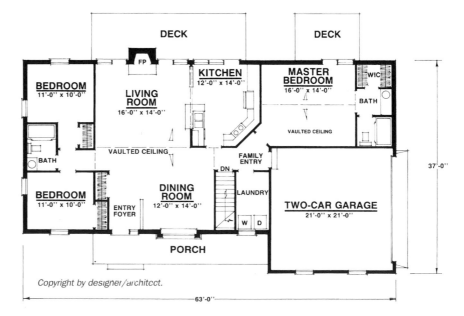

Rear View

Copyright by designer/architect.

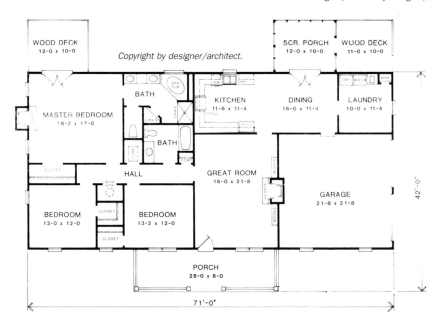

Plan #301005

Dimensions: 71' W x 42' D

Levels: 1

Square Footage: 1,930

Bedrooms: 3

Bathrooms: 2

Foundation: Crawl space, slab

Materials List Available: Yes

Price Category: D

This home features an old-fashioned rocking-chair porch that enhances the streetscape.

Features:

- Ceiling Height: 8 ft.

- Dining Room: When the weather is warm, guests can step through French doors from this elegant dining room and enjoy a breeze on the rear screened porch.

- Family Room: This family room is a warm and inviting place to gather, with its handsome fireplace and built-in bookcases.

- Kitchen: This kitchen offers plenty of counter space for preparing your favorite recipes. Its U-shape creates a convenient open traffic pattern.

- Master Suite: You'll look forward to retiring at the end of the day in this truly luxurious master suite. The bedroom has a fireplace and opens through French doors to a private rear deck. The bath features a corner spa tub, a walk-in shower, double vanities, and a linen closet.

SMARTtip

Light With Shutters

For the maximum the amount of light coming through shutters, use the largest panel possible on the window. Make sure the shutters have the same number of louvers per panel so that all of the windows in the room look unified. However, don't choose a panel that is over 48 inches high, because the shutter becomes unwieldy. Also, any window that is wider than 96 inches requires extra framing to support the shutters.

Plan #151016

Dimensions: 60'2" W x 39'10" D
Levels: 2
Square Footage: 1,783;
2,107 with bonus
Main Level Sq. Ft.: 1,124
Upper Level Sq. Ft.: 659
Bonus Room Sq. Ft.: 324
Bedrooms: 3
Bathrooms: 2½
Foundation: Basement, crawl space,
or slab
Price Category: C

Images provided by designer/architect.

An open design characterizes this spacious home built for family life and entertaining.

Features:

- **Great Room:** Enjoy the fireplace in this spacious, versatile room.

- **Dining Room:** Entertaining is easy, thanks to the open design with the kitchen.

- **Master Suite:** Luxury surrounds you in this suite, with its large walk-in closet, double vanities, and a bathroom with a whirlpool tub and separate shower.

- **Upper Bedrooms:** Window seats make wonderful spots for reading or relaxing, and a nook between the windows of these rooms is a ready-made play area.

- **Bonus Area:** Located over the garage, this space could be converted to a home office, a studio, or a game room for the kids.

- **Attic:** There's plenty of storage space here.

Main Level Floor Plan

Copyright by designer/architect.

Upper Level Floor Plan

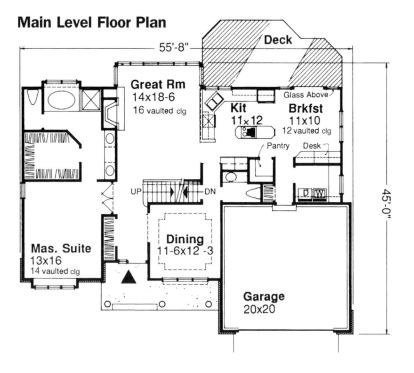

Plan #271030

Dimensions: 56' W x 45' D
Levels: 2
Square Footage: 1,926
Main Level Sq. Ft.: 1,490
Upper Level Sq. Ft.: 436
Bedrooms: 3
Bathrooms: 2½
Foundation: Basement
Materials List Available: Yes
Price Category: D

Images provided by designer/architect.

This traditional home's main-floor master suite is hard to resist, with its inviting window seat and delightful bath.

Features:

• Master Suite: Just off from the entry foyer, this luxurious oasis is entered through double doors, and offers an airy vaulted ceiling, plus a private bath that includes a separate tub and shower, dual-sink vanity, and walk-in closet.

• Great Room: This space does it all in style, with a breathtaking wall of windows and a charming fireplace.

• Kitchen: A cooktop island makes dinnertime tasks a breeze. You'll also love the roomy pantry. The adjoining breakfast room, with its deck access and built-in desk, is sure to be a popular hangout for the teens.

• Secondary Bedrooms: Two additional bedrooms reside on the upper floor and allow the younger family members a measure of desired—and necessary—privacy.

Main Level Floor Plan

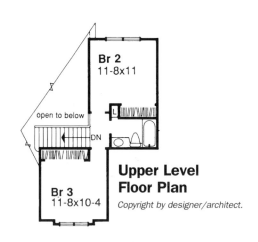

Upper Level Floor Plan
Copyright by designer/architect.

Plan #111043

Dimensions: 42' W x 49' D

Levels: 2

Square Footage: 1,737

Main Level Sq. Ft.: 1,238

Upper Level Sq. Ft.: 499

Bedrooms: 3

Bathrooms: 2½

Foundation: Crawl space

Materials List Available: No

Price Category: C

Images provided by designer/architect.

Main Level Floor Plan

Patio

Breakfast 8'10"x 11'5"

Utility

Living 20'6"x 14'

Kitchen 11'6"x 10'8"

WIC   Dressing   Ba.

1/2 Ba.

Dining 11'6"x 13'

Bedroom 16'6"x 13'6"

Porch 36'x 5'

Upper Level Floor Plan

Attic Storage

Open To Below

Bedroom 11'6"x10'

Balcony

Bath

Bedroom 11'6"x 11'4"

Attic Storage

Copyright by designer/architect.

Plan #111045

Dimensions: 41' W x 50' D

Levels: 2

Square Footage: 1,880

Main Level Sq. Ft.: 1,244

Upper Level Sq. Ft.: 636

Bedrooms: 3

Bathrooms: 2½

Foundation: Slab

Materials List Available: No

Price Category: D

Images provided by designer/architect.

Main Level Floor Plan

Deck

Bedroom 12'6"x 15'

Living 14'6"x 17'6"

Breakfast 9'8"x 10'6"

WIC

Kitch. 9'8"x 11'1"

Foyer

Dining 10'8"x 12'

Porch

Upper Level Floor Plan

Open to Below

Bedroom 12'6"x 11"

Balcony

Bedroom 10'6"x 10'9"

Copyright by designer/architect.

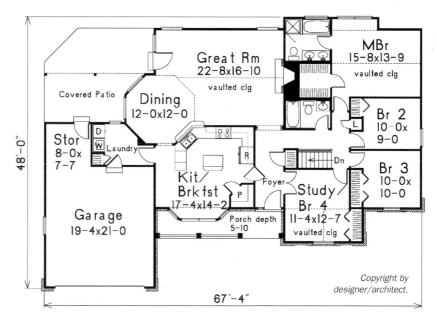

Plan #321003

Dimensions: 67'4" W x 48' D

Levels: 1

Square Footage: 1,791

Bedrooms: 4

Bathrooms: 2

Foundation: Basement

Materials List Available: Yes

Price Category: C

Images provided by designer/architect.

The traditional good looks of the exterior of this home are complemented by the stunning contemporary design of the interior.

Features:

- **Great Room:** With a vaulted ceiling to highlight its spacious dimensions, this room is certain to be the central gathering spot for friends and family.

- **Dining Room:** Also with a vaulted ceiling, this room has an octagonal shape for added interest. Windows here and in the great room look out to the covered patio.

- **Kitchen:** A center island gives a convenient work space in this well-designed kitchen, which features a pass-through to the dining room for easy serving, and large, walk-in pantry for storage.

- **Breakfast Room:** A bay window lets sunshine pour in to start your morning with a smile.

- **Master Bedroom:** A vaulted ceiling and a sitting area make you feel truly pampered in this room.

SMARTtip

Bay & Bow Windows

Occasionally too little room exists between the window frame (if there is one) and the ceiling. In this situation you might be able to use ceiling-mounted hardware. Alternatively, a cornice across the top and a rod mounted inside the cornice will give you the dual benefit of visually lowering the top of the window and concealing the hardware.

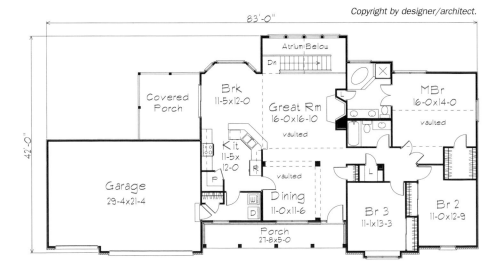

Plan #321001

Dimensions: 83' W x 42' D

Levels: 1

Square Footage: 1,721

Bedrooms: 3

Bathrooms: 2

Foundation: Basement, crawl space, or slab

Materials List Available: Yes

Price Category: C

Images provided by designer/architect.

You'll love the atrium that creates a warm, naturally lit space inside this gracious home, as well as the roof dormers that give it wonderful curb appeal from the outside.

Features:

- **Great Room:** Bathed in light from the atrium window wall, this room, with its vaulted ceiling, will be the hub of your family life.

- **Dining Room:** This room also has a vaulted ceiling and is lit by the atrium, but you can draw drapes at night to create a cozy, warm feeling.

- **Kitchen:** Designed for functionality, this step-saving kitchen is easy to organize and makes cooking a pleasure.

- **Breakfast Room:** For convenience, this room is located between the kitchen and the rear covered porch.

- **Master Suite:** Retire with pleasure to this lovely retreat, with its luxurious bath.

Rear View

Copyright by designer/architect.

Plan #131043

Dimensions: 65'8" W x 43'10" D
Levels: 2
Square Footage: 1,945
Main Level Sq. Ft.: 1,375
Upper Level Sq. Ft.: 570
Bedrooms: 3
Bathrooms: 2½
Foundation: Crawl space, slab, or basement
Materials List Available: Yes
Price Category: E

Images provided by designer/architect.

This home will delight you with its three dormers and half-round transom windows, which give a nostalgic appearance, and its amenities and conveniences that are certainly contemporary.

Features:

- Porch: This covered porch forms the entryway.
- Great Room: Enjoy the fireplace in this large, comfortable room, which is open to the dining area. A French door here leads to the

covered porch at the rear of the house.

- Kitchen: This large, country-style kitchen has a bayed nook, and oversized breakfast bar, and pass-through to the rear porch to simplify serving and make entertaining a pleasure.
- Master Suite: A tray ceiling sets an elegant tone for this room, and the bay window adds to it. The large walk in closet is convenient, and the bath is sumptuous.
- Bedrooms: These comfortable rooms have convenient access to a bath.

Main Level Floor Plan

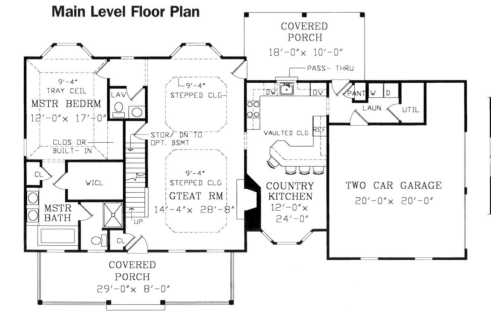

Upper Level Floor Plan

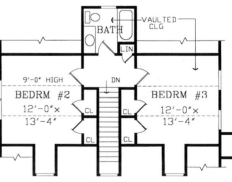

Copyright by designer/architect.

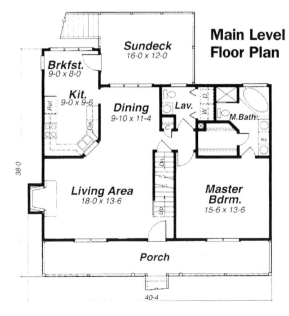

Plan #141038

Dimensions: 40'4" W x 38' D

Levels: 2

Square Footage: 1,668

Main Level Sq. Ft.: 1,057

Upper Level Sq. Ft.: 611

Bedrooms: 3

Bathrooms: 2½

Foundation: Basement with drive-under garage

Materials List Available: No

Price Category: C

Images provided by designer/architect.

If you're looking for the ideal plan for a sloping site, this could be the home of your dreams.

Features:

- Porch: Set a couple of rockers on this large porch so you can enjoy the evening views.
- Living Room: A handsome fireplace makes a lovely focal point in this large room.
- Dining Room: Three large windows over looking the sundeck flood this room with natural light.
- Kitchen: The U-shaped, step-saving layout makes this kitchen a cook's dream.
- Breakfast Room: With an expansive window area and a door to the sundeck, this room is sure to be a family favorite in any season of the year.
- Master Suite: A large walk-in closet and a private bath with tub, shower, and double vanity complement this suite's spacious bedroom.

Main Level Floor Plan

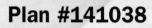

Upper Level Floor Plan

Copyright by designer/architect.

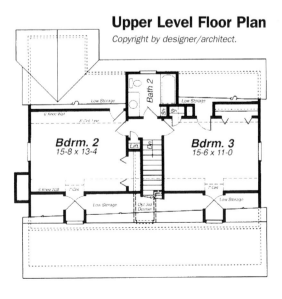

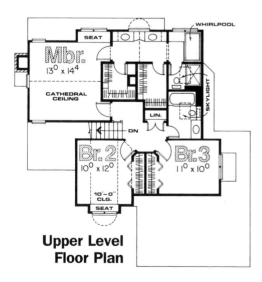

Plan #121094

Dimensions: 40'8" W x 46' D
Levels: 2
Square Footage: 1,768
Main Level Sq. Ft.: 905
Upper Level Sq. Ft.: 863
Bedrooms: 3
Bathrooms: 2½
Foundation: Basement
Materials List Available: Yes
Price Category: C

Images provided by designer/architect.

You'll love this design if you're looking for a home to complement a site with a lovely rear view.

Features:

- **Great Room:** A trio of lovely windows looks out to the front entry of this home. The French doors in this room open to the breakfast area for everyone's convenience.

- **Kitchen:** Designed to suit a gourmet cook, this kitchen includes a roomy pantry and an island with a snack bar.

- **Breakfast Area:** The boxed window here is perfect for houseplants or a collection of culinary herbs. A door leads to the rear porch, where you'll love to dine in good weather.

- **Master Suite:** On the upper level, the bedroom features a cathedral ceiling, two walk-in closets, and a window seat. The bath also has a cathedral ceiling and includes dual lavatories, a large dressing area, and a sunlit whirlpool tub.

Main Level Floor Plan

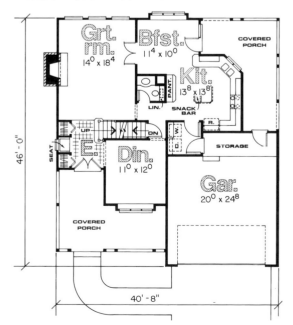

Upper Level Floor Plan

Copyright by designer/architect.

Country Crafting

The expression, "the kitchen is the heart of the house," is repeated often because it's true. Even when you plan to entertain your guests in the living room, where does everyone always end up? And where do you sit with your closest pals to chat over a cup of tea? Where do the kids do their homework? That's right, it's the kitchen, a room that's a magnet of hospitality, comfort, and warmth—and the source of the wonderful aroma of good food.

So why not enhance the welcoming ambiance with a kitchen decorating theme gathered around the bountiful fruits of the harvest? The bold shapes and bright hues of vegetables and fruits inspired these easy crafts projects. You'll notice that a warm palette was chosen for the base coat of most of the accessories to underscore the theme. A checkerboard pattern repeated throughout adds a strong visual element and serves as a cohesive component to tie all of the projects together.

Carrots, cabbage, and celery depicted in a novelty wallcovering of robust vegetables provide images for a trio of stools, pictured here. You can purchase inexpensive unfinished pine versions and treat them with an easy-to-paint gingham-check technique, on pages 160-161. After enlarging the vegetable motifs at a copy shop, just apply them to the seats and finish them with several coats of sealer so that they will be sure to stand up to all the use they are bound to get. When you're finished, compare the stools to similar versions in pricey catalogs; you'll be delighted with the savings.

Another practical and pretty project is the wooden tool caddy transformed by paint and stencils into a handy tabletop container. The easy instructions are on page 166.

Coordinating stencils extend the harvest theme to a hinged bread box, on pages 162–164, and a painted wall shelf and tiles on page 167.

Easy crafts projects that are doable in a weekend let you add personal style to your kitchen. These pages show how.

Primers, paints, and glazes

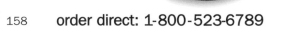

Vegetable Stools

Materials

- 3 unfinished wooden kitchen stools
- Latex paint in Linen White
- Acrylic craft paint in Sterling Green, Poppy Red, and Mystic Green
- Decoupage medium
- Vegetable-print motifs from wallpaper or decorative paper
- Flat foam paintbrushes
- Sandpaper and tack cloth
- Masking or painter's tape
- Craft knife
- Ruler or straightedge
- Sponge, natural or cellulose
- Pencil
- Cardboard tube from paper towel roll
- Sealer

Sand the kitchen stools to create a smooth surface, and wipe them with a tack cloth. After priming the stools, paint them entirely with two coats of the Linen White paint. Let the paint dry. Then follow the easy directions for painting stripes and plaid on the next page. It's as simple as masking with tape and applying acrylic paint over the unmasked areas.

For the vegetables, all you have to do is cut out the designs, which you can get from wallpaper or fabric samples. Play with them on the seats until you get the arrangement to your liking, then mark their placement with a chalk pencil.

When you're ready to apply the motifs, coat the reverse side of each cutout with decoupage medium, working on one piece at a time. Place them on the seat. Smooth

Cute as a button, these kitchen stools are inexpensive, easy to paint yourself, and look like costly boutique designs.

them down with your fingertips, and work out any air bubbles. Burnish the edges with your fingernail. When the design is complete, re-apply decoupage medium.

To create a scalloped border, pour a small amount of the Linen White paint onto a paper plate. Dip half of one end of a cardboard tube into the paint. Using the photo above as a guide and the tube as a stamp, transfer the paint to the stools, working the design all the way around each seat top. When the paint is dry, apply two or more coats of sealer.

Masking tape and painter's tapes

PAINTING STRIPES AND PLAID

Apply two base coats, and allow them to dry. The success of this technique depends largely on what you do before you begin to paint it. Measure the surface of the project, and then divide it into evenly distributed stripes. Mark their placement with a chalk pencil; then run a strip of masking tape along the outside edge of each one. To make the job easier, use masking tape that is the same width as the stripes, if possible. Smooth the tape down and burnish the edges with your fingers to secure it in place. Use a small piece of sponge or a foam brush to pull the paint over the unmasked area **(step 1)**. When the paint is thoroughly dry, remove the tape. Voilà, stripes! Creating a plaid design entails an additional step. Working perpendicular to the stripes you have just painted, mark new ones that can be the same or a different width as the originals. After masking the outside edges, paint the new stripes, which will intersect the first ones to form a crossbarred design **(step 2)**. Use the same color paint or a contrasting one. When the new paint dries thoroughly, remove the tape **(step 3)**.

STEP 1

After carefully measuring and masking, use a sponge or a foam brush to paint stripes.

STEP 2

Paint new stripes across the first ones to create a crossbarred pattern. Use the same color and stripe width for a checked plaid or various colors and widths for a traditional tartan look.

STEP 3

After the paint is completely dry, remove the tape. You can touch up any uneven edges with a fine artist's brush, or leave them as is.

How can you create a Country kitchen look? The key to a Country kitchen is coziness and a down-to-earth sensibility. This is easy to attain with wood floors and cabinets either left natural or painted and distressed. Besides the traditional American Country classic, there's the cheerful look of Vintage style, which uses graphic patterns and colors from the 1930s, '40s, and '50s. Old linens, Fiestaware, and retro appliances pull the look together. French, Italian, and English Country styles offer another approach for those with a taste for something different.

Bread Box

Sand the bread box to create a smooth surface, and wipe it with a tack cloth. Mask the hinges, and then prime the box. When the primer is dry, apply two coats of Lemon Custard paint. Let it dry.

Following the directions, on the next page, for Dragging, apply the technique using the Sunflower glaze. Let it dry.

Transfer the fruit motif to the bread box using the acrylic paints and following the directions for Hand Painting from a Stencil, on page 164. You can find a copy of the template on page 169. Refer to the photo, left, as a guide for positioning it.

To create the checkerboard pattern, use a small square foam stamp or cut a small square from a clean kitchen sponge, and apply the pattern along the edge of the box with Burnt Sienna paint. Finish with two or more coats of sealer.

A painted bread box adds a cheerful accent to this a granite countertop in a new country kitchen.

Materials

- Unfinished wooden hinged-lid bread box
- All-purpose primer
- Acrylic craft paint in Purple, Crimson, Poetry Green, Lemon Custard, Harvest Gold, Sunny Yellow, and Burnt Sienna
- Decorator glaze in Sunflower
- Fruit border stencil
- Small foam sponge
- Artist's brushes: #3 round and ½-inch flat
- Dragging brush
- Flat foam paintbrushes
- Pencil
- Sandpaper and tack cloth
- Sealer

Plastic combs

How can you give your kitchen your own "style stamp"? You don't need a big budget or professional assistance to add style to your kitchen. Because most kitchens get more use than any other room, they need frequent sprucing up, which gives you plenty of opportunity. Even with regular cleaning, kitchen surfaces get caked with grease, which attracts dust and grime after just a few years of normal living. While it's impractical to do a complete overhaul every few years, it's easy to make relatively simple changes. New paint, wallpaper, cabinet hardware, and window treatments can add a refreshing face to a kitchen at an affordable price.

DRAGGING

Paint the surface with two coats of the base color, and allow it to dry. Because the dragging technique must be worked on wet glaze, it is a good idea to work in small sections if the overall surface is large. With that in mind, apply one coat of the glaze **(step 1)**. Hold the handle of the dragging brush at a 45-degree angle above the surface, and pull the bristles through the glaze toward you **(step 2)**. (For larger surfaces, you can use a good-quality, stiff-bristled whisk broom.) Drag the brush slowly and steadily, making one uninterrupted pass. Continue onto the next section, overlapping with the wet edge of the previous one so as not to create a distinct break in the finish. The lines you make do not have to be perfectly straight. The charm of the technique is that it is supposed to look as if it was done by hand. Usually, the lines are vertical, but they can be horizontal, diagonal, or curved, as well. Make them fine or bold. Create combed, plaited, or crosshatched patterns. For success, the dragging brush must remain relatively dry at all times. When it starts to collect paint, wash and dry it before continuing.

STEP 1

After the base coat dries thoroughly, apply one coat of glaze over the surface.

STEP 2

Hold the handle of the dragging brush at a 45-degree angle above the surface, and pull the bristles through the wet glaze toward you.

HAND PAINTING FROM A STENCIL

Paint the object or surface in any desired finish coat, and allow it to dry. Position the stencil on the surface to be decorated using spray adhesive to hold it in place. For extra support, tape it down. Using a pencil, trace the outlines of the stencil's shapes **(step 1)**. Once you've traced the entire design, remove the stencil template. Even though you will not paint the design entirely freehand, it's a good idea to practice on a board before attempting the real thing.

This way, you can make brush strokes and create shading with confidence later.

Using artist's flat and round paintbrushes and the colors of your choice, fill in the outlined areas of the motif **(step 2)**. Double- or triple-load a flat paintbrush with different shades of color to add dimension. Use a stencil brush and a small amount of paint to create texture or a blush of color.

STEP 1

After mounting the stencil, trace the outlines of the design onto the object or surface you wish to paint.

STEP 2

Use an artist's brush to create shading on your design. This will give your work a professional appearance.

MAKING YOUR OWN STENCIL

Trace or photocopy the image you want to stencil, reducing or enlarging as needed. Spray the back of the paper with the image on it with spray adhesive, and adhere it to the stencil paper. Place stencil paper and the design on a clean, level surface, and cut out the design using a sharp craft knife. If you make a mistake, don't attempt to cut the same line again. Cut a new line to ensure clean, even edges. Move the stencil around as you cut, so you are always cutting at an angle that gives you the most control over the blade.

Where to Go for Inspiration

Museums and restored historic homes often contain beautiful examples of furniture and accessories that have been decorated with traditional paint techniques. Even if there's a "No Touching Allowed" policy, to actually see the authentic pieces in person is exciting and an education in itself. Remember that most of the antique examples you'll see in such places were painted and decorated with pigments and materials that are no longer available and that time has added a luster and patina newer examples just can't completely reproduce.

Antique and interior-design shops can also provide an instant education. High-end antique stores often feature fine examples of painted furniture that you can study up close. And many of today's design shops carry professionally decorated newer pieces that, while they might seem intimidating to recreate for the novice, can also be immensely inspiring.

Craft shows and boutiques usually feature some contemporary furniture makers that have mastered one or many finishing techniques. Again, the level of expertise might be way beyond what you even aspire to, but it is another good way to see what is in fashion. Sometimes you can get great

A pretty wallpaper pattern can be the starting point for your project.

ideas for using color or combining techniques just by looking at what other people have done.

With the renaissance of painted finishes that is occurring all over the world today, classes and seminars are popping up everywhere. Many classes aren't expensive to attend, either, especially if you are just looking for a basic course to get you started. Check out the course listings at local art schools or at the high schools in your area, or inquire about courses at your neighborhood craft shop.

Silverware Caddy

You don't have to have an old wooden tool caddy for your project. In fact, it's easier to work with a new, unfinished version, which you can purchase at a craft shop. Either way, make sure the wood is dirt-free, but go over the edges with sandpaper to create a slightly distressed vintage appearance.

Next, apply two coats of the Buttercream paint to both the outside and interior sections of the caddy. Let the paint dry.

Apply a small checkerboard pattern along the sides and handle using the Harvest Gold paint and a small foam stamp or a square cut from a clean kitchen sponge. Stencil the fruit motif using the red and green paints and the templates that are on page 168. With an artist's brush, apply a thin green line freehand along the edges of the handle. Finish the project with two coats of sealer.

A country-inspired silverware caddy is perfect for toting utensils and napkins outdoors to the picnic table.

Materials

- Unfinished wooden tool caddy
- Acrylic craft paint in Crimson, Buttercream, Poetry Green, Red Orange, and Harvest Gold
- Fruit stencils
- Foam sponges
- Flat foam paintbrushes
- Sandpaper and tack cloth
- Pencil
- Artist's liner brush
- Sealer

How can you add warmth to a Contemporary style kitchen in an otherwise Country home? Clean modern materials, such as stainless steel, cast concrete, and granite, are ideally suited to kitchen surfaces because they're so hard-wearing. However, they can make a kitchen appear cold. To avoid a sterile feeling in a Contemporary kitchen, counterbalance these sleek materials with wood and color. Even if your prefer a neutral color scheme, choose a warm shade, one with a slightly yellow cast.

Three-Tile Shelf

Materials

- Unfinished wooden what-not shelf
- 3 Off-White ceramic tiles, 4¼-inch square
- Acrylic craft paint in French Vanilla, Crimson, Caramel, Butter-crunch, Buttercup, and Burnt Sienna
- Fruit stencils
- Small foam block stamp
- Spray adhesive
- ⅜-inch stencil brush
- Tile surface cleaner and conditioner
- Acrylic ceramic-tile paint sets in assorted colors
- Clear satin-finish tile glaze
- Stippling paintbrush
- Tile adhesive
- Sandpaper and tack cloth
- Clean, lint-free cloth
- Paint palette
- Sealer

Stencil Brushes

Sand the shelf, and then wipe it with a tack cloth. Apply two coats of Buttercrunch paint. Let it dry.

Pour a small amount of each of the remaining acrylic paints into a paint palette. Dip the stippling brush into the paints, and dab lightly on a paper towel to remove excess paint. Lightly pounce the brush up and down on all sides of the shelf to create a fine-textured, multicolored surface, allowing the base coat to show through. Allow the paint to dry. Create a small checkered pattern all along the edges of the shelf using the Burnt Sienna paint and a small square foam stample or a small square cut from a clean kitchen sponge.

Next, go over the tiles with surface cleaner and a lint-free cloth. Make sure the tiles are dry. Then, using Yellow ceramic paint

Use this adorable shelf to store spices or small kitchen collectibles.

and a clean foam stamp or small square from a kitchen sponge, apply a checkered border along the edges of each tile.

Place a fruit template from page 168 in the center of each tile, and secure it in place with spray adhesive. Stencil a different fruit on each tile. Lightly dab a sponge with a bit of contrasting color onto each fruit. Apply lighter colors toward the center of the fruit. Paint the tiles with two or more coats of the glaze. Coat the tiles with sealer. When sealer dries, glue the tiles in place on the back of the shelf with the tile adhesive. Make sure to evenly space them.

Patterns

Follow the directions for Making Your Own Stencil (page 164), using these patterns as a guide. Enlarge or reduce these images on a copier to make them the correct scale for your project. You can also purchase ready-made stencils from a crafts store.

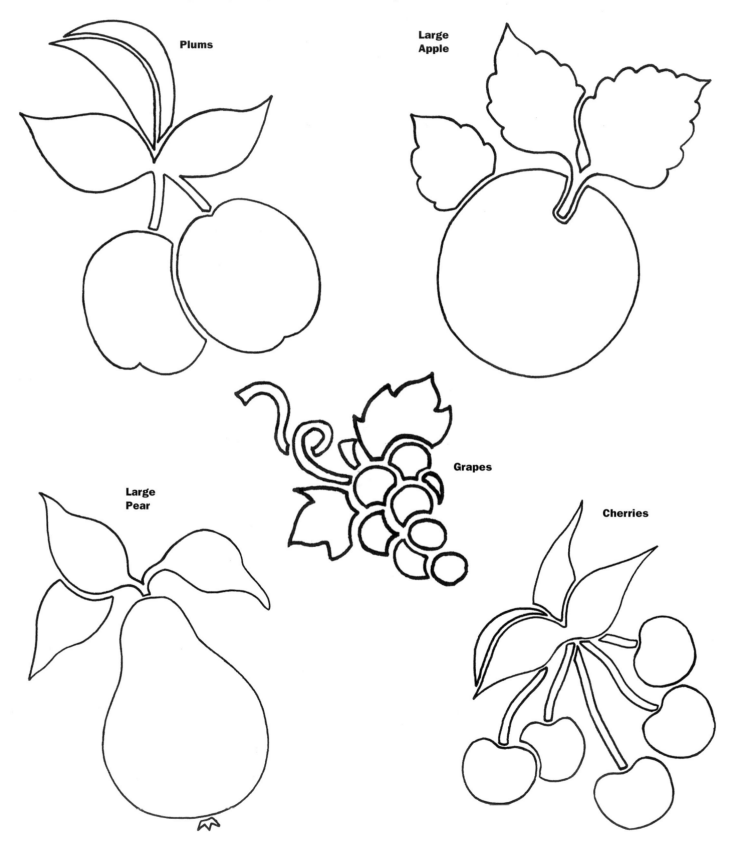

Plums

Large Apple

Grapes

Large Pear

Cherries

Fruit Border

Plan #151028

Dimensions: 36' W X 69' D
Levels: 2
Square Footage: 2,252
Main Level Sq. Ft.: 1,694
Upper Level Sq. Ft.: 558
Bedrooms: 3
Bathrooms: 3
Foundation: Crawl space, slab; optional basement plan available for extra fee
Materials List Available: Yes
Price Category: E

You'll love entertaining in this elegant home with its large covered front porch, grilling porch off the kitchen and breakfast room, and great room with a gas fireplace and media center.

Features:

- **Foyer:** A wonderful open staircase from the foyer leads you to the second floor.

- **Guest Room/Study:** A private bath makes this room truly versatile.

- **Dining Room:** Attached to the great room, this dining room features 8-in. wooden columns that you can highlight for a formal atmosphere.

- **Kitchen:** This cleverly laid-out kitchen with access to the breakfast room is ideal for informal gatherings as well as family meals.

- **Master Suite:** French doors here open to the bath, with its large walk-in closet, double vanities, corner whirlpool tub, and corner shower.

Images provided by designer/architect.

Main Level Floor Plan

Upper Level Floor Plan

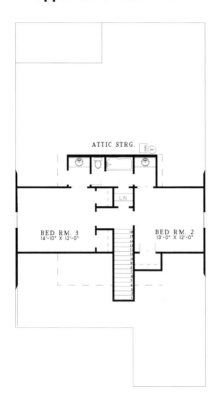

Copyright by designer/architect.

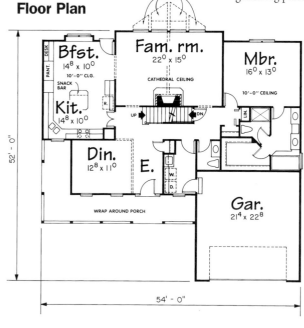

Plan #121038

Dimensions: 54' W x 52' D

Levels: 2

Square Footage: 2,332

Main Level Sq. Ft.: 1,597

Upper Level Sq. Ft.: 735

Bedrooms: 4

Bathrooms: 3½

Foundation: Basement

Materials List Available: Yes

Price Category: E

Images provided by designer/architect.

Offering plenty of architectural style, this home is designed with the busy modern lifestyle in mind.

Features:

- Ceiling Height: 8 ft. unless otherwise noted.

- Family Room: The visual spaciousness of this stylish family room is enhanced by a cathedral ceiling and light streaming through stacked windows.

- Kitchen: This is sure to be a popular informal gathering place. The kitchen features a convenient center island with a snack bar, pantry, and planning desk. The breakfast area is perfect for quick family meals.

- Master Suite: This peaceful retreat is thoughtfully located apart from the rest of the house. It includes a walk-in closet and a private bath.

- Bedrooms: Bedroom 2 has its own walk-in closet and private bath. Bedrooms 3 and 4 share a full bath.

Main Level Floor Plan

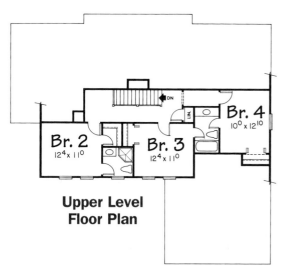

Upper Level Floor Plan

Copyright by designer/architect.

Plan #311015

Dimensions: 72'10" W x 56'6" D

Levels: 1

Square Footage: 2,197

Bedrooms: 3

Bathrooms: 2½

Foundation: Slab, crawl space, or basement

Materials List Available: No

Price Category: D

Images provided by designer/architect.

Copyright by designer/architect.

Plan #301004

Dimensions: 78'8" W x 56'4" D

Levels: 1

Square Footage: 2,344

Bedrooms: 3

Bathrooms: 2

Foundation: Crawl space, slab, or basement

Materials List Available: Yes

Price Category: E

Images provided by designer/architect.

Copyright by designer/architect.

Plan #181155

Dimensions: 50' W x 67' D

Levels: 1

Square Footage: 2,118

Bedrooms: 3

Bathrooms: 2½

Foundation: Full basement

Materials List Available: Yes

Price Category: D

Images provided by designer/architect.

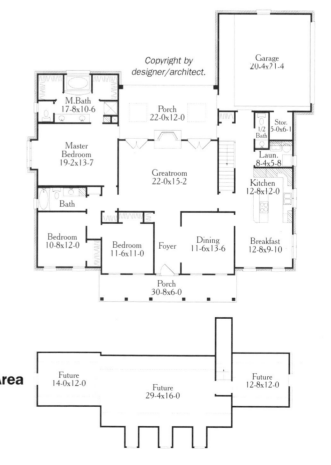

Plan #311016

Dimensions: 63'10" W x 64'7" D

Levels: 1

Square Footage: 2,089

Bedrooms: 3

Bathrooms: 2½

Foundation: Slab, crawl space, or basement

Materials List Available: Yes

Price Category: D

Images provided by designer/architect.

Bonus Area

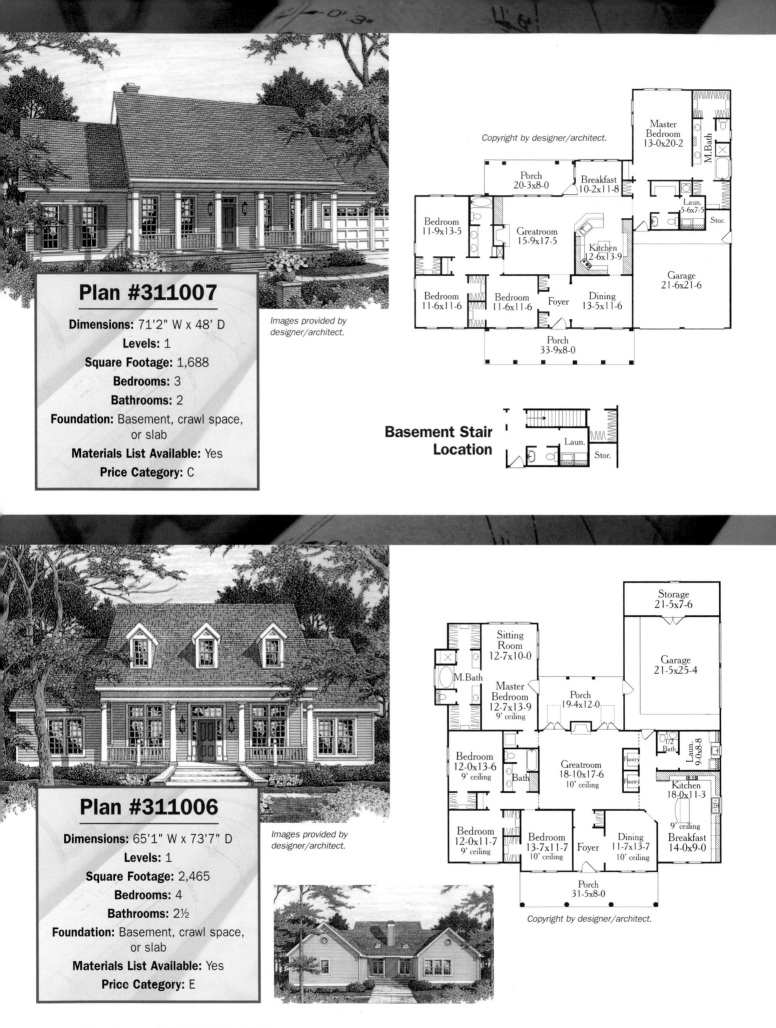

Plan #311007

Dimensions: 71'2" W x 48' D

Levels: 1

Square Footage: 1,688

Bedrooms: 3

Bathrooms: 2

Foundation: Basement, crawl space, or slab

Materials List Available: Yes

Price Category: C

Images provided by designer/architect.

Copyright by designer/architect.

Master Bedroom 13-0x20-2

M.Bath

Porch 20-3x8-0

Breakfast 10-2x11-8

Laun. 5-6x7-5

Stor.

Bedroom 11-9x13-5

Greatroom 15-9x17-5

Kitchen 12-6x13-9

Garage 21-6x21-6

Bedroom 11-6x11-6

Bedroom 11-6x11-6

Foyer

Dining 13-5x11-6

Porch 33-9x8-0

Basement Stair Location

Laun.

Stor.

Plan #311006

Dimensions: 65'1" W x 73'7" D

Levels: 1

Square Footage: 2,465

Bedrooms: 4

Bathrooms: 2½

Foundation: Basement, crawl space, or slab

Materials List Available: Yes

Price Category: E

Images provided by designer/architect.

Storage 21-5x7-6

Garage 21-5x25-4

Sitting Room 12-7x10-0

M.Bath

Master Bedroom 12-7x13-9 9' ceiling

Porch 19-4x12-0

Bedroom 12-0x13-6 9' ceiling

Bath

Greatroom 18-10x17-6 10' ceiling

Pantry

Pantry

½ Bath

Laun. 9-0x8-8

Kitchen 18-0x11-3 9' ceiling

Bedroom 12-0x11-7 9' ceiling

Bedroom 13-7x11-7 10' ceiling

Foyer

Dining 11-7x13-7 10' ceiling

Breakfast 14-0x9-0

Porch 31-5x8-0

Copyright by designer/architect.

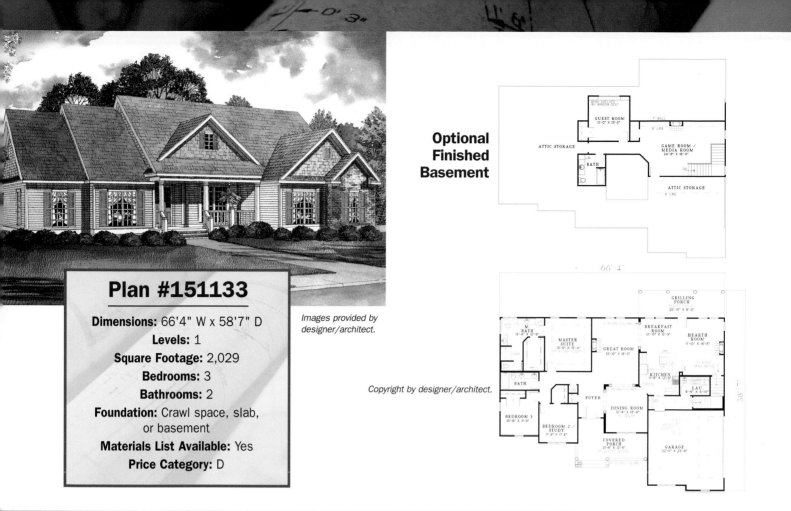

Optional Finished Basement

Images provided by designer/architect.

Copyright by designer/architect.

Plan #151133

Dimensions: 66'4" W x 58'7" D

Levels: 1

Square Footage: 2,029

Bedrooms: 3

Bathrooms: 2

Foundation: Crawl space, slab, or basement

Materials List Available: Yes

Price Category: D

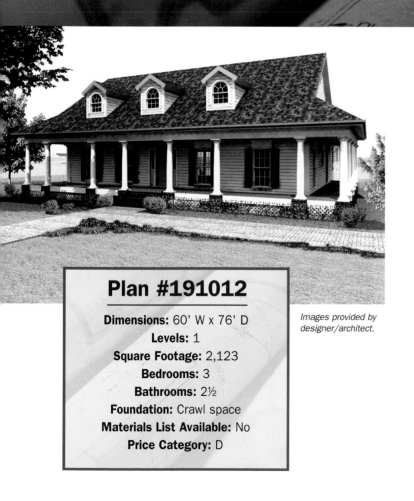

Plan #191012

Dimensions: 60' W x 76' D

Levels: 1

Square Footage: 2,123

Bedrooms: 3

Bathrooms: 2½

Foundation: Crawl space

Materials List Available: No

Price Category: D

Images provided by designer/architect.

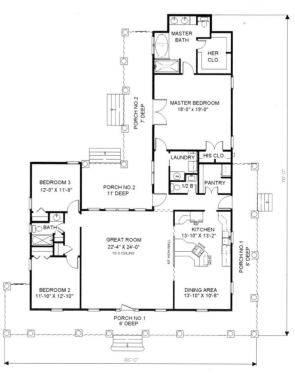

Copyright by designer/architect.

Plan #121021

Dimensions: 46' W x 48' D

Levels: 2

Square Footage: 2,270

Main Level Sq. Ft.: 1,150

Upper Level Sq. Ft.: 1,120

Bedrooms: 4

Bathrooms: 3½

Foundation: Basement

Materials List Available: Yes

Price Category: E

Images provided by designer/architect.

With its wraparound porch, this home evokes the charm of a traditional home.

Features:

• Ceiling Height: 8 ft.

• Foyer: The dramatic two-story entry enjoys views of the formal dining room and great room. A second floor balcony overlooks the entry and a plant shelf.

• Formal Dining Room: This gracious room is perfect for family holiday gatherings and for more formal dinner parties.

• Great Room: All the family will want to gather in this comfortable, informal room which features bay windows, an entertainment center, and a see-through fireplace.

• Breakfast Area: Conveniently located just off the great room, the bayed breakfast area features a built-in desk for household bills and access to the backyard.

• Kitchen: An island is the centerpiece of this kitchen. Its intelligent design makes food preparation a pleasure.

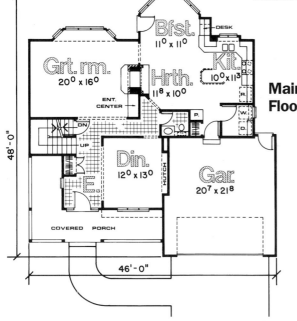

Main Level Floor Plan

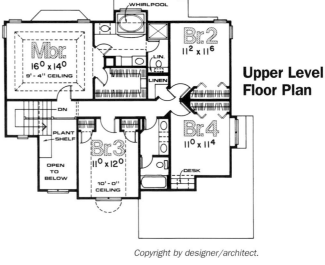

Upper Level Floor Plan

Copyright by designer/architect.

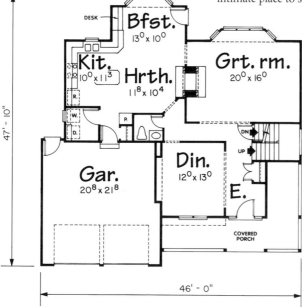

Plan #121037

Dimensions: 46' W x 47'10" D

Levels: 2

Square Footage: 2,292

Main Level Sq. Ft.: 1,158

Upper Level Sq. Ft.: 1,134

Bedrooms: 4

Bathrooms: 2½

Foundation: Basement

Materials List Available: Yes

Price Category: E

Images provided by designer/architect.

This convenient and comfortable home is filled with architectural features that set it apart.

Features:

- Ceiling Height: 8 ft. unless otherwise noted.
- Foyer: You'll know you have arrived when you enter this two-story area highlighted by a decorative plant shelf and a balcony.
- Great Room: Just beyond the entry is the great room where the warmth of the two-sided fireplace will attract family and friends to gather. A bay window offers a more intimate place to sit and converse.

- Hearth Room: At the other side of the fireplace, the hearth offers a cozy spot for smaller gatherings or a place to sit alone and enjoy a book by the fire.
- Breakfast Area: With sunlight streaming into its bay window, the breakfast area offers the perfect spot for informal family meals.
- Master Suite: This private retreat is made more convenient by a walk-in closet. It features its own tub and shower.

Main Level Floor Plan

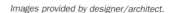
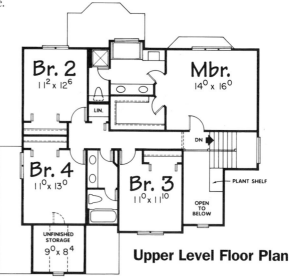

Upper Level Floor Plan

Copyright by designer/architect.

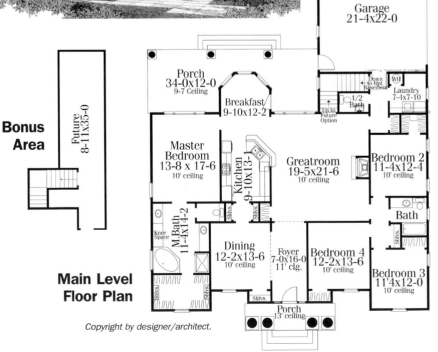

Plan #311002

Dimensions: 56'6" W x 82' D
Levels: 1
Square Footage: 2,402
Bedrooms: 4
Bathrooms: 2½
Foundation: Crawl space, slab
Materials List Available: Yes
Price Category: E

Images provided by designer/architect.

This lovely home has an open floor plan in the main living area but privacy in the bedrooms.

Features:

- **Foyer:** With an 11-ft. ceiling, this foyer opens to both the great room and the dining room.

- **Great Room:** A 10-ft. ceiling and handsome fireplace highlight this spacious room, which is open to both the kitchen and breakfast room.

- **Dining Room:** A butler's pantry and built-in china closet spell convenience in this lovely room.

- **Breakfast Room:** Bask in the sunshine flowing through the bay windows in this room, which opens to the rear porch.

- **Kitchen:** Designed for efficiency, this kitchen will charm all the cooks in the family.

- **Master Suite:** It's easy to feel pampered by the huge closet and bath with corner tub and two vanities.

Bonus Area

Future 8-11x35-0

Main Level Floor Plan

Storage 10-6x7-6
Storage 10-6x7-6
Garage 21-4x22-0
Porch 34-0x12-0 9-7 Ceiling
Breakfast 9-10x12-2
Laundry 7-4x7-10
½ Bath
Master Bedroom 13-8 x 17-6 10' ceiling
Kitchen 9-10x13-1
Greatroom 19-5x21-6 10' ceiling
Bedroom 2 11-4x12-4 10' ceiling
M.Bath 11-4x14-2
Knee Space
Dining 12-2x13-6 10' ceiling
Foyer 7-0x16-0 11' clg.
Bedroom 4 12-2x13-6 10' ceiling
Bath
Bedroom 3 11'4x12-0 10' ceiling
Porch 13' ceiling

Copyright by designer/architect.

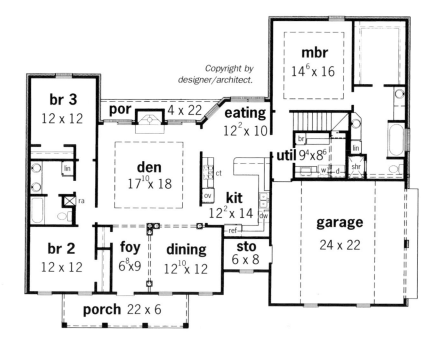

Plan #201084

Dimensions: 66'10" W x 54'5" D

Levels: 1

Square Footage: 2,056

Bedrooms: 3

Bathrooms: 2

Foundation: Crawl space, slab, or basement

Materials List Available: Yes

Price Category: D

Images provided by designer/architect.

This classic family home features beautiful country styling with lots of curb appeal.

Features:

• Ceiling Height: 8 ft.

• Open Plan: When guests arrive, they'll enter a foyer that is open to the dining room and den. This open area makes the home seem especially spacious and offers the flexibility for all kinds of entertaining and family activities.

• Kitchen: You'll love preparing meals in this large, well-designed kitchen. There's plenty of counter space, and the breakfast bar is perfect impromptu family meals.

• Master Suite: This spacious and elegant master suite is separated from the other bedroom for maximum privacy.

• Bonus Room: This unfinished bonus room awaits the time to add another bedroom or a home office.

• Garage: This attached garage offers parking for two cars, plus plenty of storage space.

Copyright by designer/architect.

Floor plan rooms:

- **br 3** 12 x 12
- **por** 4 x 22
- **eating** 12² x 10
- **mbr** 14⁶ x 16
- **den** 17¹⁰ x 18
- **util** 9⁴ x 8⁶
- **kit** 12² x 14
- **br 2** 12 x 12
- **foy** 6⁸ x 9
- **dining** 12¹⁰ x 12
- **sto** 6 x 8
- **garage** 24 x 22
- **porch** 22 x 6

bonus rm 13 x 22⁴

Bonus Room

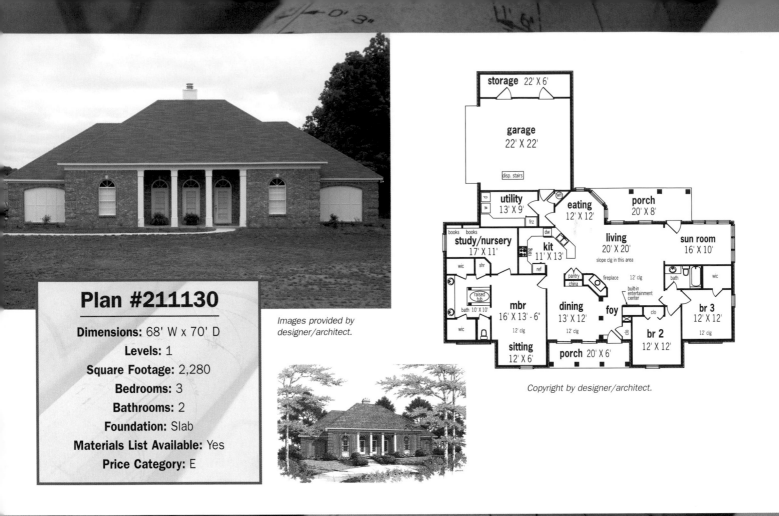

Plan #211130

Dimensions: 68' W x 70' D

Levels: 1

Square Footage: 2,280

Bedrooms: 3

Bathrooms: 2

Foundation: Slab

Materials List Available: Yes

Price Category: E

Images provided by designer/architect.

Copyright by designer/architect.

Floor plan rooms: storage 22' X 6', garage 22' X 22', disp. stairs, utility 13' X 9', eating 12' X 12', porch 20' X 8', study/nursery 17' X 11', kit 11' X 13', living 20' X 20' slope clg in this area, sun room 16' X 10', books, wic, shr, bath, wic, raised tub, bath 10' X 10', mbr 16' X 13'-6" 12 clg, pantry china, fireplace, 12' clg, built-in entertainment center, clo, br 3 12' X 12', wic, dining 13' X 12' 12 clg, foy, sitting 12' X 6', porch 20' X 6', br 2 12' X 12'

Plan #191027

Dimensions: 62' W x 42' D

Levels: 1

Square Footage: 2,354

Bedrooms: 4

Bathrooms: 2½

Foundation: Crawl space

Materials List Available: No

Price Category: E

Images provided by designer/architect.

Copyright by designer/architect.

Floor plan rooms: COVERED PORCH 2 11'-10" X 6'-0", CLOSET 8'-0" X 10'-0", LAUNDRY 8'-0" X 10'-0", BREAKFAST AREA 12'-0" X 9'-9", GREAT ROOM 20'-0" X 24'-0", BEDROOM 2 13'-10" X 13'-0", M. BATH, KITCHEN 12'-0" X 14'-3", 1/2 B, BATH 2, CLO., CLO., MASTER BEDROOM 16'-0" X 16'-0", DINING ROOM 12'-0" X 12'-0", FOYER, HALL, STUDY OR BEDROOM 4 13'-0" X 13'-0", BEDROOM 3 13'-10" X 13'-0", COVERED PORCH 1 62'-0" X 7'-0", 42'-0", 62'-0"

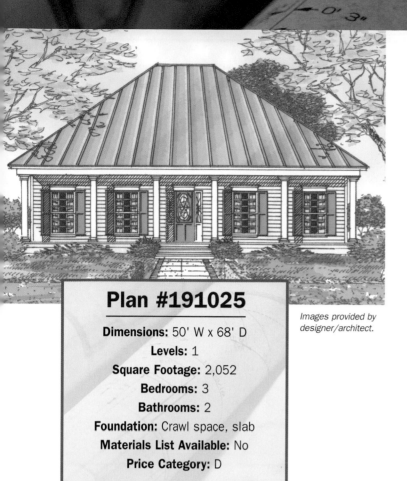

Plan #191025

Dimensions: 50' W x 68' D

Levels: 1

Square Footage: 2,052

Bedrooms: 3

Bathrooms: 2

Foundation: Crawl space, slab

Materials List Available: No

Price Category: D

Images provided by designer/architect.

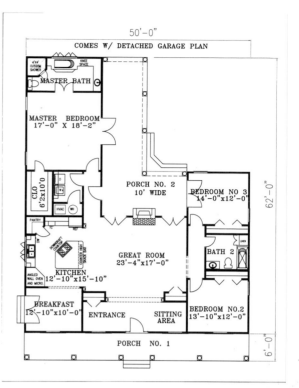

Copyright by designer/architect.

Plan #191026

Dimensions: 50' W x 62' D

Levels: 1

Square Footage: 2,052

Bedrooms: 3

Bathrooms: 2

Foundation: Crawl space, slab

Materials List Available: No

Price Category: D

Images provided by designer/architect.

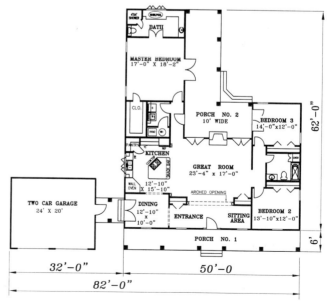

Copyright by designer/architect.

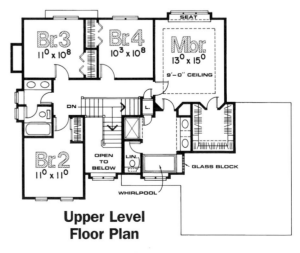

Plan #121087

Dimensions: 50' W x 40' D

Levels: 2

Square Footage: 2,103

Main Level Sq. Ft.: 1,082

Upper Level Sq. Ft.: 1,021

Bedrooms: 4

Bathrooms: 2½

Foundation: Basement

Materials List Available: Yes

Price Category: D

Images provided by designer/architect.

You'll love the comfort and the unusual design details you'll find in this home.

Features:

- **Entry:** A T-shaped staircase frames this two-story entry, giving both visual interest and convenience.

- **Family Room:** Bookcases frame the lovely fireplace here, so you won't be amiss by decorating to create a special reading nook.

- **Breakfast Area:** Pass through the cased

opening between the family room and this breakfast area, for convenience.

- **Kitchen:** Combined with the breakfast area, this kitchen features an island, pantry, and desk.

- **Master Suite:** On the upper floor, this suite has a walk-in closet and a bath with sunlit whirlpool tub, separate shower, and double vanity. A window seat makes the bedroom especially cozy, no matter what the outside weather.

Main Level Floor Plan

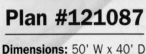

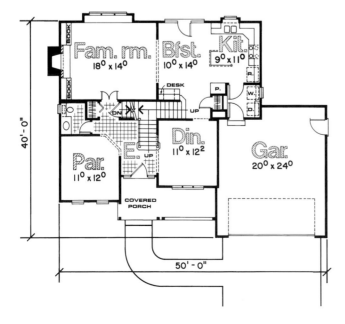

Upper Level Floor Plan

Copyright by designer/architect.

Plan #121080

Dimensions: 56' W x 49' D
Levels: 2
Square Footage: 2,384
Main Level Sq. Ft.: 1,616
Upper Level Sq. Ft.: 768
Bedrooms: 4
Bathrooms: 2½
Foundation: Slab
Materials List Available: Yes
Price Category: E

Images provided by designer/architect.

This design is ideal if you want a generously sized home now and room to expand later.

Features:

• Living Room: Your eyes will be drawn towards the ceiling as soon as you enter this lovely room. The ceiling is vaulted, giving a sense of grandeur, and a graceful balcony from the second floor adds extra interest to this room.

• Kitchen: Designed with lots of counter space to make your work convenient, this kitchen also shares an eating bar with the breakfast nook.

• Breakfast Nook: Eat here or go out to the adjoining private porch where you can enjoy your meal in the morning sunshine.

• Master Suite: The bayed area in the bedroom makes a picturesque sitting area. French doors in the bedroom open to a private bath that's fitted with a whirlpool tub, separate shower, two vanities, and a walk-in closet.

Main Level Floor Plan

Upper Level Floor Plan

Copyright by designer/architect.

Plan #151166

Dimensions: 60'8" W x 79'6" D

Levels: 1½

Square Footage: 2,140

Main Level Sq. Ft.: 1,690

Upper Level Sq. Ft.: 450

Bedrooms: 3

Bathrooms: 2½

Foundation: Crawl space, slab

Materials List Available: Yes

Price Category: D

Images provided by designer/architect.

Main Level Floor Plan

Upper Level Floor Plan

Copyright by designer/architect.

Plan #151167

Dimensions: 58' W x 85'4" D

Levels: 1½

Square Footage: 2,286

Main Level Sq. Ft.: 1,831

Upper Level Sq. Ft.: 455

Bedrooms: 4

Bathrooms: 3

Foundation: Crawl space, slab

Materials List Available: Yes

Price Category: E

Images provided by designer/architect.

Main Level Floor Plan   **Upper Level Floor Plan**

Copyright by designer/architect.

Main Level Floor Plan

Upper Level Floor Plan

Copyright by designer/architect.

Plan #151155

Dimensions: 50' W x 50' D

Levels: 1½

Square Footage: 2,296

Main Level Sq. Ft.: 1,537

Upper Level Sq. Ft.: 759

Bedrooms: 3

Bathrooms: 2½

Foundation: Crawl space, slab

Materials List Available: Yes

Price Category: E

Images provided by designer/architect.

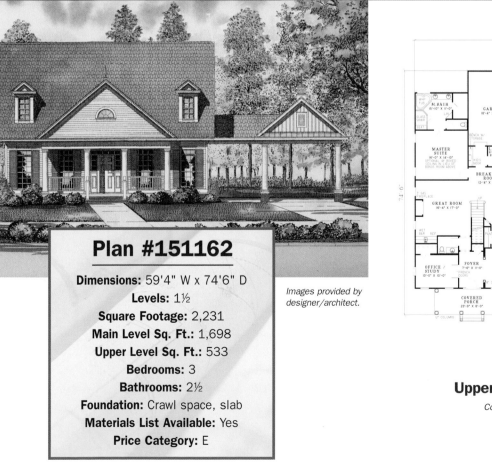

Main Level Floor Plan

Upper Level Floor Plan

Copyright by designer/architect.

Plan #151162

Dimensions: 59'4" W x 74'6" D

Levels: 1½

Square Footage: 2,231

Main Level Sq. Ft.: 1,698

Upper Level Sq. Ft.: 533

Bedrooms: 3

Bathrooms: 2½

Foundation: Crawl space, slab

Materials List Available: Yes

Price Category: E

Images provided by designer/architect.

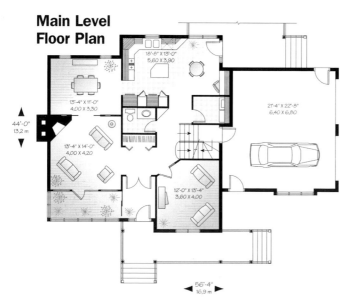

Plan #181085

Dimensions: 56'4" W x 44' D

Levels: 2

Square Footage: 2,183

Main Level Sq. Ft.: 1,232

Second Level Sq. Ft.: 951

Bedrooms: 3

Bathrooms: 2½

Foundation: Basement

Materials List Available: Yes

Price Category: D

Images provided by designer/architect.

This country home features an inviting front porch and a layout designed for modern living.

Features:

- Ceiling Height: 8 ft.

- Solarium: Sunlight streams through the windows of this solarium at the front of the house.

- Living Room: Walk through French doors, and you will enter this inviting living room. Family and friends will be drawn to the corner fireplace.

- Formal Dining Room: Usher your guests directly from the living room into this formal dining room. The kitchen is located on the other side of the dining room for convenient service.

- Kitchen: This generously sized kitchen is a delight, it offers a center island, separate eat-in area, and access to the back deck.

- Bonus Room: This room just off the entry hall can become a family room, a bedroom, or an office.

- Master Suite: Curl up by the corner fireplace in this master retreat, with its walk-in closet and lavish bath with separate shower and tub.

Main Level Floor Plan

Upper Level Floor Plan

Copyright by designer/architect.

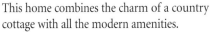

Plan #171011

Dimensions: 55' W x 61'4" D

Levels: 1

Square Footage: 2,069

Bedrooms: 3

Bathrooms: 2

Foundation: Slab, crawl space

Materials List Available: Yes

Price Category: D

Images provided by designer/architect.

This home combines the charm of a country cottage with all the modern amenities.

Features:

• Ceiling Height: 9 ft. unless otherwise noted.

• Front Porch: Watch the sun set, read a book, or just relax on this spacious front porch.

• Foyer: This gracious foyer has two closets and opens to the formal dining room and the study.

• Dining Room: This big dining room works just as well for family Sunday dinner as it does for entertaining guests on Saturday night.

• Family Room: This inviting family room features an 11-ft. ceiling, a paddle fan, and a corner fireplace.

• Kitchen: This smart kitchen includes lots of counter space, a built in desk, and a breakfast bar.

• Master Bedroom: This master bedroom is separate from the other bedrooms for added privacy. It includes a paddle fan.

• Master Bath: This master bath has two vanities, walk-in closets, a deluxe tub, and a walk-in shower.

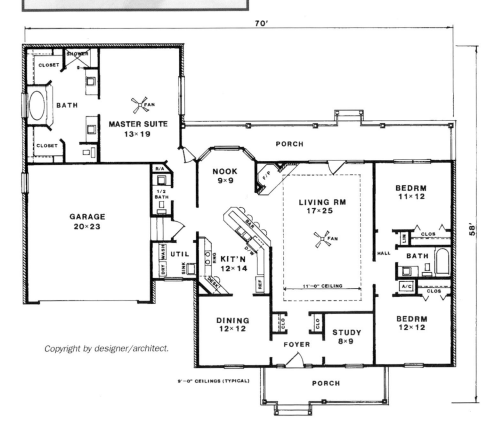

Copyright by designer/architect.

Main Level Floor Plan

Images provided by designer/architect.

Upper Level Floor Plan

Copyright by designer/architect.

Plan #151152

Dimensions: 50' W x 50' D

Levels: 1½

Square Footage: 2,297

Main Level Sq. Ft.: 1,627

Upper Level Sq. Ft.: 670

Bedrooms: 3

Bathrooms: 2½

Foundation: Crawl space, slab

Materials List Available: Yes

Price Category: E

Main Level Floor Plan

Images provided by designer/architect.

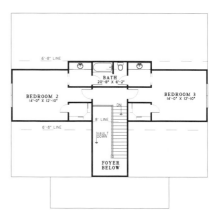

Upper Level Floor Plan

Copyright by designer/architect.

Plan #151153

Dimensions: 50' W x 50' D

Levels: 1½

Square Footage: 2,290

Main Level Sq. Ft.: 1,604

Upper Level Sq. Ft.: 686

Bedrooms: 3

Bathrooms: 2½

Foundation: Crawl space, slab

Materials List Available: Yes

Price Category: E

Main Level Floor Plan

Upper Level Floor Plan

Copyright by designer/architect.

Images provided by designer/architect.

Plan #151147

Dimensions: 76' W x 52'6" D

Levels: 1½

Square Footage: 2,422

Main Level Sq. Ft.: 1,778

Upper Level Sq. Ft.: 644

Bedrooms: 3

Bathrooms: 2½

Foundation: Crawl space, slab

Materials List Available: Yes

Price Category: E

Main Level Floor Plan

Upper Level Floor Plan

Copyright by designer/architect.

Images provided by designer/architect.

Plan #181154

Dimensions: 54' W x 42' D

Levels: 2

Square Footage: 2,406

Main Level Sq. Ft.: 1,296

Upper Level Sq. Ft.: 1,110

Bedrooms: 3

Bathrooms: 2½

Foundation: Full basement

Materials List Available: Yes

Price Category: E

Plan #201099

Dimensions: 80'5" W x 42'5" D

Levels: 2

Square Footage: 2,239

Main Level Sq. Ft.: 1,662

Upper Level Sq. Ft.: 577

Bedrooms: 3

Bathrooms: 2½

Foundation: Crawl space, slab, or basement

Materials List Available: Yes

Price Category: E

Images provided by designer/architect.

You'll enjoy the country charm of this house when you're sitting on the beautiful wraparound porch.

Features:

• Ceiling Height: 8 ft. unless otherwise noted.

• Living Room: From the elaborate foyer you are drawn into this formal living room, where you have views of the wraparound porch.

• Dining Room: This dining room, which is perfect for entertaining, flows freely into the den, where your guests can relax after they eat.

• Master Suite: This first-floor area is bursting with amenities, including a large walk-in closet and an enormous bath with separate his and her vanities.

• Storage: This home contains a large storage room that provides enough space for any size family.

Main Level Floor Plan

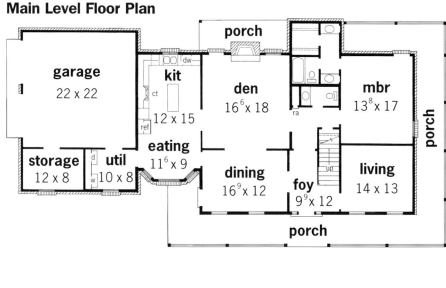

Upper Level Floor Plan

Copyright by designer/architect.

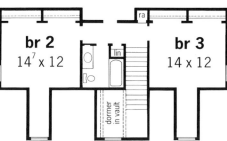

Plan #131022

Dimensions: 54'8" W x 43' D

Levels: 2

Square Footage: 2,092

Main Level Sq. Ft.: 1,152

Upper Level Sq. Ft.: 940

Bedrooms: 3

Bathrooms: 2½

Foundation: Basement, crawl space, or slab

Materials List Available: Yes

Price Category: E

You'll love the way this charming home reminds you of an old-fashioned farmhouse.

Features:

• Ceiling Height: 8 ft.

• Living Room: This large living room can be used as guest quarters when the need arises.

• Dining Room: This bayed, informal room is large enough for all your dining and entertaining needs. It could also double as an office or den.

• Garage: An expandable loft over the garage offers an ideal playroom or fourth bedroom.

Rear Elevation

Main Level Floor Plan

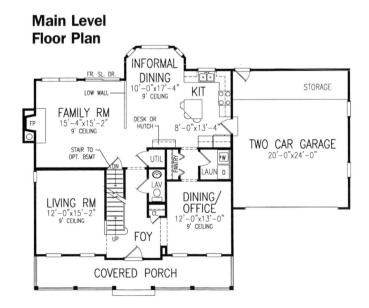

Upper Level Floor Plan

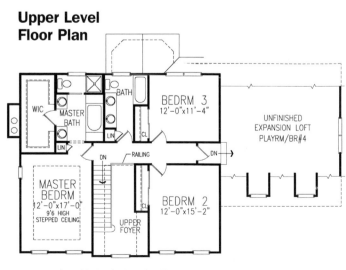

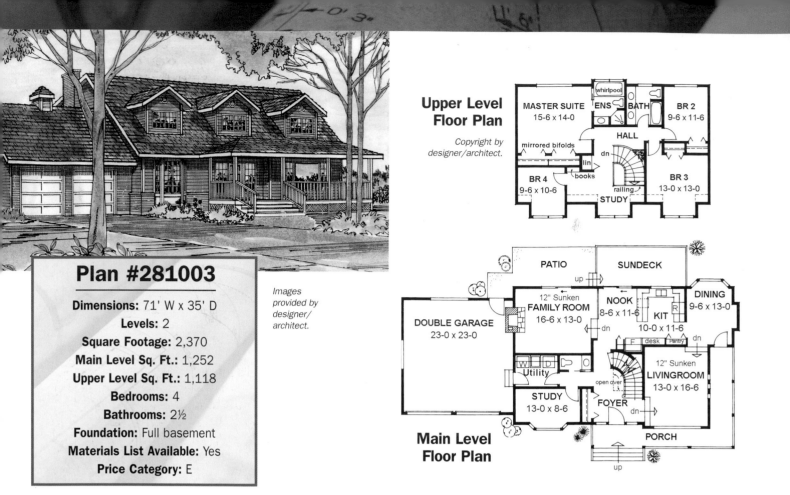

Upper Level Floor Plan

Copyright by designer/architect.

- MASTER SUITE 15-6 x 14-0
- ENS
- whirlpool
- BATH
- BR 2 9-6 x 11-6
- HALL
- mirrored bifolds
- lin
- books
- dn
- railing
- BR 4 9-6 x 10-6
- STUDY
- BR 3 13-0 x 13-0

- PATIO
- SUNDECK
- up
- 12" Sunken FAMILY ROOM 16-6 x 13-0
- NOOK 8-6 x 11-6
- DINING 9-6 x 13-0
- KIT 10-0 x 11-6
- DOUBLE GARAGE 23-0 x 23-0
- dn
- F desk Pantry dn
- W L D
- Utility
- 12" Sunken LIVINGROOM 13-0 x 16-6
- open over
- STUDY 13-0 x 8-6
- FOYER
- dn
- PORCH
- up

Main Level Floor Plan

Plan #281003

Dimensions: 71' W x 35' D

Levels: 2

Square Footage: 2,370

Main Level Sq. Ft.: 1,252

Upper Level Sq. Ft.: 1,118

Bedrooms: 4

Bathrooms: 2½

Foundation: Full basement

Materials List Available: Yes

Price Category: E

Images provided by designer/ architect.

Main Level Floor Plan

Copyright by designer/architect.

- Covered Deck
- Sundeck
- Nook 8-0 x 8-0
- Kitchen 11-3 x 15-0
- Dining Rm 10-0 x 11-4
- 9'-0" ceiling
- ovens
- wood box
- Family Room 17-5 x 15-0
- F Pantry
- 9'-0" ceiling
- W D
- Util
- dn
- Pwdr Rm
- Foyer up Open over
- Living Rm 12-0 x 16-8
- Double Garage 23-0 x 25-0
- Verandah
- dn
- Main Floor

Upper Level Floor Plan

- Balcony
- whirlpool
- Fr. door
- Ens
- MBr 18-0 x 12-0
- shwr twl
- WIC
- Bath
- linen
- niche
- laundry chute
- Hall
- railing
- dn
- Br 2 14-6 x 10-0
- Foyer below
- Br 3 12-0 x 12-4
- plant shelf

Plan #281019

Dimensions: 50' W x 55'6" D

Levels: 2

Square Footage: 2,008

Main Level Sq. Ft.: 1,023

Upper Level Sq. Ft.: 985

Bedrooms: 3

Bathrooms: 2½

Foundation: Basement

Materials List Available: Yes

Price Category: D

Images provided by designer/architect.

Rear Elevation

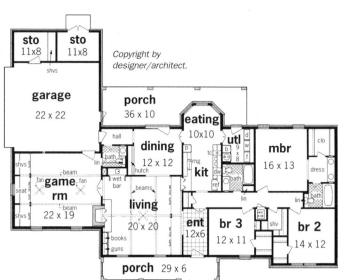

Copyright by designer/architect.

Plan #211054

Dimensions: 80' W x 62' D
Levels: 1
Square Footage: 2,358
Bedrooms: 3
Bathrooms: 2½
Foundation: Slab
Materials List Available: Yes
Price Category: E

Images provided by designer/architect.

SMARTtip

Dressing Up a Simple Fireplace

Painting a wood surround with a faux marble or faux bois (wood) is inexpensive. Adding a simple, prefabricated wooden shelf mantel can add lots of architectural character.

Plan #181158

Dimensions: 48' W x 56' D
Levels: 2
Square Footage: 2,391
Main Level Sq. Ft.: 1,405
Upper Level Sq. Ft.: 986
Bedrooms: 3
Bathrooms: 2½
Foundation: Full basement
Materials List Available: Yes
Price Category: E

Images provided by designer/architect.

Main Level Floor Plan

Upper Level Floor Plan

Copyright by designer/architect.

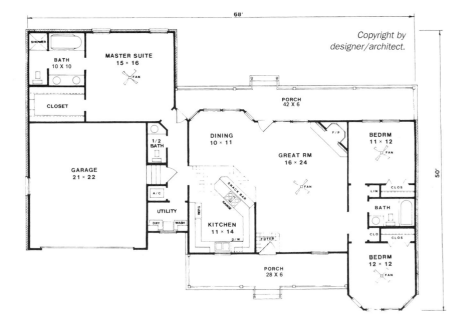

Plan #171006

Dimensions: 68' W x 50' D
Levels: 1
Square Footage: 2,296
Bedrooms: 3
Bathrooms: 2½
Foundation: Slab, crawl space
Materials List Available: Yes
Price Category: E

This classic country farmhouse features a large, open rocking-chair front porch.

Features:

• Ceiling Height: 9 ft. unless otherwise noted.

• Great Room: This spacious great room is perfect for all types of entertaining.

• Dining Room: This dining room is designed to accommodate formal dinner parties as well as less-formal family occasions. After dinner, step from the dining room onto the covered rear porch.

• Family Room: On cool evenings, enjoy the handsome fireplace in this family room. There's plenty of room for all kinds of family activities.

• Kitchen: This is truly a cook's kitchen with its cooktop range and U-shaped open traffic pattern. The snack bar will see lots of use for quick family meals.

• Master Suite: This master suite is separated from the other bedrooms for additional privacy. The large bedroom has a paddle fan and a roomy walk-in closet. The bathroom features his and her vanities, a deluxe bath, and a walk-in shower.

Window Shades

While decorative hems add interest to roller shades, they also increase the cost. If you're handy with a glue gun, choose one of the trims available at fabric and craft stores, and consider attaching it yourself. Give your shades fancy pulls for an inexpensive dash of pizzazz.

Plan #131046

Dimensions: 68' W x 57'6" D
Levels: 2
Square Footage: 2,245
Main Level Sq. Ft.: 1,720
Upper Level Sq. Ft.: 525
Bedrooms: 3
Bathrooms: 2½
Foundation: Crawl space, slab, or basement
Materials List Available: Yes
Price Category: F

You'll love the mixture of country charm and contemporary amenities in this lovely home.

Features:

- **Porch:** The covered wraparound porch spells comfort, and the arched windows spell style.

- **Great Room:** Look up at the 18-ft. vaulted ceiling and the balcony that looks over this room from the upper level, and then notice the wall of windows and the fireplace that's set into a media wall for decorating ease.

- **Kitchen:** This roomy kitchen is also designed for convenience, thanks to its ample counter space and work island.

- **Breakfast Room:** The kitchen looks out to this lovely room, with its vaulted ceiling and sliding French doors that open to the rear covered porch.

- **Master Bedroom:** A 10-ft-ceiling and a dramatic bay window give character to this charming room.

Images provided by designer/architect.

Main Level Floor Plan

Copyright by designer/architect.

Upper Level Floor Plan

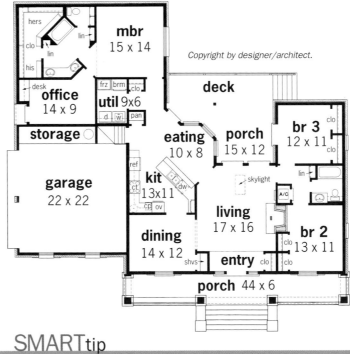

Plan #211048

Dimensions: 66' W x 60'8" D

Levels: 1

Square Footage: 2,002

Bedrooms: 3

Bathrooms: 2

Foundation: Crawl space

Materials List Available: Yes

Price Category: D

Images provided by designer/architect.

Copyright by designer/architect.

This southern-style home is filled with inviting spaces and will fit into any neighborhood.

Features:

- Ceiling Height: 8 ft.

- Front Porch: Enjoy summer breezes on this porch, which features accented shutters that are both functional and stylish.

- Living Room: From the porch, French doors lead into the side-lit entry and this gracious living room.

- Sundeck: You can bask in the summer sun on this private rear deck, or if you prefer, enjoy a cool breeze under the shade of the rear porch. Each is accessible through its own set of French doors.

- Master Suite: This suite is secluded from the rest of the house for privacy, making it the perfect retreat at the end of a busy day. From the bedroom, open double doors to gain access to the luxurious bath, with a dual sink vanity and his and her walk-in closets.

SMARTtip

Eye Appeal

Not everything in a landscaping plan needs to be in the ground. You might want to consider hanging flowering plants on a front porch or placing hardy potted plants on outdoor steps and decks or strategically along a paved walkway. Even a window box, viewed from outside, becomes a part of the landscaping.

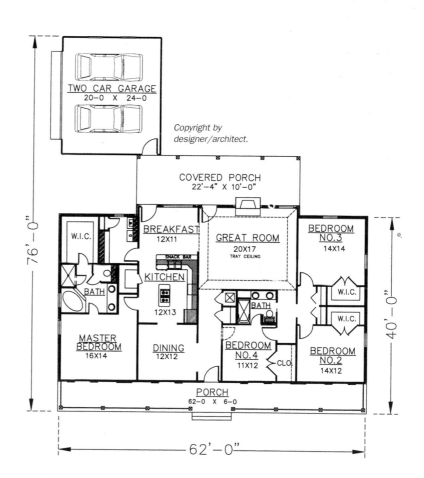

Plan #191009

Dimensions: 62' W x 76' D

Levels: 1

Square Footage: 2,172

Bedrooms: 4

Bathrooms: 2

Foundation: Crawl space, slab

Materials List Available: No

Price Category: D

This charming home is equally attractive in a rural or a settled area, thanks to its classic lines.

Features:

- **Porches:** Covered front and back porches emphasize the comfort you'll find in this home.

- **Great Room:** A tray ceiling gives elegance to this spacious room, where everyone is sure to gather. A fireplace makes a nice focal point, and French doors open onto the rear covered porch.

- **Dining Room:** Arched openings give distinction to this room, where it's easy to serve meals for the family or host a large group.

- **Kitchen:** You'll love the cooktop island, walk-in pantry, wall oven, snack bar, and view out of the windows in the adjoining breakfast area.

- **Master Suite:** The large bedroom here gives you space to spread out and relax, and the bath includes a corner whirlpool tub, shower, and dual sinks. An 8-ft. x 10-ft. walk-in closet is off the bath.

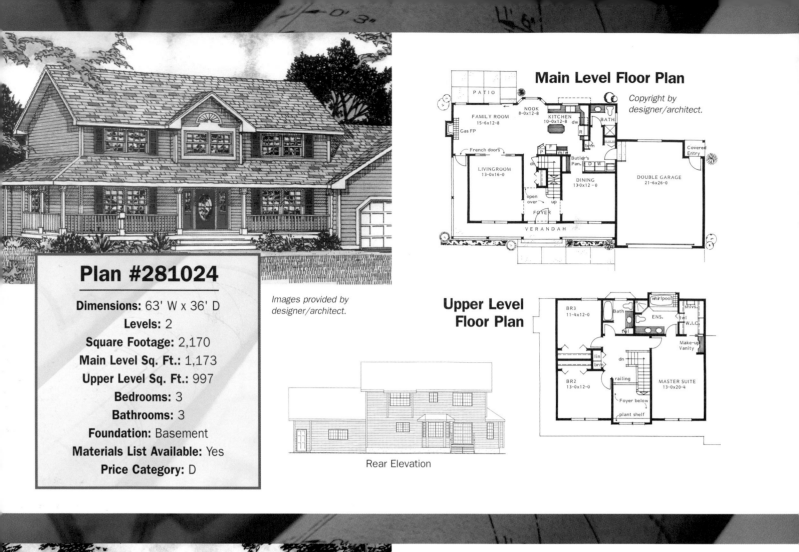

Main Level Floor Plan

Copyright by designer/architect.

Upper Level Floor Plan

Plan #281024

Dimensions: 63' W x 36' D

Levels: 2

Square Footage: 2,170

Main Level Sq. Ft.: 1,173

Upper Level Sq. Ft.: 997

Bedrooms: 3

Bathrooms: 3

Foundation: Basement

Materials List Available: Yes

Price Category: D

Images provided by designer/architect.

Rear Elevation

Copyright by designer/architect.

Main Level Floor Plan

Upper Level Floor Plan

Plan #281017

Dimensions: 50' W x 59' D

Levels: 2

Square Footage: 2,101

Main Level Sq. Ft.: 1,270

Upper Level Sq. Ft.: 831

Bedrooms: 4

Bathrooms: 2½

Foundation: Basement

Materials List Available: Yes

Price Category: D

Images provided by designer/architect.

Rear Elevation

Plan #141016

Dimensions: 64' W x 52' D

Levels: 2

Square Footage: 2,416

Main Level Sq. Ft.: 1,250

Upper Level Sq. Ft.: 1,166

Bedrooms: 4

Bathrooms: 2½

Foundation: Basement

Materials List Available: Yes

Price Category: E

Images provided by designer/architect.

Here is a classic American home with a generous wraparound front porch.

Features:

• Ceiling Height: 9 ft. unless otherwise noted.

• Formal Dining Room: Located just off the foyer you'll find this inviting dining room, which is perfect for dinner parties of all sizes.

• Formal Living Room: This room is located in close proximity to the dining room, making it easy to usher guests in to dine.

• Family Room: The whole family will want to gather in this spacious area. Columns separate it from the breakfast area while keeping an open feeling across the entire rear of the house.

• Kitchen: This warm and inviting kitchen features corner windows that look into the side yard and a rear screen porch.

• Master Bedroom: This bedroom has a modified cathedral ceiling that highlights a large Palladian window on the rear wall. Access to a second-floor deck creates the perfect master retreat.

Main Level Floor Plan

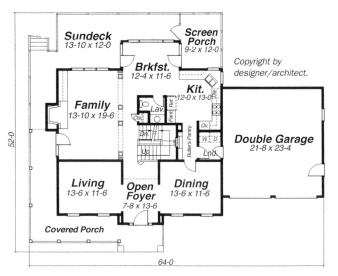

Copyright by designer/architect.

Upper Level Floor Plan

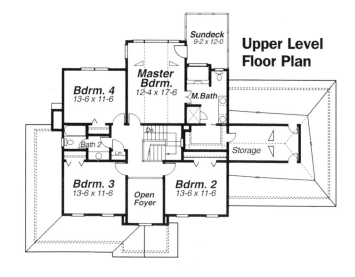

A Kitchen with Country in Mind

North Americans have always combined comfortable traditions with current inventiveness in the kitchen. Country colors, finishes, and patterns seem especially right here. As the busiest room in the house, the kitchen serves many daily needs. But it also carries symbolic weight as the place where we share work and food among familiar things and friendly faces. It's the room that most clearly says "home."

The earliest settlers recalled the kitchens of their native countries. The English colonists created rooms that glowed with wood paneling, which they painted rich red, grayed teal, and deep green. German and Dutch colonists in the New World tended toward bright colors, with high-contrast decorative painting.

An Evolving Style

The earliest North American kitchens focused on a wide fireplace. While we romantically picture a roaring fire, a skilled open-hearth cook would manage her fuel carefully, often scooping a hot pile of coals out onto the brick hearth floor to make a separate "burner." For the weekly baking, she might fire up the back oven, which was built into the fireplace wall.

Hot, laborious open-hearth cooking inspired many ingenious devices: revolving toasters, waffle irons, long-handled "spider" skillets, and Dutch ovens, with flanged lids to hold coals scooped on top. Early North Americans used a ratchet to raise and lower the large cooking pots that slow-simmered meat. Crude reflector ovens held meat on a revolving spit until it was "done to a turn." While metalwares were treasured purchases, most cooks also had a supply of homemade "treen," or wooden spoons, cups, and ladles, made by any handy whittler. Such simple early kitchenwares are evocative collectibles today.

In the mid-1800s, only the romanticists sighed over the demise of open-hearth cooking, as households quickly embraced the cast-iron cookstove that burned wood or coal. A prototype gas range appeared at the Great Exhibition of 1851 in London and at the first electric kitchen at the 1893 Chicago World's Fair. But it was well into the 1930s before these appliances came home. At that time, refrigerators arrived and by the late 1940s were considered as fundamental as the modern range and running water.

Modern Kitchen Charm

The purist, with a sufficient budget, can convincingly conceal modern appliances with specialized cabinetry. Dishwashers, microwaves, trash compactors, and refrigerators can disappear completely behind cabinet doors, perhaps with some decorative fretwork for ventilation. Some new and expensive refrigerators and freezers are modular and are installed much like drawers in various work zones instead of standing as one large unit. Dishwashers, too, are available as compact modular units. In a

This Country kitchen, above, uses the most modern appliances and fixtures.

Inviting morning sunlight floods this charming Country-style breakfast nook, opposite.

large kitchen, you can locate one near the main sink and another near a secondary bar or island sink.

For less rigorous disguise, matching-panel fronts on the major appliances help blend them into the cabinetry. Appliances can even be concealed with a colorful, washable curtain attached to the counter's overhang. In a colorful kitchen, appliances painted at a local auto body shop in sky blue or geranium red can become whimsical additions. Or apply a stenciled design or a faux finish to appliance fronts. Several manufacturers also offer modern gas and electric ranges styled like old wood-burning stoves. But to contemporary eyes, standard appliances tend to be unobtrusive. If your kitchen is rich with colors, textures, and collectibles, most observers will skim over the appliances as expected background. Appliances in standard, simple designs work best for this strategy.

The "Unfitted" Look

The informal Country-style family kitchen wasn't designed but evolved along functional lines. Individual pieces of furniture—a table, a cupboard, shelves, a hutch, or an armoire, sometimes retired from the finer "company" rooms—were added as needed. This loose, unfitted look is a hallmark of a humble Country kitchen.

Amid the current design-world hoopla about the "return of the unfitted kitchen," look critically at such plans, particularly if you're an enthusiastic cook. While unfitted designs can provide a handsome Country look, they may lack the workspace or convenient configurations that make a room a pleasure to work in.

Many Country enthusiasts find a middle ground in loosening up modern kitchen planning with selected, character-rich pieces and accessories, open shelving, and eye-catching finishes. A spacious floor plan allows leeway for idiosyncratic touches. In a large kitchen, an island styled differently from the wall cabinets or even a big farmhouse table with baskets underneath will add usable workspace with a casual, random look.

Storage Strategies

Many unsatisfactory kitchen designs spring from a lack of storage space, as appliances and ingredients proliferate and strain the capacity. When you're designing, remember that while a down-home kitchen may charmingly suggest endless bounty, bulging clutter is less appealing. There are some steps you can take to ensure efficient storage in a Country kitchen.

Zero In on Necessities

Before declaring your storage inadequate, make sure that every item is pulling its weight. If you use a fish poacher, cake decorator, and turkey platter twice a year, store them elsewhere. Watch out for needless duplication. Don't give prime storage to dozens of glasses or stacks of mixing bowls when you typically use only a few.

Great rooms, left, are typical of Country-style kitchens. Furniture that uses beadboard, above, fits right in with Country decorating.

Translucent-glass-fronted cabinets, above, provide attractive, stylish storage. Reproduction furniture, right, makes for excellent auxiliary storage.

Plan Point-of-Use Storage

Put the baking spices within reach of the mixer and the savory spices near the stove. Targeting storage may even free up room for other things such as baskets, tins, or an extra freestanding corner cabinet or work cart.

Let Practical Wares Double as Decoration

The yellowed plastic spatulas can stay in the drawer, but wooden spoons, the old sifter, canisters, skeins of herbs or garlic, or earthenware bowls can all give a room a friendly bustle while providing a useful function.

Use Open Storage Strategically

It makes sense to reserve open storage for items that you use frequently. That way they don't just gather grimy dust. Be wary of the hanging pot rack directly over the cooktop, where pots can quickly get grubby from spattering grease and liquids.

Cabinetry

Cabinetry usually costs more than any other item in a kitchen renovation, and it has the biggest impact on the room's style. Before junking existing cabinets, consider whether refinishing, perhaps with a personality-rich faux effect, or refacing with new doors can reclaim basically sound units.

Today's cabinets run a gamut of Country styles: rustic planked fronts, more formal cathedral-arched panels, or classic square panels, recessed or raised. The range of woods from which to choose is equally wide. Oak, with its rugged grain, is the most popular, adaptable choice.

Kitchen cabinet fashions oscillate between very light and very dark stain treatments, so a midtone wood is less likely to become dated in just a few short years.

If you incline toward dark, cozy woods, make sure the kitchen is well lit, and keep other elements on the light side. White-enameled cabinetry can have a cottage-fresh appeal but will require some upkeep. Among bolder choices is a color-stain or a painted finish in a Shaker blue or Nantucket green, perhaps with a distressed or antiqued finish, for example. Stenciling or free-hand painting can add still more individuality to cabinet fronts, but only if you do it sparingly.

Glass-fronted cabinets and open shelves break up the monolithic banks of cabinetry while showing off the wares inside. But don't install them if you can't make a pleasing arrangement of the contents and keep them neat.

This Country kitchen, above, with lots of work space and an eat-in area, is open and roomy.

The choice of fabrics and accessories gives this kitchen, opposite, a distinctly Country feeling.

Counter Forces

Counters can be great places for showcasing interesting collections. But unless you've got a spacious kitchen, it's more practical to keep counters clutter-free and reserve these surfaces for work. Place countertop and hand-held appliances in a convenient location where they'll be easy to retrieve, perhaps in a corner storage garage. A swing-up tray for a heavy stand mixer is a nice luxury, but it will consume considerable interior cabinet space.

Plastic Laminate. In a Country kitchen, countertop materials should appear natural or, barring that, unobtrusive. Plastic laminate is reasonably priced and easy to install or replace. High-quality plastic laminate is durable, though prone to chipping that can't be repaired, scorching, and water-infiltration at sink-side seams. More expensive solid-core laminates eliminate the dark joints and offer fancy multihued edge treatments. But in a Country setting, laminates are perhaps best presented in low-key, unfussy forms, in simple neutral colors.

Solid-Surfacing Material. The same applies to solid-surfacing material, a synthetic made from polyester or acrylic, sometimes mixed with ground stone. It generally costs three to five times as much as standard plastic laminate but is hardwearing, repairable, and good-looking. It's offered now in a rainbow of choices and faux looks, including some convincing stone impressions. Skilled professional installers can create decorative inlay effects.

Wood. Wood has natural country warmth, but as a countertop is subject to water damage and warping. You may want to limit wood to a chopping surface. Durable eastern sugar maple is common for laminated butcher-block tops. Wood countertops must be meticulously cleaned and require periodic maintenance.

Natural Stone. Stone tends to be the most expensive countertop. Marble is relatively soft and porous and requires rigorous care in a kitchen setting. Slate and soapstone are sometimes used for countertops, but the most popular choice is granite. Durable and easy to maintain, granite may suit a country mood better in a matte rather than a polished finish. Porous stone requires sealing.

Ceramic Tile. Durable, nonabsorbent glazed ceramic tile resists stains, heat, and fading, and spans the greatest range of color and pattern, from dainty florals to bold, rustic squares. But the material is unforgiving to items that are easily breakable. The grout is a weak point for tile. It's easier to maintain if the joint is tight and flush to the surface. Use a grout that's made of an impervious epoxy or a latex-modified formulation. Tiles with a rustic, handmade look may require a wider, sanded grout joint, which you should periodically seal against stains and bacteria. It's also a good idea to clean any countertop regularly with a nonabrasive antibacterial cleanser. Tile that is well maintained will last a lifetime.

Tile spans a wide price range, and the cost has to include skilled installation on a firmly reinforced backing. Countertop tiles should be specified as scratch- and acid-resistant. The countertop edge can be finished with rounded bullnose trim pieces or wood edging.

Country Kitchen Flooring

No floor takes more abuse than the kitchen's, which is subject to high traffic, dropped kitchenware, spills, grease, water, and harsh cleansers. Yet it's still expected to make a stylish contribution to the room's overall design. In any material, light-colored floors add an airy look but will require more scrupulous housekeeping. A floor that is dark tends to be less demanding, visually and logistically, but it may make a small room feel confining. You'll have to weigh your choice against how much time you have for upkeep and the actual size of the space. Whatever your circumstances, here are the most popular flooring products today.

Wood. Classic hardwood flooring and newer wood-look laminate floors evoke a Country feeling in any room. For kitchen use, wood must be particularly well sealed to avoid moisture damage. Pine and fir are the less expensive options, but they aren't as durable as costlier maple, birch, oak, and ash. Color stains or stenciled patterns may be appropriate, especially in a rustic Country kitchen.

Authentic wood floors will probably take a beating in a busy kitchen. That means refinishing periodically—sanding and recoating with a tough polyurethane, for example. Laminate products are easy to keep clean, using a damp mop. But they won't hold up as long as a well-maintained real wood floor.

Vinyl. For kitchens, resilient vinyl flooring is a standard choice. It's cost effective, comfortable underfoot, potentially more merciful on dropped breakables, and available in myriad designs. Though easy to maintain with a damp mop, most resilients will eventually need a liquid polish if you want a floor that shines. Vinyl products simulating wood, brick, stone, or tile aren't necessarily going to fool anyone, but they feature easy-to-live-with, dirt-hiding patterns with a pleasant Country attitude. Abstract or speckled patterns can add visual texture.

Ceramic Tile. Beyond its countertop applications, ceramic tile makes a long-lasting, easy-to-keep floor with a handsome aura of authenticity and history. Like any hard floor, however, it is cold and tiring to stand on, echoes noise, and is unkind to a dropped teacup. Some judiciously placed rugs can help overcome these disadvantages. Unglazed tiles are simply the hard-fired clay body, the same natural color throughout, from pale sand to deep umber or tinted with minerals.

The more highly fired the product, the denser, harder, and less absorbent it becomes. Low-fired earthenware terra-

cotta tiles are rugged and rustic but porous. They require frequent sealing and extra maintenance in a kitchen setting. Higher-fired stoneware quarry tiles still provide a handsome, earthy look and bear up to heavy use if well sealed. Most highly fired and more expensive tiles are smooth, impervious porcelain pavers, which require no sealing.

To enliven unglazed tiles without losing their neutral earthiness, lay them in intriguing overall patterns, such as octagons, squares, herringbones, or basket weaves. Standard floor mosaics, usually with porcelain bodies, can be factory mounted on mesh sheets in custom patterns. Plain mosaics have a charming retro flair.

Glazed tiles, permanently sealed with a thin, impervious glasslike layer, open up even more decorative possibilities. Tile industry organizations test and rate glazes for durability, so make sure your choice is specified for a demanding floor application, particularly if the kitchen has an exterior entrance.

Finishing Touches

After assembling the kitchen's working parts, add the flourishes that make the whole less workaday. Paint is often the cheapest form of embellishment. Wainscoting, applied with precut tongue-and-groove planks or scored panels, can effectively dress walls, too. Of course, wallpaper is the easiest way to add pattern and print to your kitchen. You can choose from florals, checks, plaids, ticking stripes, or themed motifs, or look for designs that reinforce your Country decorating style. Many manufacturers carry different lines that might include American, English, French, Italian, or Swedish Country style, as well as Victorian, Shaker, and Arts and Crafts motifs, among others.

Light-colored wood cabinets and natural-finish pine table and benches, opposite, shout Country.

The Modern Country look is sustained by a copper-finish faucet and solid-wood cabinets, right top and bottom.

Plan #151027

Dimensions: 37' W x 73' D

Levels: 2

Square Footage: 2,332

Main Level Sq. Ft.: 1,713

Upper Level Sq. Ft.: 619

Bedrooms: 3

Bathrooms: 3

Foundation: Crawl space, slab; optional basement plan available for extra fee

Materials List Available: Yes

Price Category: E

A traditional design with a covered front porch and high ceilings in many rooms gives this home all the space and comfort you'll ever need.

Features:

- **Foyer:** A formal foyer with 8-in. wood columns will lead you to an elegant dining area.

- **Great Room:** This wonderful gathering room has 10-ft. boxed ceilings, a built-in media center, and an atrium door leading to a rear grilling porch.

- **Kitchen:** Functional yet cozy, this kitchen opens to the breakfast area with built-in computer desk and is open to the great room as well.

- **Master Suite:** Pamper yourself in this luxurious bedroom with 10-ft. boxed ceilings, large walk-in closets, and a bath area with a whirlpool tub, shower, and double vanity.

- **Second Level:** A game room and two bedrooms with walk-thru baths make this floor special.

Images provided by designer/architect.

Main Level Floor Plan

Upper Level Floor Plan

Copyright by designer/architect.

Plan #271082

Dimensions: 71' W x 62' D

Levels: 1

Square Footage: 2,074

Bedrooms: 4

Bathrooms: 2

Foundation: Crawl space or slab

Materials List Available: No

Price Category: D

Images provided by designer/architect.

Magnificent pillars and a huge transom window add stature to the impressive entry of this traditional home.

Features:

- **Living Room:** A corner fireplace warms this spacious room, which shares a 12-ft. ceiling with the dining room and the kitchen.

- **Backyard:** A French door provides direct access to a covered porch, which in turn flows into a wide deck and a sunny patio.

- **Master Suite:** A cathedral ceiling enhances the master bedroom, which offers a large walk-in closet. The private bath is certainly luxurious, with its whirlpool tub and two vanities

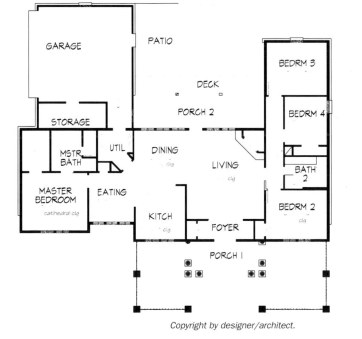

Copyright by designer/architect.

SMARTtip

Making a Cornice

Any new cornice or cornice shelf includes mounting hardware and directions for its installation. But you'll probably need to purchase mounting brackets to install older or homemade cornices. If you're not comfortable with the idea of working on a ladder, especially while handling the cornice and various tools, call a pro. A professional installer will charge a flat rate for coming to your house plus an additional fee for each treatment. Prices vary, but your location, the size of the treatment (measured by the foot), and the difficulty of the job will determine its price.

Plan #331002

Dimensions: 62'2" W x 66'8" D

Levels: 2

Square Footage: 2,299

Main Level Sq. Ft.: 1,517

Upper Level Sq. Ft.: 782

Bedrooms: 3

Bathrooms: 2½

Foundation: Basement, crawl space, or slab

Materials List Available: No

Price Category: E

Images provided by designer/architect.

Main Level Floor Plan

Upper Level Floor Plan

Copyright by designer/architect.

Plan #271057

Dimensions: 66' W x 41' D

Levels: 2

Square Footage: 2,195

Main Level Sq. Ft.: 1,095

Upper Level Sq. Ft.: 1,100

Bedrooms: 3

Bathrooms: 2½

Foundation: Daylight basement

Materials List Available: No

Price Category: D

Images provided by designer/architect.

Main Level Floor Plan

Upper Level Floor Plan

Copyright by designer/architect.

Main Level Floor Plan

Patio

Porch

Master Bedroom 15'x 13'6"

WIC

Living 19'4"x 17'4"

Breakfast 10'8"x 10'

Two-Car Garage 21'8"x 23'4"

Kit. 10'8"x 12'

Ma. Bath

Bedroom 11'10"x 11'7"

Dining 11'10"x 13'3"

Utility

Copyright by designer/architect.

Images provided by designer/architect.

Upper Level Floor Plan

Unfin. Bedroom 10'8"x 12'

Bath

Balcony

Bedroom 11'10"x 11'

Open to Below

Bedroom 11'10"x 13'

Plan #111050

Dimensions: 77' W x 51' D

Levels: 2

Square Footage: 2,333

Main Level Sq. Ft.: 1,685

Upper Level Sq. Ft.: 648

Bedrooms: 4

Bathrooms: 3

Foundation: Basement

Materials List Available: No

Price Category: E

Porch 22'1"x 8'

Breakfast 10'x 10'

Utility

Living 20'5"x 15'6"

Kitchen 12'x 13'6"

Two Car Garage 22'8"x 21'4"

Ma. Ba.

Master Bedroom 13'x 17'8"

Dining 12'x 12'8"

Foyer

Porch 34'10"x 6'

Main Level Floor Plan

Copyright by designer/architect.

Images provided by designer/architect.

Computer Area

Future Gameroom 18'9"x 12'6"

Bedroom 12'3"x 14'

Bedroom 12'5"x 14'

Upper Level Floor Plan

Plan #111022

Dimensions: 62' W x 36'4" D

Levels: 2

Square Footage: 3,105

Main Level Sq. Ft.: 1,470

Upper Level Sq. Ft.: 1,635

Bedrooms: 4

Bathrooms: 2½

Foundation: Finished basement

Materials List Available: Yes

Price Category: G

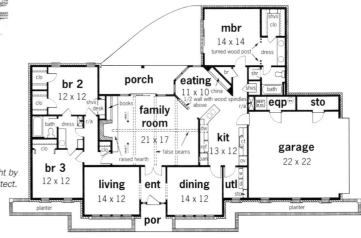

Plan #211047

Dimensions: 74'6" W x 50' D

Levels: 1

Square Footage: 2,009

Bedrooms: 3

Bathrooms: 2

Foundation: Slab

Materials List Available: Yes

Price Category: D

Images provided by designer/architect.

Copyright by designer/architect.

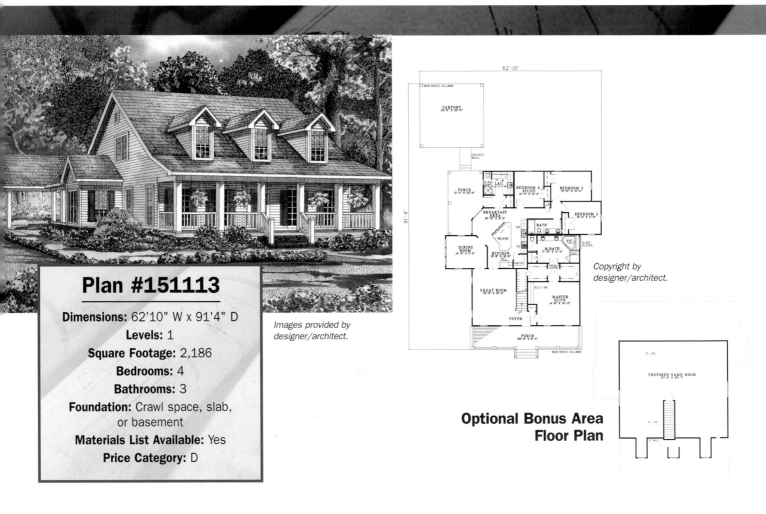

Plan #151113

Dimensions: 62'10" W x 91'4" D

Levels: 1

Square Footage: 2,186

Bedrooms: 4

Bathrooms: 3

Foundation: Crawl space, slab, or basement

Materials List Available: Yes

Price Category: D

Images provided by designer/architect.

Copyright by designer/architect.

Optional Bonus Area Floor Plan

Plan #241002

Dimensions: 65' W x 59'8" D

Levels: 1

Square Footage: 2,154

Bedrooms: 4

Bathrooms: 2½

Foundation: Slab

Materials List Available: No

Price Category: D

Images provided by designer/architect.

Copyright by designer/architect.

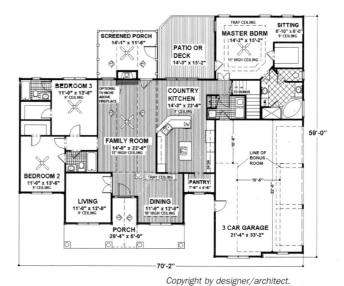

Plan #101009

Dimensions: 70'2" W x 59' D

Levels: 1

Square Footage: 2,097

Bedrooms: 3

Bathrooms: 3

Foundation: Slab

Materials List Available: No

Price Category: D

Images provided by designer/architect.

Copyright by designer/architect.

SMARTtip

Single-Level Decks

A single-level deck can use a strong vertical element, such as a pergola or a gazebo, to make it interesting. A simple and less-expensive option is a potted conical shrub or a clematis growing on a trellis.

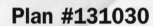

Plan #131030

Dimensions: 51' W x 41'10" D
Levels: 2
Square Footage: 2,470
Main Level Sq. Ft.: 1,290
Upper Level Sq. Ft.: 1,180
Bedrooms: 4
Bathrooms: 2½
Foundation: Crawl space, slab, basement, or walk-out basement
Materials List Available: Yes
Price Category: F

Images provided by designer/architect.

Master Bedroom

Master Bathroom

Entry

If high ceilings and spacious rooms make you happy, you'll love this gorgeous home.

Features:

- Family Room: An 18-ft. vaulted ceiling that's open to the balcony above, a corner fireplace, and a wall of windows make this room feel special.

- Dining Room: This formal room, which flows into the living room, also opens to the front porch and optional backyard deck.

- Kitchen: A bright breakfast room joins with this kitchen and opens to the backyard deck.

- Master Suite: You'll smile when you see the 11-ft. vaulted ceiling, stunning arched window, and two walk-in closets in the bedroom. A skylight lets natural light into the private bath, with its spa tub, separate shower, and dual-sink vanity.

- Bedrooms: To reach these three charming bedrooms, you'll admire the view into the family room below as you walk along the balcony hall.

Main Level Floor Plan

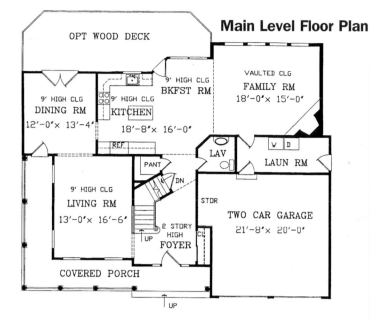

OPT WOOD DECK

FAMILY RM
VAULTED CLG
18'-0" × 15'-0"

9' HIGH CLG
BKFST RM

DINING RM
9' HIGH CLG
12'-0" × 13'-4"

KITCHEN
9' HIGH CLG
18'-8" × 16'-0"

REF

LAV

LAUN RM
W D

PANT

DN

LIVING RM
9' HIGH CLG
13'-0" × 16'-6"

STOR

TWO CAR GARAGE
21'-8" × 20'-0"

UP

2 STORY HIGH
FOYER
CL

COVERED PORCH

UP

Upper Level Floor Plan

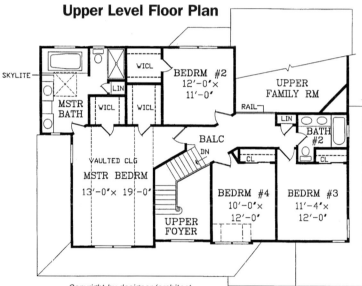

SKYLITE

WICL

BEDRM #2
12'-0" × 11'-0"

UPPER FAMILY RM

LIN

MSTR BATH

WICL

WICL

RAIL

LIN

BATH #2

BALC

DN

CL

CL

MSTR BEDRM
VAULTED CLG
13'-0" × 19'-0"

UPPER FOYER

BEDRM #4
10'-0" × 12'-0"

BEDRM #3
11'-4" × 12'-0"

Copyright by designer/architect.

Kitchen/Breakfast Area

Dining Room

Living Room

Kitchen/Breakfast Area

Copyright by designer/architect.

Plan #321030

Dimensions: 61' W x 51' D
Levels: 1
Square Footage: 2,029
Bedrooms: 4
Bathrooms: 2
Foundation: Basement
Materials List Available: Yes
Price Category: D

Images provided by designer/architect.

Plan #321019

Dimensions: 70'8" W x 70' D
Levels: 1
Square Footage: 2,452
Bedrooms: 4
Bathrooms: 2½
Foundation: Basement
Materials List Available: Yes
Price Category: E

Images provided by designer/architect.

Copyright by designer/architect.

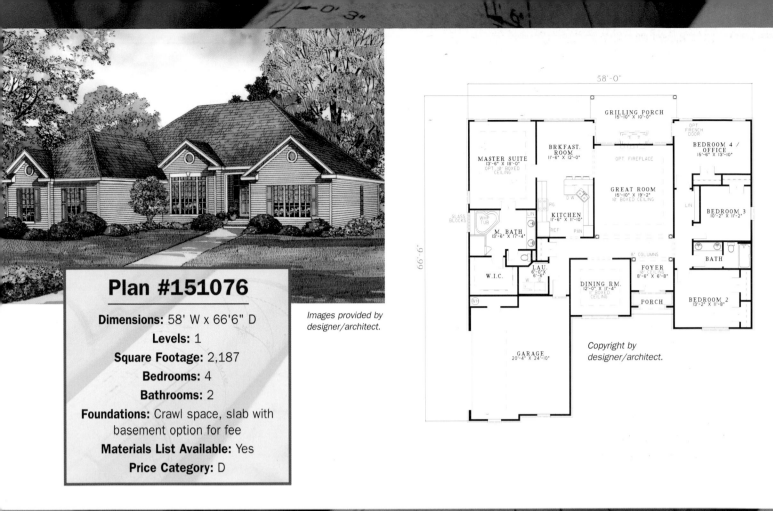

Plan #151076

Dimensions: 58' W x 66'6" D

Levels: 1

Square Footage: 2,187

Bedrooms: 4

Bathrooms: 2

Foundations: Crawl space, slab with basement option for fee

Materials List Available: Yes

Price Category: D

Images provided by designer/architect.

Copyright by designer/architect.

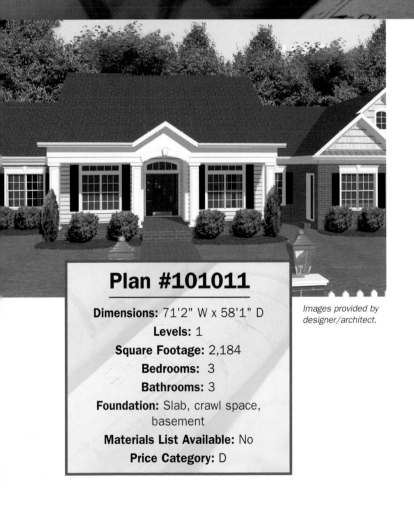

Plan #101011

Dimensions: 71'2" W x 58'1" D

Levels: 1

Square Footage: 2,184

Bedrooms: 3

Bathrooms: 3

Foundation: Slab, crawl space, basement

Materials List Available: No

Price Category: D

Images provided by designer/architect.

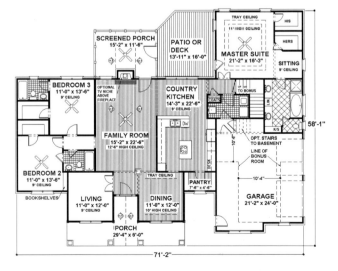

Copyright by designer/architect.

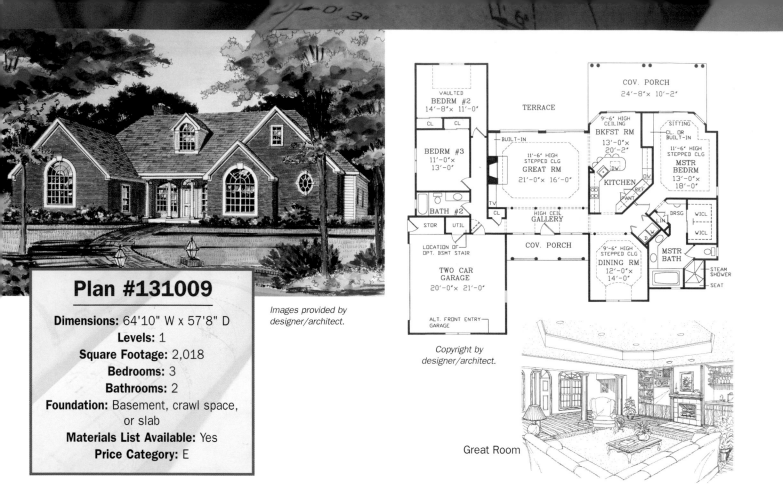

Images provided by designer/architect.

Copyright by designer/architect.

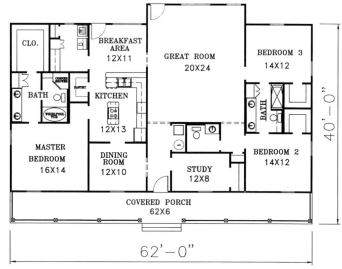

Great Room

Plan #131009

Dimensions: 64'10" W x 57'8" D

Levels: 1

Square Footage: 2,018

Bedrooms: 3

Bathrooms: 2

Foundation: Basement, crawl space, or slab

Materials List Available: Yes

Price Category: E

Plan #191010

Dimensions: 62' W x 40' D

Levels: 1

Square Footage: 2,189

Bedrooms: 3

Bathrooms: 2½

Foundation: Crawl space, slab

Materials List Available: No

Price Category: D

Images provided by designer/architect.

Copyright by designer/architect.

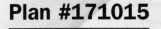

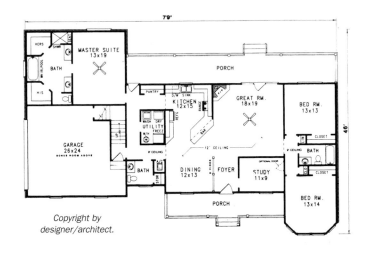

Plan #171015

Dimensions: 79' W x 46' D

Levels: 1

Square Footage: 2,089

Bedrooms: 3

Bathrooms: 2½

Foundation: Slab, crawl space

Materials List Available: Yes

Price Category: D

*Images provided by
designer/architect.*

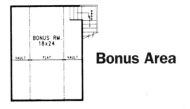

Bonus Area

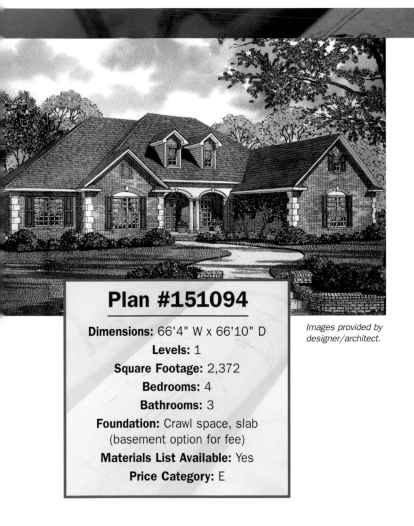

Plan #151094

Dimensions: 66'4" W x 66'10" D

Levels: 1

Square Footage: 2,372

Bedrooms: 4

Bathrooms: 3

Foundation: Crawl space, slab
(basement option for fee)

Materials List Available: Yes

Price Category: E

*Images provided by
designer/architect.*

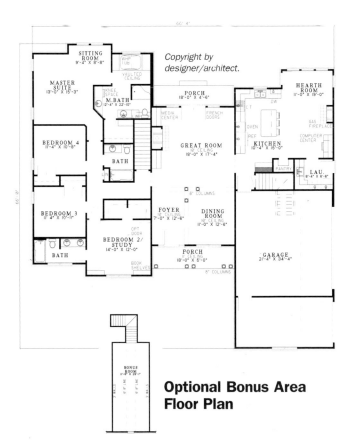

**Optional Bonus Area
Floor Plan**

Plan #181151

Dimensions: 50' W x 46' D

Levels: 2

Square Footage: 2,283

Main Level Sq. Ft.: 1,274

Second Level Sq. Ft.: 1,009

Bedrooms: 3

Bathrooms: 2½

Foundation: Basement

Materials List Available: Yes

Price Category: E

Images provided by designer/architect.

Multiple porches, stately columns, and arched multi-paned windows adorn this country home.

Features:

- Ceiling Height: 8 ft. unless otherwise noted.

- Great Room: The second-floor mezzanine overlooks this great room. With its soaring ceiling, this dramatic room is the centerpiece of a spacious and flowing design that is just as suited to entertaining as it is to family life.

- Dining Area: Guests will naturally flow into this dining area when it is time to eat. After dinner they can step directly out onto the porch to enjoy coffee and dessert when the weather is fair.

- Kitchen: This efficient and well-designed kitchen has double sinks and offers a separate eating area for those impromptu family meals.

- Master Bedroom: This master retreat has a walk-in closet and its own sumptuous bath.

- Home Office: Whether you work at home or just need a place for the family computer and keeping track of family finances, this home office fills the bill.

Main Level Floor Plan

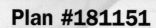

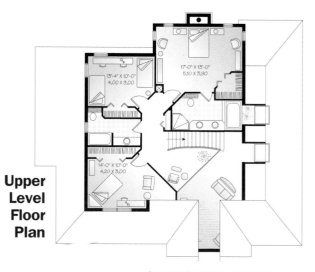

Upper Level Floor Plan

Copyright by designer/architect.

Plan #271074

Dimensions: 68' W x 86' D
Levels: 1
Square Footage: 2,400
Bedrooms: 4
Bathrooms: 3
Foundation: Crawl space or slab
Materials List Available: No
Price Category: C

Images provided by designer/architect.

Perfect for families with aging relatives or boomerang children, this home includes a completely separate suite at the rear.

Features:

- **Living Room:** A corner fireplace casts a friendly glow over this gathering space.
- **Kitchen:** This efficient space offers a serving bar that extends toward the eating nook

and the formal dining room.

- **Master Suite:** A cathedral ceiling presides over this deluxe suite, which boasts a whirlpool tub, dual-sink vanity, and walk-in closet.
- **In-law Suite:** This separate wing has its own vaulted living room, plus a kitchen, a dining room, and a bedroom suite.

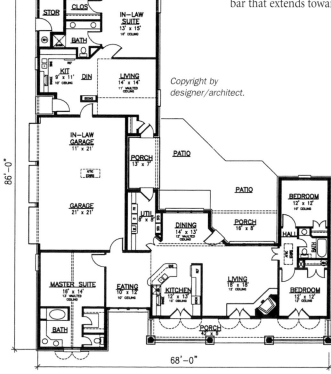

Copyright by designer/architect.

SMARTtip

Adding Professional Flair to Window Treatments

You can give your window treatment designs a professional look by using decorator tricks to customize readymades or dress your own home-sewn designs. These could include contrast linings, tassels, cording, ribbons, or couture trimmings such as buttons, coins, or bows applied to edges. Another trick is to sew a fine wire into the hem of curtains or valances to create a pliable edge that you can shape yourself. Small weights that you can sew into the hem of drapery panels or jabots will make them hang better. For more inspiration look at fashion magazines and visit showrooms.

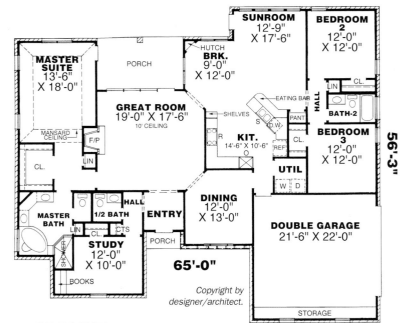

Plan #241001

Dimensions: 65' W x 56'3" D

Levels: 1

Square Footage: 2,350

Bedrooms: 3

Bathrooms: 2½

Foundation: Slab

Materials List Available: No

Price Category: E

Images provided by designer/architect.

Classic, traditional rooflines combine with arched windows to draw immediate attention to this lovely three-bedroom home.

Features:

- **Great Room:** The foyer introduces you to this impressive great room, with its grand 10-ft. ceiling and handsome fireplace.

- **Kitchen:** Certain to become the hub of such a family-oriented home, this spacious kitchen, which adjoins the breakfast area and a delightful sunroom, features an abundance of counter space, a pantry, and a convenient eating bar.

- **Master Suite:** You will enjoy the privacy and comfort of this master suite, which features a whirlpool tub, split vanities, and a separate shower.

- **Study:** Adjourn to the front of the house, and enjoy the quiet confines of this private study with built-in bookshelves to work, read, or just relax.

Copyright by designer/architect.

SMARTtip

Kitchen Counters

Make use of counter inserts to help with the cooking chores. For example, ceramic tiles inlaid in a laminate counter create a heat-proof landing zone near the range. A marble or granite insert is tailor-made for pastry chefs. And a butcher-block inlay is a great addition to the food prep area.

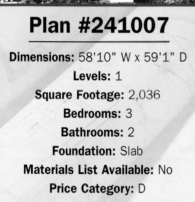

Plan #241007

Dimensions: 58'10" W x 59'1" D

Levels: 1

Square Footage: 2,036

Bedrooms: 3

Bathrooms: 2

Foundation: Slab

Materials List Available: No

Price Category: D

Images provided by designer/architect.

Enjoy summer breezes while relaxing on the large front porch of this charming country cottage.

Features:

- **Great Room:** Whether you enter from the front door or from the kitchen, you will feel welcome in this comfortable great room, which features a corner fireplace.

- **Kitchen:** This well-designed kitchen with extensive counter space offers a delightful eating bar, perfect for quick or informal meals.

- **Master Suite:** This luxurious master suite, located on the first floor for privacy, features his and her walk-in closets, separate vanities, a deluxe corner tub, a linen closet, and a walk-in shower.

- **Additional Bedrooms:** Two secondary bedrooms and an optional, large game room —well suited for a growing family— are located on the second floor.

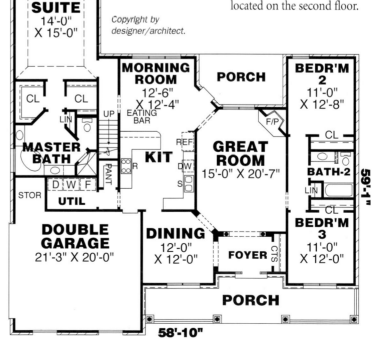

Copyright by designer/architect.

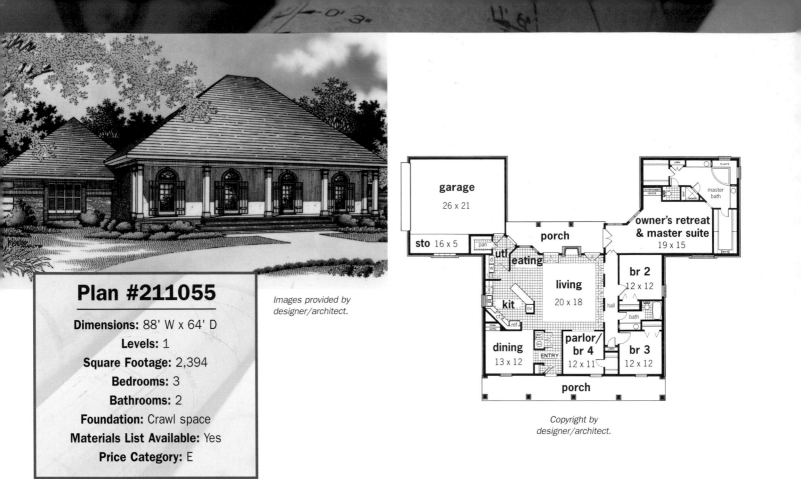

Plan #211055

Dimensions: 88' W x 64' D

Levels: 1

Square Footage: 2,394

Bedrooms: 3

Bathrooms: 2

Foundation: Crawl space

Materials List Available: Yes

Price Category: E

Images provided by designer/architect.

Copyright by designer/architect.

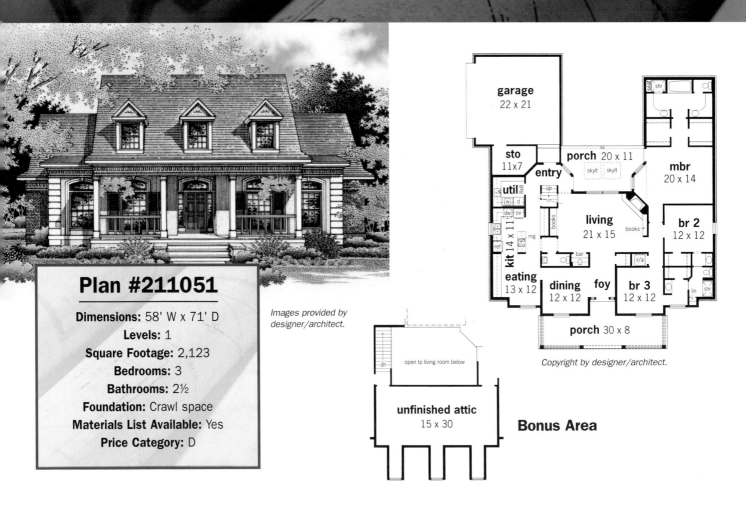

Plan #211051

Dimensions: 58' W x 71' D

Levels: 1

Square Footage: 2,123

Bedrooms: 3

Bathrooms: 2½

Foundation: Crawl space

Materials List Available: Yes

Price Category: D

Images provided by designer/architect.

Copyright by designer/architect.

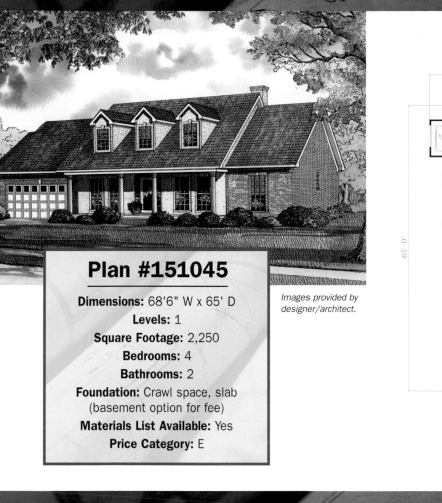

Plan #151045

Dimensions: 68'6" W x 65' D

Levels: 1

Square Footage: 2,250

Bedrooms: 4

Bathrooms: 2

Foundation: Crawl space, slab (basement option for fee)

Materials List Available: Yes

Price Category: E

Images provided by designer/architect.

Copyright by designer/architect.

Rear Elevation

Plan #131019

Dimensions: 83'6" W x 53'4" D

Levels: 1

Square Footage: 2,243

Bedrooms: 3

Bathrooms: 2½

Foundation: Basement, crawl space, or slab

Materials List Available: Yes

Price Category: F

Images provided by designer/architect.

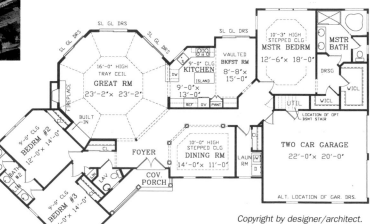

Copyright by designer/architect.

Plan #271049

Dimensions: 74' W x 44' D

Levels: 2

Square Footage: 2,464

Main Level Sq. Ft.: 1,288

Upper Level Sq. Ft.: 1,176

Bedrooms: 4

Bathrooms: 2½

Foundation: Basement, crawl space

Materials List Available: Yes

Price Category: E

Images provided by designer/architect.

This classic farmhouse design features a wraparound porch for enjoying conversation on warm afternoons.

Features:

• Living Room: A central fireplace warms this spacious gathering place, while French doors offer porch access.

• Dining Room: On formal occasions, this room is perfect for hosting elegant meals.

• Country Kitchen: An island workstation and a handy pantry keep the family chef organized and productive.

• Family Room: The home's second fireplace warms this cozy area, which is really an extension of the kitchen. Set up a kitchen table here, and enjoy casual meals near the crackling fire.

• Master Suite: The master bedroom is certainly vast. The walk-in closet is large as well. The private, compartmentalized bath offers a sit-down shower and a separate dressing area.

Main Level Floor Plan

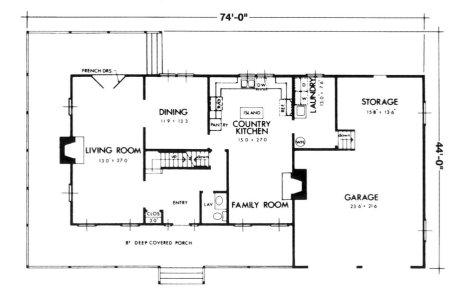

Upper Level Floor Plan

Copyright by designer/architect.

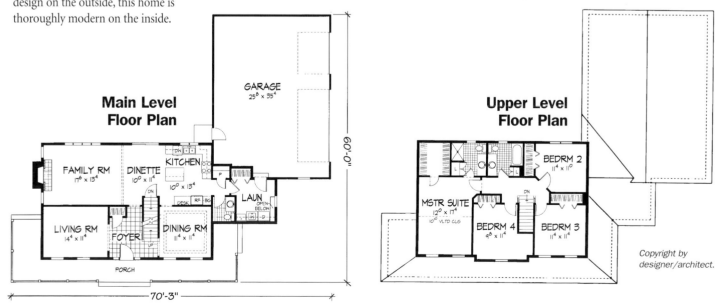

Plan #271070

Dimensions: 71' W x 60' D

Levels: 2

Square Footage: 2,144

Main Level Sq. Ft.: 1,156

Upper Level Sq. Ft.: 988

Bedrooms: 4

Bathrooms: 2½

Foundation: Basement, crawl space

Materials List Available: No

Price Category: D

Images provided by designer/architect.

A nice example of a country farmhouse design on the outside, this home is thoroughly modern on the inside.

Features:

- Living Room: To the left of the foyer, this secluded space offers a moment of peace and quiet after a long day at the office.

- Dining Room: An interesting ceiling treatment makes this elegant room even more sophisticated.

- Kitchen: You won't find a more well-appointed space than this! You'll love the central work island, this useful menu desk

and nearby pantry. The adjacent dinette hosts casual meals and offers outdoor access via sliding glass doors.

- Family Room: A handsome fireplace sets the mood in this expansive area.

- Master Suite: A vaulted ceiling presides over the sleeping room, while a walk-in closet organizes your entire wardrobe. The private bath boasts a refreshing shower and a linen closet.

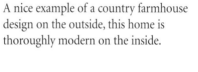

Main Level Floor Plan

GARAGE
25⁸ x 35⁴

FAMILY RM
17⁶ x 13⁴

DINETTE
10⁰ x 11⁴

KITCHEN
10⁰ x 13⁴

LAUN
OPEN-BELOW

LIVING RM
14⁴ x 11⁴

FOYER

DINING RM
11⁴ x 11⁴

DESK RF

PORCH

70'-3"

60'-0"

Upper Level Floor Plan

MSTR SUITE
12⁰ x 17⁴
10⁰ VLTD CLG

BEDRM 2
11⁴ x 11⁰

BEDRM 4
9⁸ x 11⁴

BEDRM 3
11⁴ x 11⁴

Copyright by designer/architect.

Main Level Floor Plan

Two Car Garage
21'2"x 21'1"

Patio

Porch

Storage

1/2 Ba

Master Bedroom
15'x 15'

WIC

Living
19'4"x 17'1"

Breakfast
13'8"x 10'7"

Ma. Bath

Bath

WIC

Kitchen
10'8"x 12'3"

Bedroom
12'x 11'7"

Dining
12'x 13'6"

Utility

Porch

Images provided by designer/architect.

Open to Below

Bath

Balcony

Upper Level Floor Plan

Bedroom
12'x 11'7"

Bedroom
12'x 13'

Copyright by designer/architect.

Plan #111026

Dimensions: 66' W x 65' D

Levels: 2

Square Footage: 2,406

Main Level Sq. Ft.: 1,796

Upper Level Sq. Ft.: 610

Bedrooms: 4

Bathrooms: 3½

Foundation: Crawlspace

Materials List Available: No

Price Category: E

Two Car Garage
22'x 23'6"

Porch

Breakfast

Main Level Floor Plan

Master Bedroom
15'x 15'4"

Dining
13'6"x 12'

Living
18'x 17'6"

Porch

Images provided by designer/architect.

Bedroom
14'x 11'

Bedroom
15'5"x 12'

Bedroom
14'x 11'6"

Open To Below

Upper Level Floor Plan

Copyright by designer/architect.

Plan #111023

Dimensions: 46'11" W x 73'5" D

Levels: 2

Square Footage: 2,356

Main Level Sq. Ft.: 1,516

Upper Level Sq. Ft.: 840

Bedrooms: 4

Bathrooms: 2½

Foundation: Slab

Materials List Available: No

Price Category: E

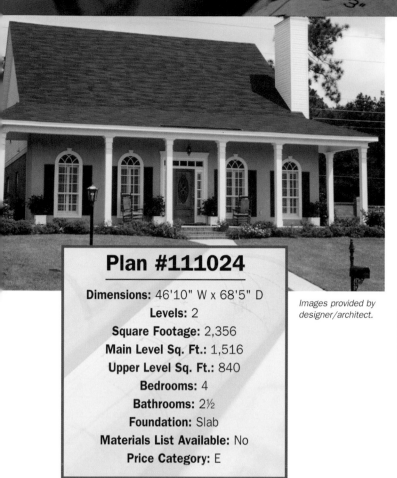

Plan #111024

Dimensions: 46'10" W x 68'5" D

Levels: 2

Square Footage: 2,356

Main Level Sq. Ft.: 1,516

Upper Level Sq. Ft.: 840

Bedrooms: 4

Bathrooms: 2½

Foundation: Slab

Materials List Available: No

Price Category: E

Images provided by designer/architect.

Main Level Floor Plan

Upper Level Floor Plan

Copyright by designer/architect.

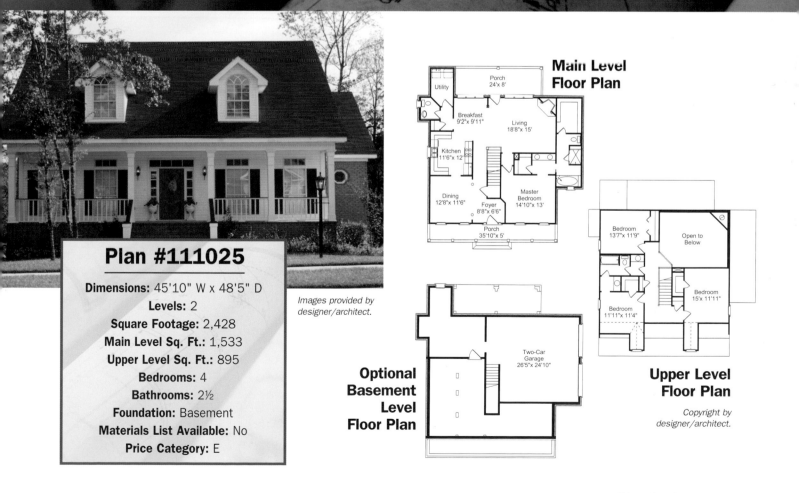

Plan #111025

Dimensions: 45'10" W x 48'5" D

Levels: 2

Square Footage: 2,428

Main Level Sq. Ft.: 1,533

Upper Level Sq. Ft.: 895

Bedrooms: 4

Bathrooms: 2½

Foundation: Basement

Materials List Available: No

Price Category: E

Images provided by designer/architect.

Main Level Floor Plan

Optional Basement Level Floor Plan

Upper Level Floor Plan

Copyright by designer/architect.

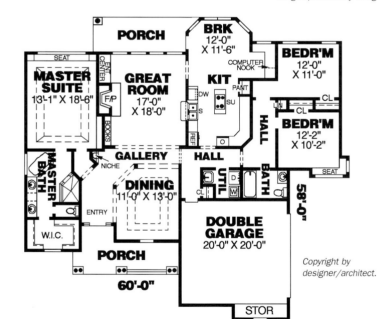

Plan #241003

Dimensions: 60' W x 58' D
Levels: 1
Square Footage: 2,080
Bedrooms: 3
Bathrooms: 2
Foundation: Slab
Materials List Available: No
Price Category: D

Striking rooflines combine with a stone-and-shingle exterior to give this lovely country home immediate appeal.

Features:

- **Great Room:** Certain to become a favorite gathering place for friends and family, this great room features a fireplace, bookshelves, and an entertainment center.

- **Kitchen:** This well-designed kitchen—with ample counter space and cabinets—features a pantry, island, and large breakfast area. It also includes a convenient computer nook, well suited for managing today's complexities.

- **Master Suite:** Separated for privacy, this master suite features his and her vanities, a corner tub, a separate shower, a large walk-in closet, and a delightful window seat for your relaxing pleasure.

- **Garage:** Use the extra space in this garage for storage.

SMARTtip

Color Basics for Kids' Rooms

Use color effectively to enhance the perception of the space itself. Make a large room feel cozy with warm colors, which tend to advance. Conversely, open up a small room with cool colors or neutrals, which tend to recede. The less-intense version of a color will generally reduce its tendency to advance or recede, as well. Other tricks: Sharp contrasts often have the same impact as a dark color, reducing perceived space. Monochromatic schemes enlarge space. Neutrals of similar value make walls appear to retreat.

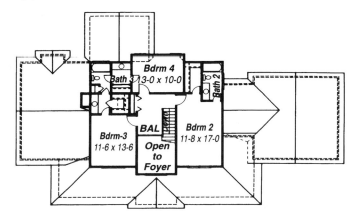

Plan #141017

Dimensions: 82' W x 49' D

Levels: 2

Square Footage: 2,480

Main Level Sq. Ft.: 1,581

Upper Level Sq. Ft.: 899

Bedrooms: 4

Bathrooms: 3½

Foundation: Basement, crawl space, or slab

Materials List Available: No

Price Category: E

You'll enjoy cool summer breezes on the wraparound porch of this spacious home.

Features:

- Ceiling Height: 9 ft.

- Family Room: Through French doors leading from the living room you will enter the family domain. This large and open space features a handsome fireplace.

- Rear Porch: Accessible from the family room, this porch is screened in to create a comfortable, private warm-weather retreat.

- Master Suite: This luxurious suite is located on the first floor for added privacy. The master bath features separate walk-in closets and vanities.

- Kitchen: This open sunny kitchen has an island for food preparation.

- Laundry: This large laundry is conveniently located between the kitchen and the garage.

Images provided by designer/architect.

Main Level Floor Plan

Copyright by designer/architect.

Upper Level Floor Plan

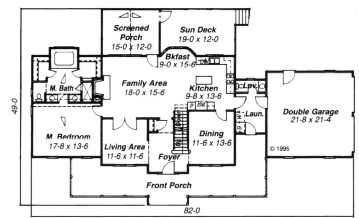

**Main Level
Floor Plan**

**Upper Level
Floor Plan**

Copyright by designer/architect.

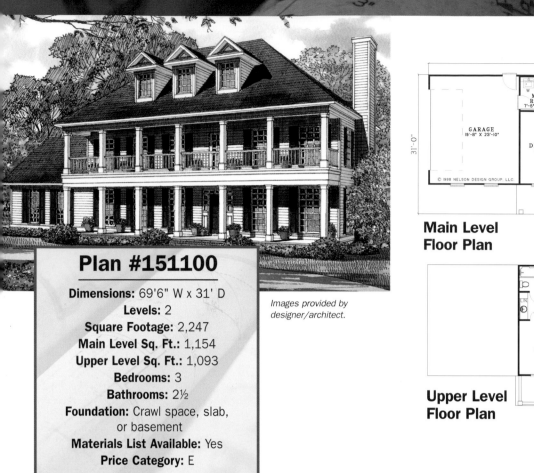

Plan #151100

Dimensions: 69'6" W x 31' D

Levels: 2

Square Footage: 2,247

Main Level Sq. Ft.: 1,154

Upper Level Sq. Ft.: 1,093

Bedrooms: 3

Bathrooms: 2½

Foundation: Crawl space, slab, or basement

Materials List Available: Yes

Price Category: E

Images provided by designer/architect.

Plan #181136

Dimensions: 52' W x 46'8" D

Levels: 2

Square Footage: 2,426

Main Level Sq. Ft.: 1,319

Upper Level Sq. Ft.: 1,107

Bedrooms: 3

Bathrooms: 1½

Foundation: Full basement

Materials List Available: Yes

Price Category: E

Images provided by designer/architect.

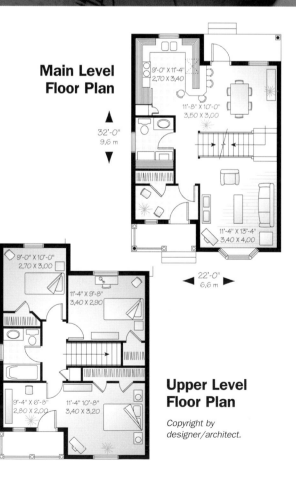

**Main Level
Floor Plan**

**Upper Level
Floor Plan**

Copyright by designer/architect.

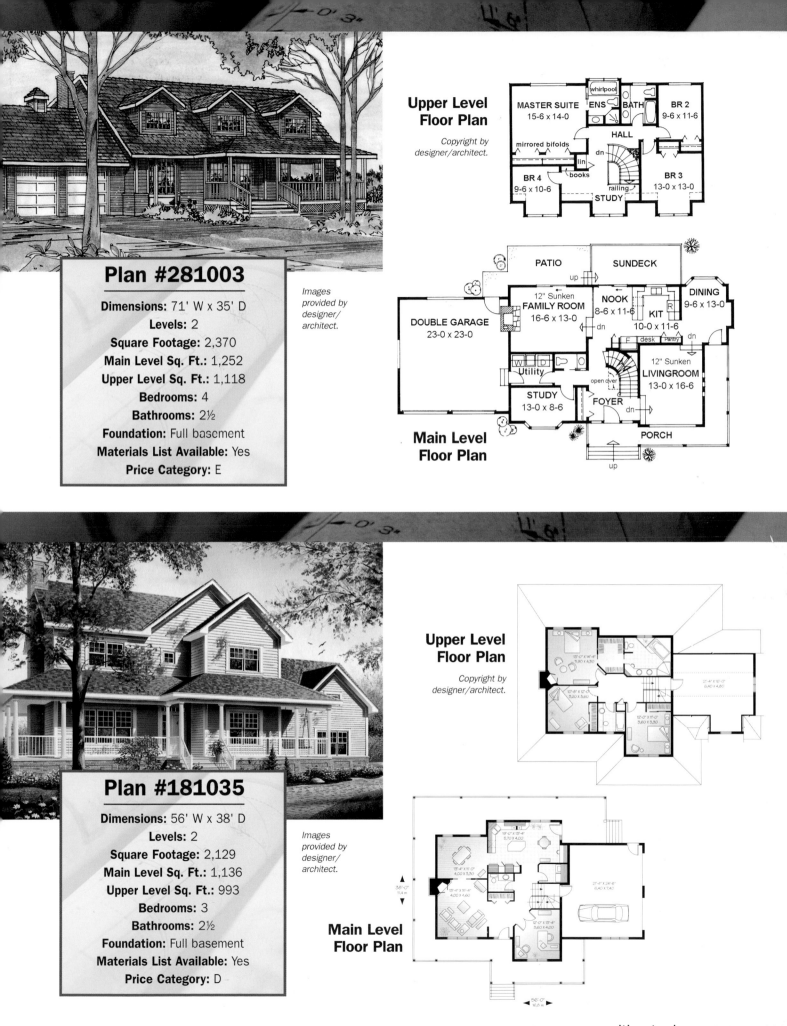

Plan #281003

Dimensions: 71' W x 35' D

Levels: 2

Square Footage: 2,370

Main Level Sq. Ft.: 1,252

Upper Level Sq. Ft.: 1,118

Bedrooms: 4

Bathrooms: 2½

Foundation: Full basement

Materials List Available: Yes

Price Category: E

Images provided by designer/architect.

Upper Level Floor Plan

Copyright by designer/architect.

MASTER SUITE 15-6 x 14-0 — whirlpool — ENS — BATH — BR 2 9-6 x 11-6

mirrored bifolds — HALL — dn — lin — books — railing — BR 3 13-0 x 13-0

BR 4 9-6 x 10-6 — STUDY

Main Level Floor Plan

PATIO — SUNDECK — up

12" Sunken FAMILY ROOM 16-6 x 13-0 — NOOK 8-6 x 11-6 — KIT 10-0 x 11-6 — DINING 9-6 x 13-0 — R

DOUBLE GARAGE 23-0 x 23-0 — dn — F — desk — Pantry — dn

Utility — W D — open over — 12" Sunken LIVINGROOM 13-0 x 16-6

STUDY 13-0 x 8-6 — FOYER — dn — PORCH — up

Plan #181035

Dimensions: 56' W x 38' D

Levels: 2

Square Footage: 2,129

Main Level Sq. Ft.: 1,136

Upper Level Sq. Ft.: 993

Bedrooms: 3

Bathrooms: 2½

Foundation: Full basement

Materials List Available: Yes

Price Category: D

Images provided by designer/architect.

Upper Level Floor Plan

Copyright by designer/architect.

Main Level Floor Plan

Plan #311003

Dimensions: 70'10" W x 65'4" D

Levels: 2

Square Footage: 2,428

Main Level Sq. Ft.: 2,348

Upper Level Sq. Ft.: 80

Bedrooms: 3

Bathrooms: 2½

Foundation: Crawl space, slab

Materials List Available: Y

Price Category: E

If you admire the gracious colonnaded porch, curved brick steps, and stunning front windows, you'll fall in love with the interior of this home.

Features:

- Great Room: Enjoy the vaulted ceiling, balcony from the upper level, and fireplace with flanking windows that let you look out to the patio.

- Dining Room: Columns define this formal room, which is adjacent to the breakfast room.

- Kitchen: A bayed sink area and extensive curved bar provide visual interest in this well-designed kitchen, which every cook will love.

- Breakfast Room: Huge windows let the sun shine into this room, which is open to the kitchen.

- Master Suite: The sitting area is open to the rear porch for a special touch in this gorgeous suite. Two walk-in closets and a vaulted ceiling and double vanity in the bath will make you feel completely pampered.

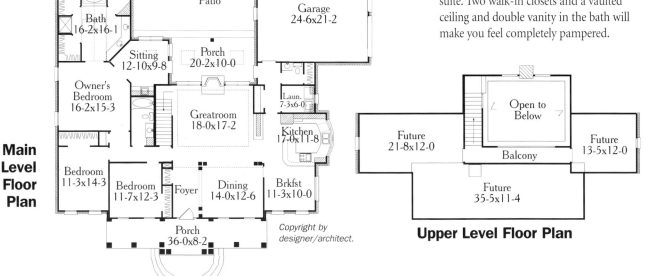

Main Level Floor Plan

Upper Level Floor Plan

Copyright by designer/architect.

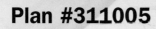

Plan #311005

Dimensions: 87' W x 57'3" D

Levels: 1

Square Footage: 2,497

Bedrooms: 3

Bathrooms: 3½

Foundation: Crawl space, slab

Materials List Available: Yes

Price Category: E

Images provided by designer/architect.

You'll love this home, which mixes practical features with a gracious appearance.

Features:

- **Great Room:** A handsome fireplace and flanking windows that give a view of the back patio are the highlights of this gracious room.

- **Kitchen:** A curved bar defines the perimeter of this well-planned kitchen.

- **Breakfast Room:** Open to both the great room and the kitchen, this sunny spot leads to the rear porch, which in turn, leads to the patio beyond.

- **Master Suite:** Vaulted ceilings, a huge walk-in closet, and deluxe bath create luxury here.

- **Bonus Room:** Finish this 966-sq.-ft. area as a huge game room, or divide it into a game room, study, and sewing or craft room.

- **Additional Bedrooms:** Each bedroom has a private bath and good closet space.

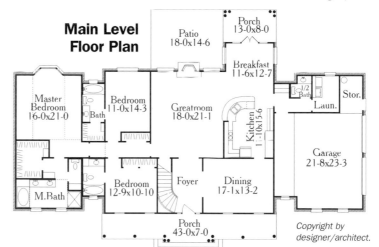

Main Level Floor Plan

Copyright by designer/architect.

Bonus Area Floor Plan

SMARTtip

Front Porch

A front porch proclaims you to the outside world, so furnish it in a way that expresses what you want the world to know about you. Use the walls of your porch to hang interesting items such as sundials or old shutters. Set a mirror into an old window to reflect a portion of the garden.

Plan #321052

Dimensions: 57' W x 48'8" D

Levels: 2

Square Footage: 2,182

Main Level Sq. Ft.: 1,112

Upper Level Sq. Ft.: 1,070

Bedrooms: 3

Bathrooms: 3½

Foundation: Basement

Materials List Available: Yes

Price Category: D

Images provided by designer/architect.

Main Level Floor Plan

Great Rm 19-4x15-0
Breakfast 11-8x13-0
Kit 12-0x14-6
Entry
Porch Depth 7-8
Dining 15-0x12-0
Garage 21-4x21-10

57'-0"
48'-8"

Upper Level Floor Plan

Copyright by designer/architect.

MBr 19-4x13-0 Vaulted
Br 2 14-0x11-0
Dn
Br 3 12-9x12-0 Vaulted

Plan #291012

Dimensions: 58' W x 44' D

Levels: 2

Square Footage: 1,898

Main Level Sq. Ft.: 1,182

Upper Level Sq. Ft.: 716

Bedrooms: 4

Bathrooms: 2½

Foundation: Basement

Materials List Available: No

Price Category: D

Images provided by designer/architect.

Main Level Floor Plan

Copyright by designer/architect.

35'-0"

PORCH
FAMILY ROOM 18'-0"x19'-6"
MORNING ROOM 8'-0"x11'-6"
KITCHEN 10'-0"x11'-6"
DINING ROOM 13'-9"x14'-4"
VAULTED CEILING
FAMILY ENTRY
FP
PANTRY
LAV.
LAUNDRY W D
LIVING ROOM 13'-9"x18'-6"
ENTRY FOYER
UP
TWO-CAR GARAGE 23'-4"x23'-2"
PORCH

44'-0"
58'-0"

Upper Level Floor Plan

BEDROOM 13'-0"x8'-10"
BEDROOM 12'-8"x11'-0"
WIC
LIN
BATH
UPPER HALL
DN
MASTER BATH
BEDROOM 12'-0"x11'-0"
WIC
MASTER BEDROOM 13'-9"x14'-2"

32'-0"
35'-0"

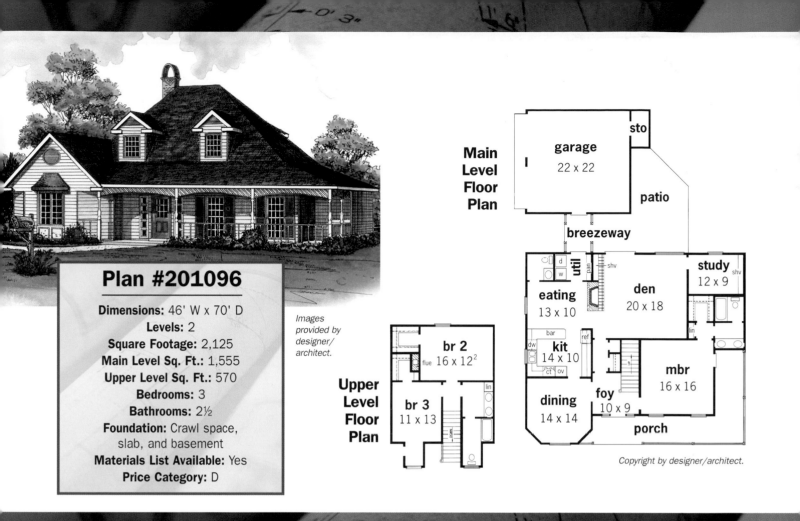

Plan #201096

Dimensions: 46' W x 70' D

Levels: 2

Square Footage: 2,125

Main Level Sq. Ft.: 1,555

Upper Level Sq. Ft.: 570

Bedrooms: 3

Bathrooms: 2½

Foundation: Crawl space, slab, and basement

Materials List Available: Yes

Price Category: D

Images provided by designer/architect.

Copyright by designer/architect.

Main Level Floor Plan

garage 22 x 22

sto

patio

breezeway

util

eating 13 x 10

den 20 x 18

study 12 x 9

Upper Level Floor Plan

br 2 16 x 12²

br 3 11 x 13

kit 14 x 10

bar

mbr 16 x 16

dining 14 x 14

foy 10 x 9

porch

Plan #311014

Dimensions: 64'4" W x 66'1" D

Levels: 2

Square Footage: 2,344

Main Level Sq. Ft.: 1,791

Upper Level Sq. Ft.: 553

Bedrooms: 3

Bathrooms: 2½

Foundation: Slab, crawl space, or basement

Materials List Available: Yes

Price Category: E

Images provided by designer/architect.

Copyright by designer/architect.

Main Level Floor Plan

Garage 23-4x23-4

Patio 22-0x12-0

Laun. 8-4x6-0

M. Bath 17-7x10-6

Greatroom 22-0x15-6

1/2 Bath

Kitchen 12-8x12-0

Master Bedroom 14-0x17-0

Study 11-6x11-0

Foyer 5-8x13-6

Dining 11-6x13-6

Breakfast 12-8x9-10

Porch 30-8x6-0

Upper Level Floor Plan

Future 11-8x10-5

Bedroom 10-6x12-6

Bedroom 9-8x10-2

Bath 8-6x7-2

Future 12-7x10-5

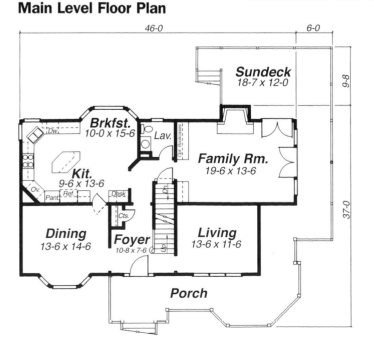

Images provided by designer/architect.

Plan #141015

Dimensions: 46' W x 36'8" D

Levels: 2

Square Footage: 2,350

Main Level Sq. Ft.: 1,155

Upper Level Sq. Ft.: 1,195

Bedrooms: 4

Bathrooms: 2½

Foundation: Basement

Materials List Available: Yes

Price Category: E

This home offers classic Victorian details combined with modern amenities.

Features:

- Ceiling Height: 9 ft. unless otherwise noted.

- Porch: Enjoy summer breezes on this large wraparound porch, with its classic turret corner.

- Family Room: This room has a fireplace and two sets of French doors. One set of doors

leads to the porch; the other leads to a rear sun deck.

- Living Room: This large room at the front of the house is designed for formal entertaining.

- Kitchen: This convenient kitchen features an island and a writing desk.

- Master Bedroom: Enjoy the cozy sitting area in the turret corner. The bedroom offers access to a second story balcony.

- Laundry: The second-floor laundry means you won't have to haul clothing up and down stairs.

Main Level Floor Plan

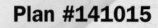

Upper Level Floor Plan

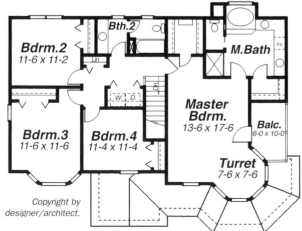

Copyright by designer/architect.

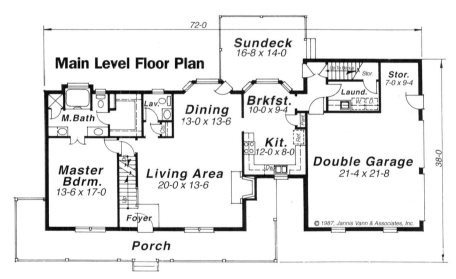

Plan #141014

Dimensions: 72' W x 38' D

Levels: 2

Square Footage: 2,091

Main Level Sq. Ft.: 1,362

Upper Level Sq. Ft.: 729

Bedrooms: 3

Bathrooms: 2½

Foundation: Basement

Materials List Available: Yes

Price Category: D

The wraparound front porch and front dormers evoke an old-fashioned country home.

Features:

- Ceiling Height: 8 ft. unless otherwise noted.

- Living Room: This spacious area has an open flow to the dining room, so you can graciously usher guests when it is time to eat.

- Dining Room: This elegant dining room has a bay that opens to the sun deck.

- Kitchen: This warm and inviting kitchen looks out to the front porch. Its bayed breakfast area is perfect for informal family meals.

- Master Suite: The bedroom enjoys a view through the front porch and features a master bath with all the amenities.

- Flexible Room: A room above the two-bay garage offers plenty of space that can be used for anything from a home office to a teen suite.

- Study Room: The two second-floor bedrooms share a study that is perfect for homework.

Images provided by designer/architect.

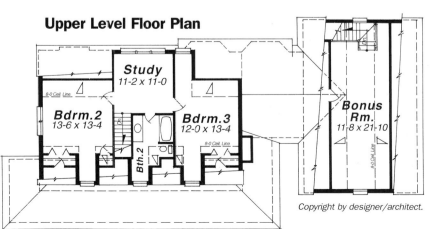

Copyright by designer/architect.

Plan #181078

Dimensions: 58' W x 42'2" D

Levels: 2

Square Footage: 2,292

Main Level Sq. Ft.: 1,266

Upper Level Sq. Ft.: 1,026

Bedrooms: 4

Bathrooms: 2½

Foundation: Full basement

Materials List Available: Yes

Price Category: E

Images provided by designer/architect.

Main Level Floor Plan

Upper Level Floor Plan

Copyright by designer/architect.

Plan #181094

Dimensions: 50' W x 39' D

Levels: 2

Square Footage: 2,099

Main Level Sq. Ft.: 1,060

Upper Level Sq. Ft.: 1,039

Bedrooms: 4

Bathrooms: 2½

Foundation: Full basement

Materials List Available: Yes

Price Category: D

Images provided by designer/architect.

Main Level Floor Plan

Upper Level Floor Plan

Copyright by designer/architect.

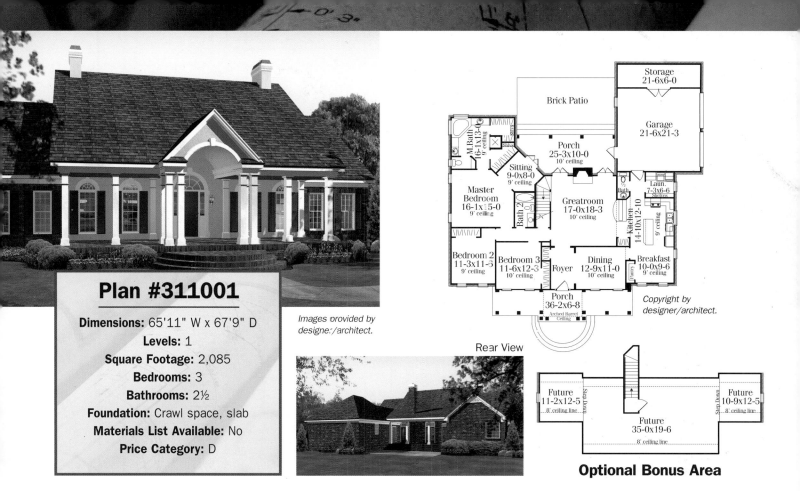

Storage
21-6x6-0

Brick Patio

Garage
21-6x21-3

Porch
25-3x10-0
10' ceiling

M.Bath
16-1x13-0
9' ceiling

Sitting
9-0x8-0
9' ceiling

Master Bedroom
16-1x15-0
9' ceiling

Bath 2

Greatroom
17-0x18-3
10' ceiling

Bath

Kitchen
14-10x12-10
9' ceiling

Laun.
7-3x6-6

Bedroom 2
11-3x11-5
9' ceiling

Bedroom 3
11-6x12-3
10' ceiling

Foyer

Dining
12-9x11-0
10' ceiling

Breakfast
10-0x9-6
9' ceiling

Porch
36-2x6-8

Arched Barrel Ceiling

Copyright by designer/architect.

Plan #311001

Dimensions: 65'11" W x 67'9" D

Levels: 1

Square Footage: 2,085

Bedrooms: 3

Bathrooms: 2½

Foundation: Crawl space, slab

Materials List Available: No

Price Category: D

Images provided by designer/architect.

Rear View

Future
11-2x12-5
8' ceiling line

Future
10-9x12-5
8' ceiling line

Future
35-0x19-6
8' ceiling line

Step Down

Optional Bonus Area

Copyright by designer/architect.

Porch
32-2x8-0

Breakfast
11-8x10-6

Master Bedroom
14-0x17-6

Bath
9.0x15.3

Bedroom
11-10x11-6

Greatroom
17-6x17-6

Kitchen
11-8x14-11

Laundry
11-6x7-6

Storage
11-6x7-10

shelving   linen   shelving

Bath

Bedroom
11-10x11-6

Foyer

Dining
13-0x11-6

½ Bath

Garage
23-4x21-8

Porch
36-4x8-0

Plan #311004

Dimensions: 68'2" W x 57'4" D

Levels: 1

Square Footage: 2,046

Bedrooms: 3

Bathrooms: 2½

Foundation: Crawl space, slab

Materials List Available: Yes

Price Category: D

Images provided by designer/architect.

Rear View

Plan #321041

Dimensions: 64' W x 34' D

Levels: 2

Square Footage: 2,286

Main Level Sq. Ft.: 1,283

Upper Level Sq. Ft.: 1,003

Bedrooms: 4

Bathrooms: 2½

Foundation: Basement

Materials List Available: Yes

Price Category: E

Images provided by designer/architect.

If you love the way these gorgeous windows look from the outside, you'll be thrilled with the equally gracious interior of this home.

Features:

- **Entryway:** This two-story entryway shows off the fine woodworking on the railing and balustrades.

- **Living Room:** The large front windows form a glamorous background in this spacious room.

- **Family Room:** A handsome fireplace and a sliding glass door to the backyard enhance the open design of this room.

- **Breakfast Room:** Large enough for a crowd, this room makes a perfect dining area.

- **Kitchen:** The angled bar and separate pantry are highlights in this step-saving design.

- **Master Suite:** Enjoy this suite's huge walk-in closet, vaulted ceiling, and private bath, which features a double vanity, tub, and shower stall.

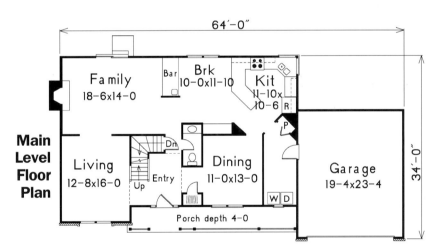

Main Level Floor Plan

Upper Level Floor Plan

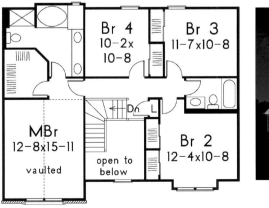

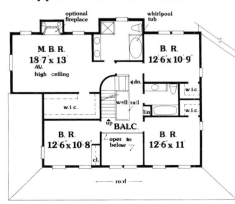

Plan #131051

Dimensions: 64'4" W x 53'4" D

Levels: 2

Square Footage: 2,431

Main Level Sq. Ft.: 1,293

Upper Level Sq. Ft.: 1,138

Bedrooms: 4

Bathrooms: 2½

Foundation: Basement, crawl space, or slab

Materials List Available: Yes

Price Category: F

Gracious and charming with a wraparound front porch and a backyard terrace, this home also has a ready-to-finish third floor all-purpose room and a full bath.

Features:

- Main Level Ceiling Height: 8 ft.

- Family Room: A comfortable space for the entire family to gather, this delightful room can be warmed by a heat-circulating fireplace.

- Dining Room: A cozy dinette boasts a sliding glass door with access to a gorgeous backyard terrace with an optional calm reflecting pool.

- Kitchen: Adjoining the dining area, the kitchen offers plenty of storage and counter space. The laundry room and half-bath are nearby for convenience.

- Garage: The garage is tucked way back to keep it from intruding into the traditional facade.

Images provided by designer/architect.

Main Level Floor Plan

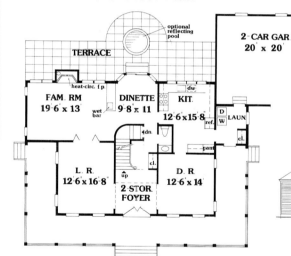

Rear Elevation

Upper Level Floor Plan

Optional 3rd Level Floor Plan

Copyright by designer/architect.

Landscape Plans and Ideas

Landscapes change over the years. As plants grow, the overall look evolves from sparse to lush. Trees cast cool shade where the sun used to shine. Shrubs and hedges grow tall and dense enough to provide privacy. Perennials and ground covers spread to form colorful patches of foliage and flowers. Meanwhile, paths, arbors, fences, and other structures gain the patina of age.

Constant change over the years—sometimes rapid and dramatic, sometimes slow and subtle—is one of the joys of landscaping. It is also one of the challenges. Anticipating how fast plants will grow and how big they will eventually get is difficult, even for professional designers.

To illustrate the kinds of changes to expect in a planting, these pages show a landscape design at three different "ages." Even though a new planting may look sparse at first, it will soon fill in. And because of careful spacing, the planting will look as good in 10 to 15 years as it does after 3 to 5. It will, of course, look different, but that's part of the fun.

At Planting

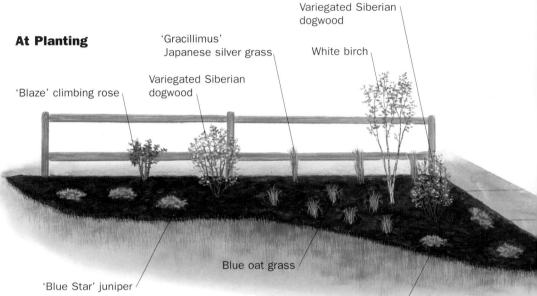

Variegated Siberian dogwood

'Gracillimus' Japanese silver grass

White birch

'Blaze' climbing rose

Variegated Siberian dogwood

'Blue Star' juniper

Blue oat grass

'Blue Star' juniper

Three to Five Years

At Planting—Here's how the corner might appear in early summer immediately after planting. The white birch tree is only 5 to 6 ft. tall, with trunks no thicker than broomsticks. The variegated Siberian dogwoods each have a few main stems about 3 to 4 ft. tall. The 'Blaze' rose has just short stubs where the nursery cut back the old stems, but it will grow fast and may bloom the first year. The 'Blue Star' junipers are low mounds about 6 to 10 in. wide. The blue oat grass forms small, thin clumps of sparse foliage. The 'Gracillimus' Japanese silver grass may still be dormant, or it may have a short tuft of new foliage. Both grasses will grow vigorously the first year.

Three to Five Years—The birch tree has grown 1 to 2 ft. taller every year but is still quite slender. Near the base, it's starting to show the white bark typical of maturity. The variegated Siberian dogwoods are well established now. If you cut them to the ground every year or two in spring, they grow back 4 to 6 ft. tall by midsummer, with strong, straight stems. The 'Blaze' rose covers the fence, and you need to prune out a few of its older stems every spring. The slow-growing 'Blue Star' junipers make a series of low mounds. you still see them as individuals, not a continuous patch. The grasses have reached maturity and form lush, robust clumps. It would be a good idea to divide and replant them now, to keep them vigorous.

Ten to Fifteen Years—The birch tree is becoming a fine specimen, 20 to 30 ft. tall, with gleaming white bark on its trunks. Prune away the lower limbs up to 6 to 8 ft. above ground to expose its trunks and to keep it from crowding and shading the other plants. The variegated dogwoods and 'Blaze' rose continue to thrive and respond well to regular pruning. The 'Blue Star' junipers have finally merged into a continuous mass of glossy foliage. The blue oat grass and Japanese silver grass will still look good if they have been divided and replanted over the years. If you get tired of the grasses, you could replace them with cinnamon fern and astilbe, as shown here, or other perennials or shrubs.

Ten to Fifteen Years

Cinnamon fern

Astilbe

Country Lane of Your Own

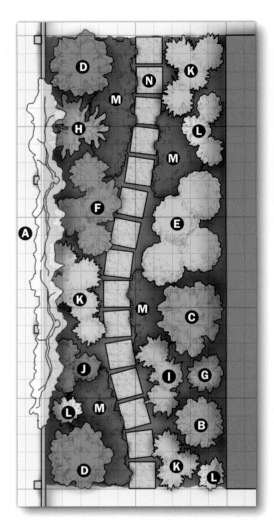

Many residential lots include a slim strip of land between the house and a property line. Usually overlooked by everyone except children and dogs racing between the front yard and the back, this often shady corridor can become a valued addition to the landscape. In the design shown here, a steppingstone path curves gently through a selection of shade-loving shrubs and perennials to make a garden that invites adults (as well as children) to linger as they stroll from one part of the property to another.

The wall of the house and a tall, opaque fence on the property line shade the space most of the day and give it a closed-in feeling, like a long empty hallway or narrow room. The design uses plants to enlarge these confines in the same way that comfortable furniture, floor coverings, and pictures on the walls seem to enlarge a small room in a house.

Large shrubs with striking foliage and spring flowers mark each entrance to this narrow "outdoor room." Handsome vines hang from the fence like three-dimensional floral prints. The foliage and flowers of good-size shrubs are nicely displayed against the wall opposite. (In spring the daphne's pale flowers fill the entire area with a delicious aroma.) On the "floor," the steppingstones are flanked by broad-leaved and grassy ground-cover "throw rugs" along the path. Ferns and perennials with pretty flowers and interesting foliage complete the furnishings.

Plants and Projects

Foliage distinguishes this planting in all seasons, from brilliant emerging leaves in spring to glossy summer greens and winter-defying evergreens. Flowers bloom from spring through fall in white, lilac, and shades of pink. Maintenance includes seasonal cleanup and shrub pruning to direct growth and to control size.

A **Climbing hydrangea** *Hydrangea petiolaris* (use 2 plants)
This deciduous vine brightens June with mildly fragrant white flowers. Glossy leaves and dark brown papery bark look good the rest of the year.

B **'Carol Mackie' daphne** *Daphne x burkwoodii* (use 1)
An evergreen shrub prized for its intensely fragrant bursts of starry light pink spring flowers and beautiful variegated green- and-cream leaves.

C **Garden hydrangea** *Hydrangea macrophylla* (use 1)
A deciduous shrub with shiny green leaves and large clusters of pink or blue flowers throughout the summer.

D **'Mountain Fire' Japanese andromeda** *Pieris japonica* (use 2)
The leaves of this evergreen shrub emerge fiery red, then mature to glossy green. In spring, clusters of buds that have dangled from branch tips since autumn open in a blizzard of white flowers.

E **White evergreen azalea** *Rhododendron* (use 4)
This shrub's semievergreen, fine-textured leaves contrast nicely with nearby foliage. Large, frilly white flowers lighten the shade in early summer.

F **'Halcyon' hosta** *Hosta* (use 4)
Grown for its low mounding foliage, this perennial's large, lush blue leaves become greener as the season progresses.

G **'Royal Standard' hosta** *Hosta* (use 1)
Another hosta with lovely foliage, this time bright green. In addition, this cultivar's trumpetlike white flowers will perfume the path in August and September.

H **Japanese autumn fern** *Dryopteris erythrosora* (use 3)
Tall clumps of glossy fronds start out copper-colored and turn dark green as they mature. Semievergreen.

I **Japanese painted fern** *Athyrium goeringianum* 'Pictum' (use 3)
Eye-catching deciduous fern. The delicately painted fronds blend gray-green, silver, and maroon.

J **'Palace Purple' heuchera** *Heuchera* (use 3)
A tough perennial with unusually dark purple-bronze foliage. Forms low mounds of large, lobed leaves and wiry stalks of tiny flowers in summer.

K **Variegated lilyturf** *Liriope muscari* 'Variegata' (use 12)
The grassy evergreen foliage of this low mounding perennial is striped green and yellow. Small spikes of lilac flowers appear in late summer.

L **White astilbe** *Astilbe x arendsii* (use 5)
The white spires of this perennial brighten the shade in early summer. Dark green, lacy foliage is pleasing all season. The 18-in.-tall 'Deutschland' is a good size for this planting.

M **Pachysandra** *Pachysandra terminalis* (as needed)
This durable perennial ground cover forms a dense mat of glossy evergreen leaves.

N **Path**
Use pavers or flagstones 18 in. square. Bluestone is attractive with the blue-tinted foliage of the planting.

Site: Shady

Season: Early summer

Concept: Plants with colorful foliage of varying textures make an enticing stroll garden in a frequently neglected area.

See site plan for **G** **J**

H Japanese autumn fern

F 'Halycon' hosta

A Climbing hydrangea

D 'Mountain Fire' Japanese andromeda

C Garden hydrangea

E White evergreen azalea

K Variegated lilyturf

N Path

D 'Mountain Fire' Japanese andromeda

I Japanese painted fern

K Variegated lilyturf

L White astilbe

M Pachysandra

B 'Carol Mackie' daphne

Note: *All plants are appropriate for USDA Hardiness Zones 5, 6, and 7.*

Dressed-Up "Farmyard" Fence

A 'Autumn Light'
Japanese silver grass

A perennial border can be one of the most delightful of all gardens. Indeed, that's usually its sole purpose. Unlike many other types of landscape plantings, a traditional border is seldom yoked to any function beyond that of providing as much pleasure as possible. From the first neat mounds of foliage in the spring to the fullness of summer bloom and autumn color, the mix of flowers, foliage, textures, tones, and hues brings enjoyment.

This border is designed for a beginning perennial gardener, using durable plants that are easy to establish and care for. Behind the planting, screening out distraction, is a simple fence. The planting is meant to be viewed from the front, so tall plants go at the back. A pair of graceful grasses mark the rear corners of the symmetrical design, with a slightly shorter grass as a leafy backdrop between them. Front corners are defined by the swordlike leaves of yucca.

Within this frame, a handsome collection of flowering perennials offers a long season of bloom and attractive foliage in a range of greens and grays. Low-growing plants edge the front of the border with blue and yellow flowers all summer. In the middle of the bed, loose spikes of catmint, upright spires of veronica, and the airy lavender flowers of Russian sage continue the blue theme. Autumn flowers add a burst of color, with deep purple asters, pink mums, and rosy sedums set against a tan and gold backdrop of grasses.

Plants and Projects

No perennial garden is carefree, but this one comes very close. Veronica blooms longer and pincushion flowers look better when spent flowers are clipped off. If you cut back catmint by about one-third after flowering, it will make a return performance, but don't cut back the grasses or sedum until spring, or you'll miss their buff and brown winter hues.

A **'Autumn Light' Japanese silver grass** *Miscanthus sinensis* (use 2 plants)
Tall clumps of narrow leaves produce silvery flower plumes in late summer that mature to fluffy seed heads.

B **'Karl Foerster' feather reed grass** *Calamagrostis x acutiflora* (use 5)
In midsummer, thin stalks rise high above upright clumps of slender green leaves, carrying narrow flower spikes that ripen, along with the leaves, to a warm tan color.

C **Yucca** *Yucca filamentosa* (use 4)
A dramatic shrub with spiky evergreen leaves and clusters of creamy white flowers that tower over the foliage in June on thick, branched stalks.

D **Russian sage** *Perovskia atriciplifolia* (use 4)
This shrubby perennial's sparse, fragrant gray-green leaves and tiers of small blue late-summer flowers hover like an airy cloud in the border.

E **'Purple Dome' New England aster** *Aster novae-angliae* (use 2)
A perennial whose mound of handsome deep green foliage is blanketed with rich purple flowers in early fall.

F **'Sheffield' chrysanthemum** *Dendranthema x grandiflorum* (use 2)

The large, single, light pink flowers produced by this perennial last from late September to early November.

G **'Sunny Border Blue' veronica** *Veronica* (use 3)
At the center of the planting, this perennial blooms all summer, with intense blue-purple flower spikes rising above a low bushy clump of glossy green foliage.

H **'Goodness Grows' veronica** *Veronica* (use 6)
A shorter veronica, its low mat of lustrous foliage defining the front edge of the bed. Slender spikes of lavender-blue flowers bloom all summer.

I **'Butterfly Blue' pincushion flower** *Scabiosa columbaria* (use 6)
Another season-long bloomer, this perennial produces masses of light blue flowers on neat, compact clumps of bright green leaves.

J **'Dropmore' catmint** *Nepeta x faassenii* (use 5)
This perennial's soft gray leaves are nicely set off by the foliage and flowers of its neighbors. Clusters of small blue flowers repeat (if sheared) from early summer on.

K **'Vera Jameson' sedum** *Sedum* (use 4)
Short sturdy stalks with succulent purplish leaves support flat-topped clusters of rosy pink flowers in late summer. A perennial, it forms neat, compact clumps near the front of the bed.

L **'Moonbeam' coreopsis** *Coreopsis verticillata* (use 3)
This perennial's tiny pale yellow flowers float over a mound of delicate dark green foliage from midsummer into fall.

M **Fence**
A 6-ft.-tall fence provides a backdrop for the border and privacy.

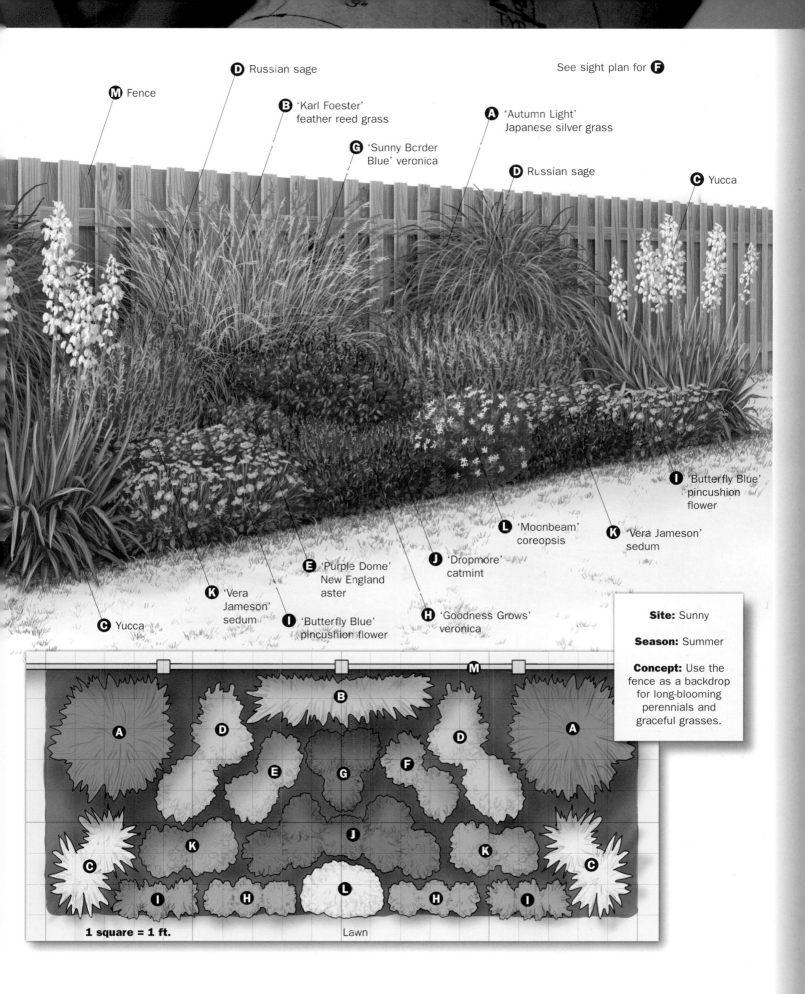

M Fence

D Russian sage

B 'Karl Foester' feather reed grass

G 'Sunny Border Blue' veronica

See sight plan for **F**

A 'Autumn Light' Japanese silver grass

D Russian sage

C Yucca

I 'Butterfly Blue' pincushion flower

L 'Moonbeam' coreopsis

K 'Vera Jameson' sedum

J 'Dropmore' catmint

H 'Goodness Grows' veronica

E 'Purple Dome' New England aster

K 'Vera Jameson' sedum

I 'Butterfly Blue' pincushion flower

C Yucca

Site: Sunny

Season: Summer

Concept: Use the fence as a backdrop for long-blooming perennials and graceful grasses.

1 square = 1 ft.

Lawn

Country Garden

Plantings in domestic landscapes are usually "attached" to something. Beds and borders hew to property lines, walls, or patios; foundation plantings skirt the house, garage, or deck. Most are meant to be viewed from the front, rather like a wall-mounted sculpture in raised relief.

On the other hand, the planting shown here is only loosely moored to a low fence, forming a peninsula jutting into the lawn. It is an excellent option for those who want to squeeze more gardening space from a small lot, add interest to a rectangular one, or divide a large area into smaller "outdoor rooms." Because you can walk around most of the bed, plants can be displayed "in the round," and they can be combined to present different scenes from several vantage points.

Without a strong connection to a structure or other landscape feature, a bed like this (or its close cousin, the island bed, which floats free of any anchors) requires a particular sensitivity to scale. To be successful, the bed must neither dominate its surroundings nor be lost in them. This planting was designed with a modest or larger suburban property in mind. A combination of large and small, subtle and bold plants makes this attractive up close or viewed from a distance, and there's always something to admire as you stroll by.

See sight plan for **C** **I**

E 'Little Princess' Japanese spirea

H 'Kashmir White' geranium

J 'Bath's Pink' dianthus

Plants and Projects

A handsome collection of woody plants garnished by complementary perennials gives this bed its character. There are flowers from spring to fall (and sometimes in winter), in whites, pinks, and purples. All of the plants have attractive foliage, including a number with evergreen leaves, and all grow well with a minimum of fuss.

A Japanese stewartia *Stewartia pseudocamellia* (use 1 plant)
This small tree offers new spring shoots tinged with purple and white camellia-like flowers in summer (perhaps even the first year after transplanting). Multicolored fall foliage gives way in winter to distinctive flaking bark.

B 'Black Knight' butterfly bush *Buddleia davidii* (use 3)
From midsummer on, spikes of fragrant purple flowers bloom on the arching shoots of this large deciduous shrub. Cut back hard each spring; fresh shoots quickly reach 5 ft. tall.

C 'Bonica' rose *Rosa* (use 3)
This shrub rose forms a large mound that's covered with small, scentless, double pink flowers all summer. A reliable plant, free of common rose ailments.

D White evergreen azalea *Rhododendron* (use 3)
Masses of lovely flowers cover these neat, compact shrubs in mid- to late spring. The small green leaves are attractive all year.

E 'Little Princess' Japanese spirea *Spiraea japonica* (use 1)
This compact rounded shrub, wider than tall, with fine-textured, deciduous dark green leaves is a good companion for the vase-shaped butterfly bush nearby. Clusters of pink flowers last for weeks in June.

F Southernwood *Artemisia abrotanum* (use 3)
Sweet-scented, feathery, silver-gray leaves are the attraction of this shrubby perennial, which rarely flowers. Prune it back halfway every spring to keep it compact and bushy.

G White Japanese anemone *Anemone x hybrida* (use 5)
In late summer, this perennial displays enchanting clear white, single or double flowers held on branched stalks above dark green mounds of foliage.

H 'Kashmir White' geranium *Geranium clarkei* (use 17)
Edging two portions of the bed, this perennial forms a low mound of beautiful deeply lobed leaves. In early summer, white flowers with lilac veins completely cover the plant, making it look like a bouquet. If you can't find this one at your local nursery, try 'Album', a white cultivar of Geranium sanguineum.

I Christmas rose *Helleborus niger* (use 5)
This perennial's large pure white flowers may be a Christmas present nestled under the stewartia in December. Dark, finely cut evergreen leaves turn bronze in winter. Although the plant takes a few years to get established, it then persists happily for decades.

J 'Bath's Pink' dianthus *Dianthus* (use 7)
Edging the end of the bed, these low-growing perennials form a mat of grassy evergreen foliage and produce clear pink carnation-like flowers that have a marvelous scent. Flowers appear in late spring; when they fade, shear the plants back halfway and new foliage will form.

K Foamflower *Tiarella cordifolia* (use 15)
A native woodland perennial that spreads to form an airy evergreen ground cover under the stewartia. Clumps of maple-shaped leaves are topped with soft spikes of tiny white flowers in late spring.

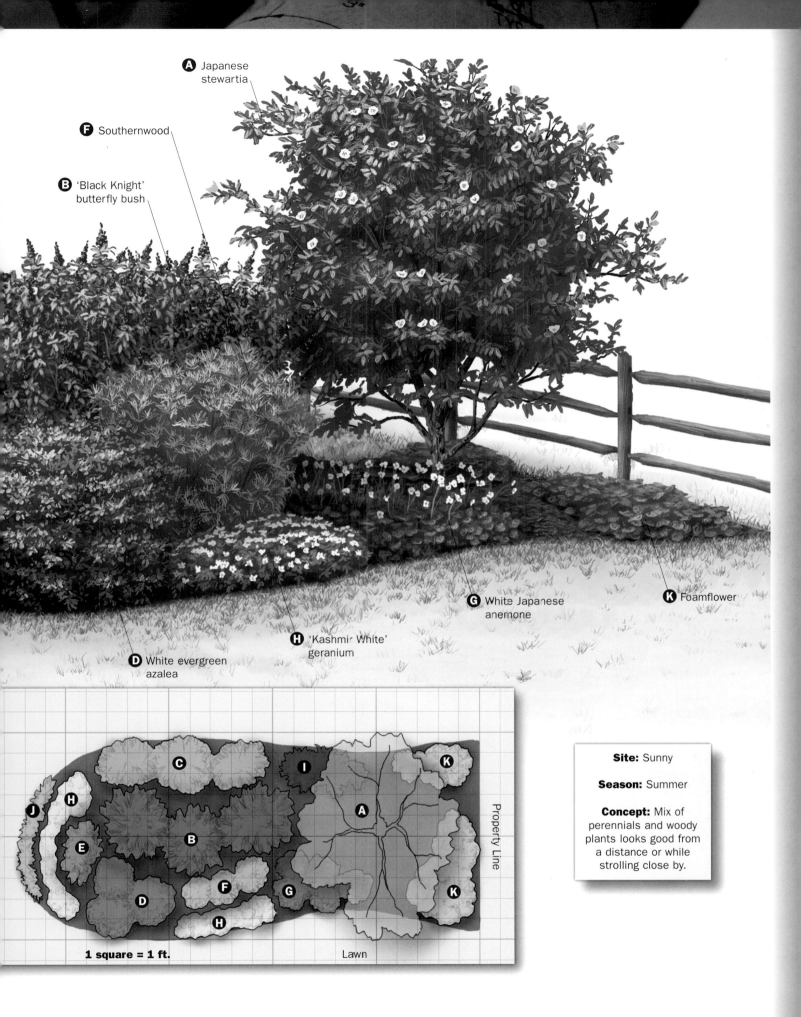

A Japanese stewartia

F Southernwood

B 'Black Knight' butterfly bush

G White Japanese anemone

K Foamflower

H 'Kashmir White' geranium

D White evergreen azalea

Site: Sunny

Season: Summer

Concept: Mix of perennials and woody plants looks good from a distance or while strolling close by.

1 square = 1 ft.

Property Line

Lawn

Plan #151015

Dimensions: 72'4" W x 48'4" D
Levels: 2
Square Footage: 2,789
Main Level Sq. Ft.: 1,977
Upper Level Sq. Ft.: 812
Bedrooms: 4
Bathrooms: 3
Foundation: Basement, crawl space, or slab
Price Category: F

Images provided by designer/architect.

The spacious kitchen that opens to the breakfast room and the hearth room make this family home ideal for entertaining.

Features:

- Great Room: The fireplace will make a cozy winter focal point in this versatile space.

- Hearth Room: Enjoy the built-in entertainment center, built-in shelving, and fireplace here.

- Dining Room: A swing door leading to the kitchen is as attractive as it is practical.

- Study: A private bath and walk-in closet make this room an ideal spot for guests when needed.

- Kitchen: An island work area, a computer desk, and an eat-in bar add convenience and utility.

- Master Bath: Two vanities, two walk-in closets, a shower with a seat, and a whirlpool tub highlight this private space.

Main Level Floor Plan

Upper Level Floor Plan

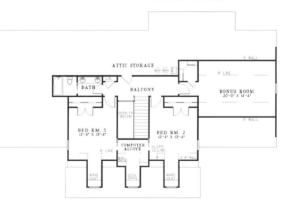

Copyright by designer/architect.

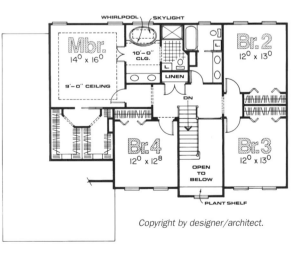

Plan #121028

Dimensions: 54'8" W x 42' D

Levels: 2

Square Footage: 2,644

Main Level Sq. Ft.: 1,366

Upper Level Sq. Ft.: 1,278

Bedrooms: 4

Bathrooms: 2½

Foundation: Basement

Materials List Available: Yes

Price Category: F

Images provided by designer/architect.

This home is filled with special touches and amenities that add up to gracious living.

Features:

- Ceiling Height: 8 ft.
- Formal Living Room: This large, inviting room is the perfect place to entertain guests.
- Family Room: This cozy, comfortable room is accessed through elegant French doors in the living room. It is sure to be the favorite family gathering place with its bay window, see-through fireplace, and bay window.

- Breakfast Area: This area is large enough for the whole family to enjoy a casual meal as they are warmed by the other side of the see-through fireplace. The area features a bay window and built-in bookcase.
- Master Bedroom: Upstairs, enjoy the gracious and practical master bedroom with its boxed ceiling and two walk-in closets.
- Master Bath: Luxuriate in the whirlpool bath as you gaze through the skylight framed by ceiling accents.

Main Level Floor Plan

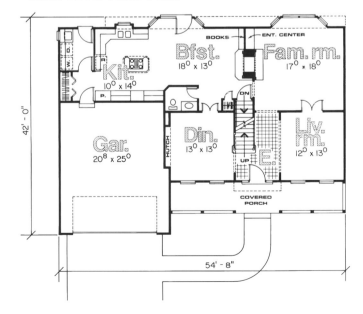

Upper Level Floor Plan

Copyright by designer/architect.

Plan #181064

Dimensions: 91'4" W x 40'8" D

Levels: 2

Square Footage: 2,802

Main Level Sq. Ft.: 2,219

Upper Level Sq. Ft.: 583

Bedrooms: 4

Bathrooms: 2½

Foundation: Crawl space

Materials List Available: Yes

Price Category: F

Images provided by designer/architect.

Upper Level Floor Plan

Copyright by designer/architect.

Main Level Floor Plan

Plan #271058

Dimensions: 68' W x 53' D

Levels: 2

Square Footage: 2,924

Main Level Sq. Ft.: 1,579

Upper Level Sq. Ft.: 1,345

Bedrooms: 3

Bathrooms: 2½

Foundation: Daylight basement

Materials List Available: No

Price Category: F

Images provided by designer/architect.

Main Level Floor Plan

Upper Level Floor Plan

Copyright by designer/architect.

Plan #191028

Dimensions: 80' W x 63' D

Levels: 1

Square Footage: 2,669

Bedrooms: 4

Bathrooms: 3½

Foundation: Basement, slab

Materials List Available: No

Price Category: F

Images provided by designer/architect.

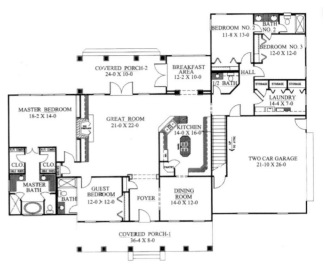

Copyright by designer/architect.

Plan #191029

Dimensions: 78' W x 67' D

Levels: 1

Square Footage: 2,726

Bedrooms: 4

Bathrooms: 3½

Foundation: Basement, crawl space, or slab

Materials List Available: No

Price Category: F

Images provided by designer/architect.

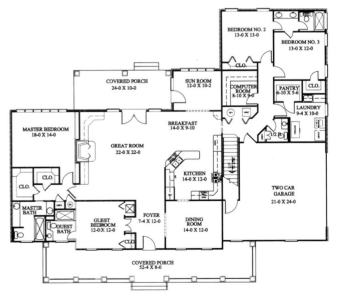

Copyright by designer/architect.

Plan #311019

Dimensions: 76'2" W x 66'4" D

Levels: 1

Square Footage: 2,506

Bedrooms: 4

Bathrooms: 2½

Foundation: Slab, crawl space, or basement

Materials List Available: Yes

Price Category: E

Images provided by designer/architect.

Basement Stair Location

Plan #151154

Dimensions: 50' W x 50' D

Levels: 1½

Square Footage: 2,533

Main Level Sq. Ft.: 1,768

Upper Level Sq. Ft.: 765

Bedrooms: 3

Bathrooms: 2½

Foundation: Crawl space, slab

Materials List Available: Yes

Price Category: E

Images provided by designer/architect.

Main Level Floor Plan

Upper Level Floor Plan

Copyright by designer/architect.

Main Level Floor Plan

Upper Level Floor Plan

Images provided by designer/architect.

Copyright by designer/architect.

Plan #181160

Dimensions: 54' W x 42' D

Levels: 2

Square Footage: 2,768

Main Level Sq. Ft.: 1,296

Upper Level Sq. Ft.: 1,472

Bedrooms: 4

Bathrooms: 3½

Foundation: Basement

Materials List Available: Yes

Price Category: F

Plan #211132

Dimensions: 58' W x 76' D

Levels: 2

Square Footage: 2,535

Main Level Sq. Ft.: 1,647

Upper Level Sq. Ft.: 888

Bedrooms: 4

Bathrooms: 3½

Foundation: Basement

Materials List Available: No

Price Category: E

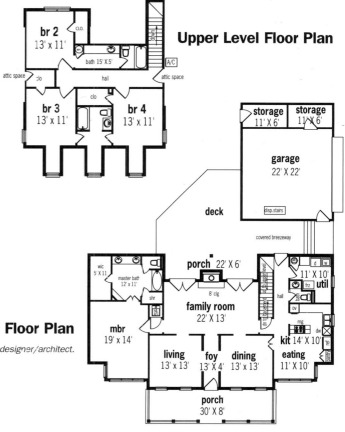

Upper Level Floor Plan

Main Level Floor Plan

Images provided by designer/architect.

Copyright by designer/architect.

Plan #121030

Dimensions: 58' W x 45' D

Levels: 2

Square Footage: 2,613

Main Level Sq. Ft.: 1,333

Upper Level Sq. Ft.: 1,280

Bedrooms: 4

Bathrooms: 2½

Foundation: Basement

Materials List Available: Yes

Price Category: F

Images provided by designer/architect.

This home is packed with all the amenities you need for a gracious and comfortable lifestyle.

Features:

- Ceiling Height: 8 ft. unless otherwise noted.

- Foyer: The elegant entry opens into the living room and formal dining room.

- Adaptable Space: An area linking the formal living room and the family room would make a great area for the family computer. Alternately, it can become a wet bar with window seat.

- Breakfast Area: The family will enjoy informal meals in this sun-bathed area.

- Snack Bar: Perfect for a quick bite, this angled area joins the kitchen to the breakfast area.

- Master Suite: Two walk-in closets make this suite convenient as well as luxurious. The bayed whirlpool tub under a cathedral ceiling invites you to unwind and relax.

- Bonus Room: The second level includes a large room that could become an extra bedroom, a guest room, or a home office.

Main Level Floor Plan

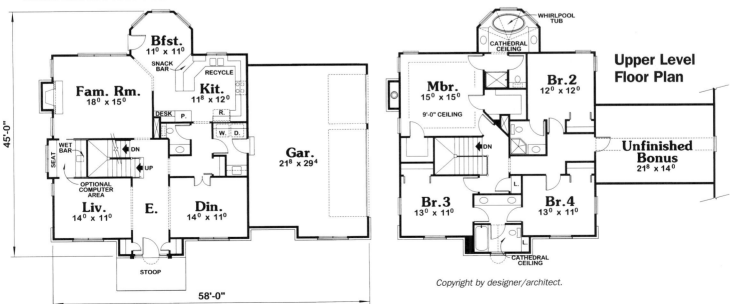

Copyright by designer/architect.

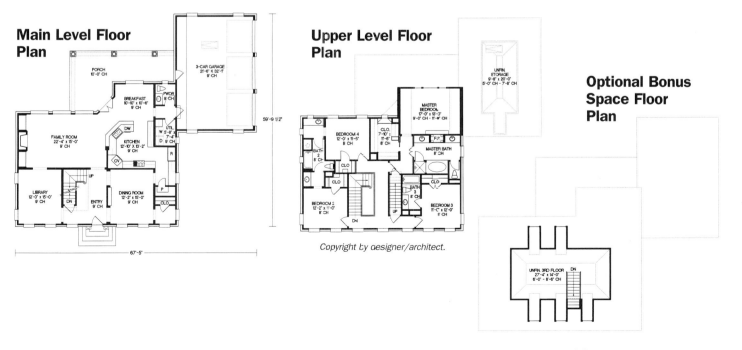

Plan #121048

Dimensions: 67'5" W x 59'9½" D
Levels: 2
Square Footage: 2,975
Main Level Sq. Ft.: 1,548
Upper Level Sq. Ft.: 1,427
Bedrooms: 4
Bathrooms: 3½
Foundation: Slab
Materials List Available: Yes
Price Category: F

The classic good looks on the exterior of this impressive home are matched by an interior that's as beautiful as it is comfortable.

Features:

- Dining Room: A built-in hutch adds elegance to this formal dining room.
- Library: Shut the doors to this large room, and you'll make it into a quiet retreat.
- Family Room: A fireplace and a wall of windows highlight this spacious, open room.

- Breakfast Room: This room features a door to the rear covered porch and large window area.
- Kitchen: The angled bar adds convenience to this well-planned kitchen.
- Master Suite: Enjoy this suite's fireplace, which is open to the bedroom and the bath. A large tub, separate shower, and two vanities highlight the bathroom, and a huge walk-in closet completes the area.

Main Level Floor Plan

Upper Level Floor Plan

Copyright by designer/architect.

Optional Bonus Space Floor Plan

Plan #211131

Dimensions: 58' W x 76' D

Levels: 2

Square Footage: 2,598

Main Level Sq. Ft.: 1,647

Upper Level Sq. Ft.: 951

Bedrooms: 4

Bathrooms: 3½

Foundation: Basement

Materials List Available: No

Price Category: E

Images provided by designer/architect.

Upper Level Floor Plan

Main Level Floor Plan

Copyright by designer/architect.

Plan #151158

Dimensions: 60'8" W x 82' D

Levels: 2

Square Footage: 2,990

Main Level Sq. Ft.: 1,796

Upper Level Sq. Ft.: 1,194

Bedrooms: 4

Bathrooms: 3½

Foundation: Crawl space, slab

Materials List Available: Yes

Price Category: F

Images provided by designer/architect.

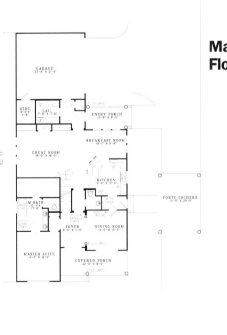

Main Level Floor Plan

Upper Level Floor Plan

Copyright by designer/architect.

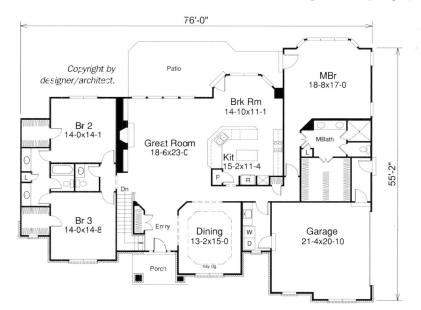

Plan #321007

Dimensions: 76' W x 55'2" D
Levels: 1
Square Footage: 2,695
Bedrooms: 3
Bathrooms: 2½
Foundation: Basement
Materials List Available: Yes
Price Category: F

Images provided by designer/architect.

You'll love the way this spacious ranch reminds you of a French country home.

Features:

- **Foyer:** Come into this lovely home's foyer, and be greeted with a view of the gracious staircase and the great room just beyond.

- **Great Room:** Settle down by the cozy fireplace in cool weather, and reach for a book on the built-in shelves that surround it.

- **Kitchen:** Designed for efficient work patterns, this large kitchen is open to the great room.

- **Breakfast Room:** Just off the kitchen, this sunny room will be a family favorite all through the day.

- **Master Suite:** A bay window, walk-in closet, and shower built for two are highlights of this area.

- **Additional Bedrooms:** These large bedrooms both have walk-in closets and share a Jack-and-Jill bath for total convenience.

SMARTtip

Decorative Poles

Drapery poles are supported by the brackets fastened to the window frame or wall. The brackets that are provided with the poles generally coordinate and blend in with the pole finish. Brackets can be simple but also decorative. If you opt for a spectacular, attention-grabbing bracket, consider choosing less showy finials for the ends of the pole.

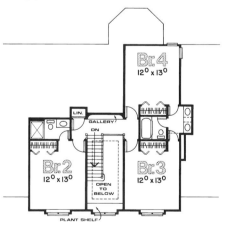

Plan #121083

Dimensions: 72' W x 45'4" D
Levels: 2
Square Footage: 2,695
Main Level Sq. Ft.: 1,881
Upper Level Sq. Ft.: 814
Bedrooms: 4
Bathrooms: 3½
Foundation: Basement
Materials List Available: Yes
Price Category: F

Images provided by designer/architect.

You'll love this home for its soaring entryway ceiling and well-designed layout.

Features:

- Entry: A balcony from the upper level looks down into this two-story entry, which features a decorative plant shelf.
- Great Room: Comfort is guaranteed in this large room, with its built-in bookcases framing a lovely fireplace and trio of transom-topped windows along one wall.
- Living Room: Save both this formal room and the formal dining room, both of which flank the entry, for guests and special occasions.
- Kitchen: This convenient work space includes a gazebo-shaped breakfast area where friends and family will gather at any time of day.

Main Level Floor Plan

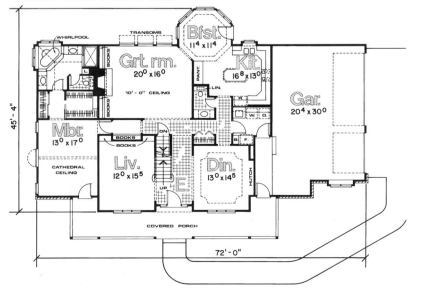

Upper Level Floor Plan

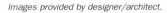

Copyright by designer/architect.

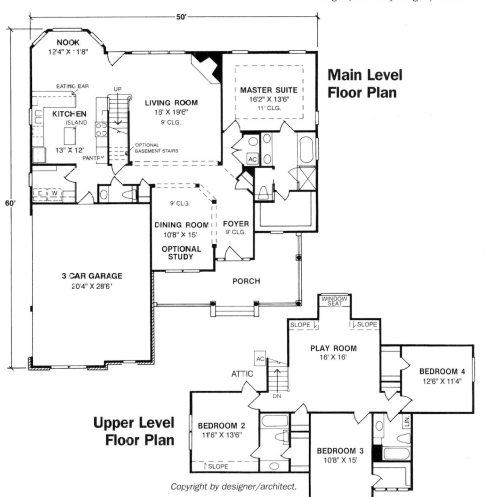

Plan #121079

Dimensions: 50' W x 60' D

Levels: 2

Square Footage: 2,688

Main Level Sq. Ft.: 1,650

Upper Level Sq. Ft.: 1,038

Bedrooms: 4

Bathrooms: 3½

Foundation: Slab

Materials List Available: Yes

Price Category: F

You'll love this open design if you're looking for a home that gives a spacious feeling while also providing private areas.

Features:

• **Entry:** The cased openings and corner columns here give an attractive view into the dining room.

• **Living Room:** Another cased opening defines the entry to this living room but lets traffic flow into it.

• **Kitchen:** This well-designed kitchen is built around a center island that gives you extra work space. A snack bar makes an easy, open transition between the sunny dining nook and the kitchen.

• **Master Suite:** An 11-ft. ceiling sets the tone for this private space. With a walk-in closet and adjoining full bath, it will delight you.

Images provided by designer/architect.

Copyright by designer/architect.

Rear View

Plan #321017

Dimensions: 77' W x 36'8" D

Levels: 1

Square Footage: 2,531

Bedrooms: 1-4

Bathrooms: 1-2½

Foundation: Daylight basement

Materials List Available: Yes

Price Category: E

Images provided by designer/architect.

Optional Basement Level Floor Plan

Copyright by designer/architect.

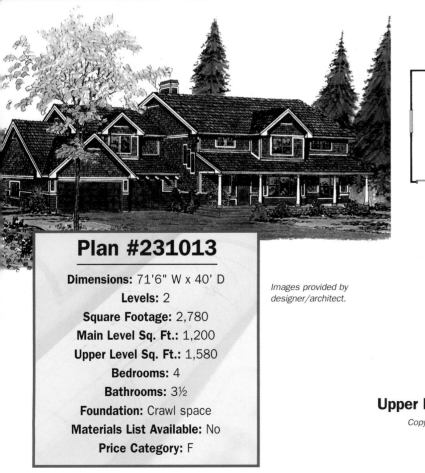

Plan #231013

Dimensions: 71'6" W x 40' D

Levels: 2

Square Footage: 2,780

Main Level Sq. Ft.: 1,200

Upper Level Sq. Ft.: 1,580

Bedrooms: 4

Bathrooms: 3½

Foundation: Crawl space

Materials List Available: No

Price Category: F

Images provided by designer/architect.

Main Level Floor Plan

Upper Level Floor Plan

Copyright by designer/architect.

Main Level Floor Plan

Gathering 18x17

Nook 9-6x9

Kitchen

Utility

Garage 27-8x23-4

Pantry

Dining 11x12

Den 12-6x12

Covered Porch

Upper Level Floor Plan

Balcony

Sitting

M.Br. 18x16

Bonus Rm. 14x13-6

Lin

Br. #3 10-8x11

Br. #2 12-6x12

Images provided by designer/architect.

Copyright by designer/architect.

Plan #231025

Dimensions: 66' W x 46' D

Levels: 2

Square Footage: 2,501

Main Level Sq. Ft.: 1,170

Upper Level Sq. Ft.: 1,331

Bedrooms: 3

Bathrooms: 2½

Foundation: Crawl space

Materials List Available: No

Price Category: E

Main Level Floor Plan

70'-0"

Patio

Storage 13-6x10-6

Kitchen

Brk 9-0x 14-8

Family 20-6x14-8

sloped clg

Garage 23-4x25-0

Dining 12-9x14-2

Living 12-9x14-2

Up

Foyer

Porch depth 6-0

40'-0"

Upper Level Floor Plan

Br 2 12-6x11-6

MBr 12-9x18-0

open to below

Br 3 12-9x12-0

Images provided by designer/architect.

Copyright by designer/architect.

Plan #321055

Dimensions: 70' W x 40' D

Levels: 2

Square Footage: 2,505

Main Level Sq. Ft.: 1,436

Upper Level Sq. Ft.: 1,069

Bedrooms: 3

Bathrooms: 2½

Foundation: Basement

Materials List Available: Yes

Price Category: E

Images provided by designer/architect.

Plan #121016

Dimensions: 52' W x 47'4" D
Levels: 2
Square Footage: 2,594
Main Level Sq. Ft.: 1,322
Upper Level Sq. Ft.: 1,272
Bedrooms: 4
Bathrooms: 3
Foundation: Basement
Materials List Available: Yes
Price Category: E

A huge wraparound porch gives this home warmth and charm.

Features:

- Ceiling Height: 8 ft. except as noted.
- Family Room: This informal sunken room's beamed ceiling and fireplace flanked by windows makes it the perfect place for family gatherings.
- Formal Dining Room: Guests will enjoy gathering in this large elegant room.
- Master Suite: The second-floor master bedroom features its own luxurious bathroom.
- Compartmented Full Bath: This large bathroom serves the three secondary bedrooms on the second floor.
- Optional Play Area: This special space, included in one of the bedrooms, features a cathedral ceiling.
- Kitchen: A large island is the centerpiece of this modern kitchen's well-designed food-preparation area.

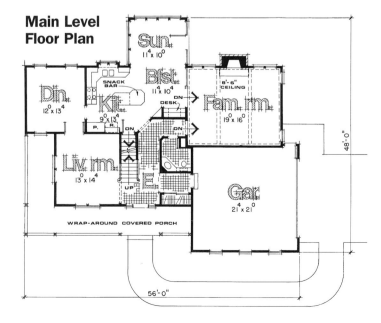

Main Level Floor Plan

Upper Level Floor Plan

Copyright by designer/architect.

Plan #151029

Dimensions: 59'4" W x 74'2" D

Levels: 1½

Square Footage: 2,777

Main Level Sq. Ft.: 2,082

Upper Level Sq. Ft.: 695

Bedrooms: 4

Bathrooms: 2½

Foundation: Crawl space, slab; optional basement plan available for extra fee

Materials List Available: Yes

Price Category: F

This grand home combines historic Southern charm with modern technology and design. A two-car garage and covered front porch allow for optimum convenience.

Features:

- Foyer: This marvelous foyer leads directly to an elegant dining room and comfortable great room.

- Great Room: With high ceilings, a built-in media center, and a fireplace, this will be your favorite room during the chilly fall months.

- Kitchen: An eat-in-bar with an optional island, computer area, and adjoining breakfast room with a bay window make a perfect layout.

- Master Suite: Relax in comfort with a corner whirlpool tub, a separate glass shower, double vanities, and large walk-in closets.

- Upper Level Bedrooms: 2 and 3 both have window seats.

Main Level Floor Plan

Upper Level Floor Plan

Main Level Floor Plan

Plan #171017

Dimensions: 84' W x 54' D

Levels: 2

Square Footage: 2,558

Main Level Sq. Ft.: 1,577

Upper Level Sq. Ft.: 981

Bedrooms: 4

Bathrooms: 2½

Foundation: Slab, crawl space

Materials List Available: Yes

Price Category: E

Images provided by designer/architect.

Upper Level Floor Plan

Copyright by designer/architect.

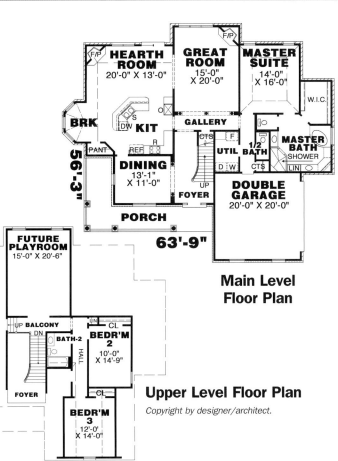

Plan #241012

Dimensions: 64' W x 56' D

Levels: 2

Square Footage: 2,743

Main Level Sq. Ft.: 2,153

Upper Level Sq. Ft.: 590

Bedrooms: 3

Bathrooms: 2½

Foundation: Slab

Materials List Available: No

Price Category: E

Images provided by designer/architect.

Main Level Floor Plan

Upper Level Floor Plan

Copyright by designer/architect.

Upper Level Floor Plan

Copyright by designer/architect.

Plan #341006

Dimensions: 86'3" W x 35'4" D

Levels: 2

Square Footage: 2,588

Main Level Sq. Ft.: 1,660

Upper Level Sq. Ft.: 928

Bedrooms: 4

Bathrooms: 3

Foundation: Crawl space, slab, or basement

Materials List Available: Yes

Price Category: E

Images provided by designer/architect.

Main Level Floor Plan

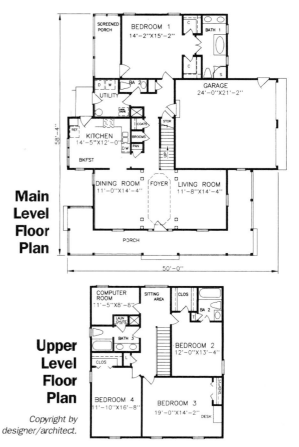

Plan #341011

Dimensions: 50' W x 58'4" D

Levels: 2

Square Footage: 2,560

Main Level Sq. Ft.: 1,387

Upper Level Sq. Ft.: 1,173

Bedrooms: 4

Bathrooms: 3½

Foundation: Crawl space, slab, or basement

Materials List Available: Yes

Price Category: E

Images provided by designer/architect.

Main Level Floor Plan

Upper Level Floor Plan

Copyright by designer/architect.

Plan #131029

Dimensions: 56'4" W x 46'6" D
Levels: 2
Square Footage: 2,936
Main Level Sq. Ft.: 1,680
Upper Level Sq. Ft.: 1,256
Bedrooms: 4
Bathrooms: 2½
Foundation: Crawl space, slab, or basement
Materials List Available: Yes
Price Category: G

Images provided by designer/architect.

This home is ideal if you love the look of a country-style farmhouse.

Features:

• Foyer: Walk across the large wraparound porch that defines this home to enter this two-story foyer.

• Living Room: French doors from the foyer lead into this living room.

• Family Room: The whole family will love this room, with its vaulted ceiling, fireplace, and sliding glass doors that open to the wooden rear deck.

• Kitchen: A beautiful sit-down center island opens to the family room. There's also a breakfast nook with a lovely bay window.

• Master Suite: Luxury abounds with vaulted ceilings, walk-in closets, private bath with whirlpool tub, separate shower, and dual sinks.

• Loft: A special place with vaulted ceiling and view into the family room below.

Main Level Floor Plan

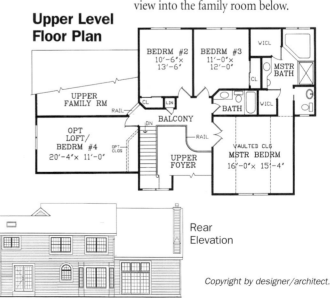

Upper Level Floor Plan

Rear Elevation

Copyright by designer/architect.

Dining Room

Breakfast Area

Kitchen Island

Kitchen

Master Bathroom

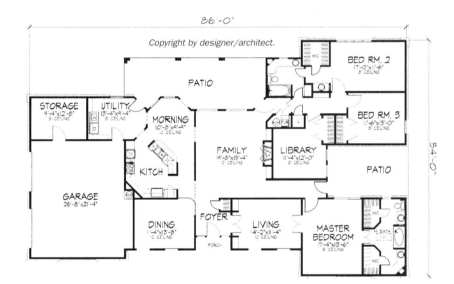

Images provided by designer/architect.

Plan #271081

Dimensions: 86' W x 54' D

Levels: 1

Square Footage: 2,539

Bedrooms: 4

Bathrooms: 2

Foundation: Slab

Materials List Available: No

Price Category: E

This traditional home is sure to impress your guests and even your neighbors.

Features:

- Living Room: This quiet space off the foyer is perfect for pleasant conversation.

- Family Room: A perfect gathering spot, this room is nicely enhanced by a fireplace.

- Kitchen: This room easily serves the bayed morning room and the formal dining room.

- Master Suite: The master bedroom overlooks a side patio, and boasts a private bath with a skylight and a whirlpool tub.

- Library: This cozy room is perfect for curling up with a good novel. It would also make a great extra bedroom.

SMARTtip

Determining Curtain Length

Follow length guidelines for foolproof results, but remember that they're not rules. Go ahead and play with curtain and drapery lengths. Instead of shortening long panels at the hem, for instance, take up excess material by blousing them over tiebacks for a pleasing effect.

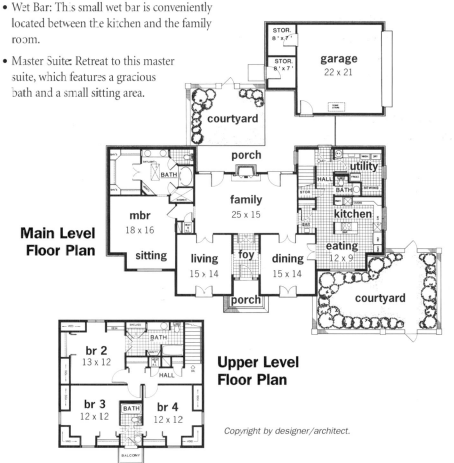

Plan #211108

Dimensions: 66' W x 66' D
Levels: 2
Square Footage: 2,954
First Level Sq. Ft.: 1,984
Second Level Sq. Ft.: 970
Bedrooms: 4
Bathrooms: 3½
Foundation: Slab, crawl space, or basement
Materials List Available: Yes
Price Category: F

This home is designed with the feel of a European cottage and will nestle nicely in any neighborhood.

Features:

• Ceiling Height: 8 ft.

• Living Room: This formal living room offers plenty of space for all kinds of entertaining and family activities.

• Eating Area: This eating area adjacent to the kitchen is the perfect spot for informal family meals, with its panoramic view of an intimate private courtyard through a graceful Palladian-style window.

• Family Room: Relax with the family in this cozy family room, which opens to the rear covered porch and the formal living room and dining room via pairs of French doors.

• Wet Bar: This small wet bar is conveniently located between the kitchen and the family room.

• Master Suite: Retreat to this master suite, which features a gracious bath and a small sitting area.

Main Level Floor Plan

STOR. 8' x 7'
STOR. 8' x 7'
garage 22 x 21
courtyard
porch
utility
HALL
family 25 x 15
STOR
BATH
SEWING
mbr 18 x 16
BATH
kitchen
sitting
living 15 x 14
foy
dining 15 x 14
eating 12 x 9
porch
courtyard

Upper Level Floor Plan

br 2 13 x 12
BATH
HALL
br 3 12 x 12
BATH
br 4 12 x 12
BALCONY

Images provided by designer/architect.

Plan #131050

Dimensions: 72'8" W x 47' D
Levels: 2
Square Footage: 2,874
Main Level Sq. Ft.: 2,146
Upper Level Sq. Ft.: 728
Bedrooms: 4
Bathrooms: 3
Foundation: Crawl space, slab, or basement
Materials List Available: Yes
Price Category: G

A gazebo and long covered porch at the entry let you know that this is a spectacular design.

Features:

• **Foyer:** This vaulted foyer divides the formal living room and dining room, setting the stage for guests to feel welcome in your home.

• **Great Room:** This large room is defined by several columns; a corner fireplace and vaulted ceiling add to its drama.

• **Kitchen:** An island work space

separates this area from the bayed breakfast nook.

• **Master Suite:** You'll have privacy in this main-floor suite, which features two walk-in closets and a compartmented bath with a dual-sink vanity.

• **Upper Level:** The two large bedrooms share a bath and a dramatic balcony.

• **Bonus Room:** Walk down a few steps into this large bonus room over the 3-car garage.

Main Level Floor Plan

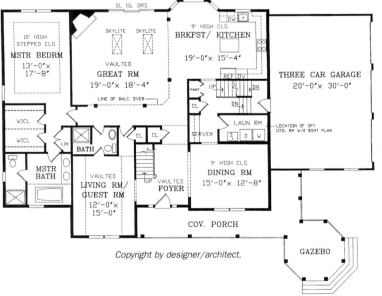

Copyright by designer/architect.

Upper Level Floor Plan

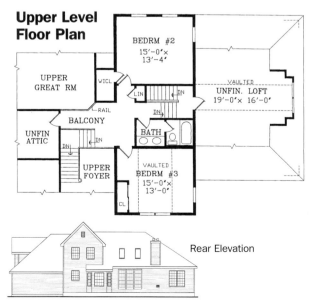

Rear Elevation

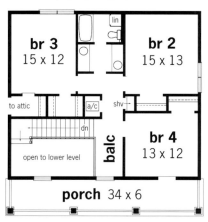

Plan #211103

Dimensions: 77' W x 56' D

Levels: 2

Square Footage: 2,605

Main Level Sq. Ft.: 1,770

Upper Level Sq. Ft.: 855

Bedrooms: 4

Bathrooms: 2½

Foundation: Slab

Materials List Available: Yes

Price Category: F

Images provided by designer/architect.

This grand plantation-style home has all the amenities you need for gracious modern living.

Features:

- Ceiling Height: 9 ft.
- Kitchen: You'll love cooking in this huge gourmet kitchen. It boasts a large island for plenty of food-preparation space. Linger over coffee and the Sunday paper as you enjoy the sunlight streaming into the breakfast nook.
- Living Room: Family and guests alike will be drawn to this central living room, with its

handsome fireplace. Pluck a book from the built-in bookcases, and settle into your favorite chair for a read by the fire.

- Back Porch: When the weather warms, step through the elegant French doors in the living room and catch a breeze on this back porch.
- Energy-Efficient Structure: Expect lower heating and cooling bills thanks to the 2x6 framing that allows room for more insulation in the walls.

Main Level Floor Plan

Upper Level Floor Plan

Copyright by designer/architect.

Main Level Floor Plan

BRK 11'-0" X 13'-6"

SUNROOM 20'-7" X 12'-4"

UTIL

REAR ENTRY

46'-0"

MASTER BATH

GREAT ROOM 19'-1" X 16'-1"

EATING BAR

UP STOR 1/2 BATH

MASTER SUITE 15'-1" X 16'-0"

KIT.

DOUBLE GARAGE 20'-1" X 21'-0"

HALL

CL.

LANDING

UP

DINING 10'-8" X 13'-0"

STUDY 7'-8" X 9'-1"

FOYER

DROP CEILING

PORCH

68'-0"

Images provided by designer/architect.

Plan #241013

Dimensions: 68' W x 46' D

Levels: 2

Square Footage: 2,779

Main Level Sq. Ft.: 1,918

Upper Level Sq. Ft.: 861

Bedrooms: 4

Bathrooms: 3½

Foundation: Slab

Materials List Available: No

Price Category: F

BEDROOM 2 11'-2" X 16'-6"

BEDROOM 3 12'-9" X 12'-0"

BATH-3

LANDING DN

PLAYROOM 14'-0" X 15'-1"

SEAT

Upper Level Floor Plan

CL.

BATH 2

BALCONY

LANDING DN

CL.

CL.

SHOWER

LIN

FOYER BELOW

BEDROOM 4 11'-0" X 11'-3"

SEAT

LANDING

BALCONY

Copyright by designer/architect.

Plan #181034

Dimensions: 60' W x 44' D

Levels: 2

Square Footage: 2,687

Main Level Sq. Ft.: 1,297

Upper Level Sq. Ft.: 1,390

Bedrooms: 3

Bathrooms: 2½

Foundation: Full basement

Materials List Available: Yes

Price Category: F

Images provided by designer/architect.

Main Level Floor Plan

44'-0" 13.2 m

11'-8" X 16'-4" 3,50 x 4,90

26'-0" X 15'-0" 7,80 x 4,50

20'-4" X 21'-4" 6,10 x 6,40

12'-4" X 14'-0" 3,70 x 4,20

18'-4" X 20'-0" 5,50 x 6,20

60'-0" 18,0 m

Upper Level Floor Plan

11'-0" X 11'-0" 3,50 x 3,30

11'-8" X 16'-4" 3,50 x 4,90

18'-0" X 15'-0" 5,40 x 4,50

12'-0" X 21'-4" 3,60 x 6,40

11'-8" X 9'-8" 3,50 x 2,90

12'-4" X 13'-4" 3,70 x 4,00

12'-4" X 14'-0" 3,70 x 4,20

Copyright by designer/architect.

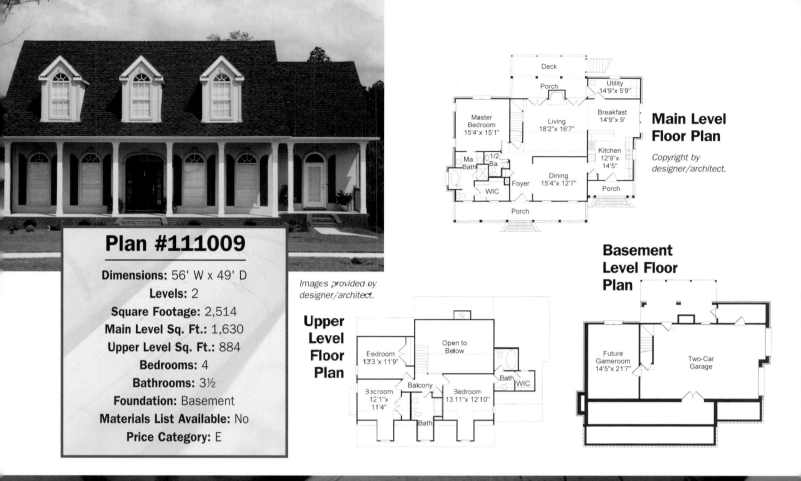

Main Level Floor Plan

Copyright by designer/architect.

Deck

Porch

Utility 14'9"x 5'9"

Master Bedroom 15'4'x 15'1"

Living 18'2"x 16'7"

Breakfast 14'9"x 9'

Kitchen 12'9"x 14'5"

Ma. Bath

1/2 Ba.

Dining 15'4"x 12'7"

Foyer

WIC

Porch

Porch

Basement Level Floor Plan

Upper Level Floor Plan

Images provided by designer/architect.

Bedroom 13'3'x 11'9"

Open to Below

Bath

WIC

Bedroom 12'1"x 11'4"

Balcony

Bedroom 13 11'x 12'10"

Bath

Future Gameroom 14'5"x 21'7"

Two-Car Garage

Plan #111009

Dimensions: 56' W x 49' D

Levels: 2

Square Footage: 2,514

Main Level Sq. Ft.: 1,630

Upper Level Sq. Ft.: 884

Bedrooms: 4

Bathrooms: 3½

Foundation: Basement

Materials List Available: No

Price Category: E

Plan #321054

Dimensions: 70'6" W x 55'6" D

Levels: 2

Square Footage: 2,828

Main Level Sq. Ft.: 2,006

Upper Level Sq. Ft.: 822

Bedrooms: 5

Bathrooms: 3½

Foundation: Basement

Materials List Available: Yes

Price Category: F

Images provided by designer/architect.

Main Level Floor Plan

Family 16-4x19-4 vaulted

Patio

Kitchen 13-0x12-8

Brk 13-2x10-9

Bar

up Dn

MBr 15-0x16-11 vaulted

Garage 20-4x21-10

Dining 12-2x13-0

Study 13-5x13-0

Foyer

Porch Depth 6-0

55'-6"

70'-6"

Upper Level Floor Plan

Copyright by designer/architect.

open to below

Br 5 10-7x11-0

Br 2 10-7x11-0

Dn

Br 4 10-7x10-7

open to below

Br 3 10-7x10-7

Plan #271099

Dimensions: 71' W x 75' D

Levels: 2

Square Footage: 2,949

Main Level Sq. Ft.: 2,000

Upper Level Sq. Ft.: 949

Bedrooms: 3

Bathrooms: 2½

Foundation: Crawl space

Materials List Available: No

Price Category: F

Images provided by designer/architect.

Gracious symmetry highlights the lovely facade of this traditional two-story home.

Features:

- Foyer: With a high ceiling and a curved staircase, this foyer gives a warm welcome to arriving guests.
- Family Room: At the center of the home, this room will host gatherings of all kinds. A fireplace adds just the right touch.
- Kitchen: An expansive island with a cooktop anchors this space, which easily serves the adjoining nook and the nearby dining room.
- Master Suite: A cozy sitting room with a fireplace is certainly the highlight here. The private bath is also amazing, with its whirlpool tub, separate shower, dual vanities, and walk-in closet.
- Bonus Room: This generous space above the garage could serve as an art studio or as a place for your teenagers to play their electric guitars.

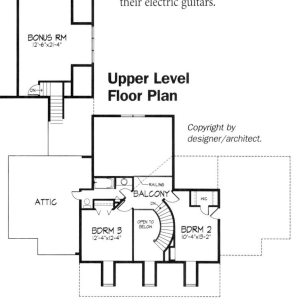

Images provided by designer/architect.

Plan #271064

Dimensions: 76' W x 54' D
Levels: 2
Square Footage: 2,864
Main Level Sq. Ft.: 1,610
Upper Level Sq. Ft.: 1,254
Bedrooms: 4
Bathrooms: 2½
Foundation: Daylight basement
Materials List Available: No
Price Category: E

Tall windows and a colonnaded porch lend a touch of style to this traditional home.

Features:

- Family Room: A bay window enhances this sizable family room, which shares a see-through fireplace with a cozy hearth room.
- Kitchen: This room's island presents a unique serving bar that facilitates meals and entertaining. The versatile

dinette incorporates sliding glass doors for easy access to a nice backyard deck.

- Dining Room: This formal space is the perfect locale for holiday feasts and special meals.
- Study: Double doors introduce this quiet study, which could easily serve as a guest-room or a home office.
- Master Suite: This fabulous area boasts a tray ceiling and a bay window in the sleeping chamber. The deluxe private bath offers a whirlpool tub, separate shower, dual-sink vanity, and walk-in closet.

Main Level Floor Plan

Copyright by designer/architect.

Upper Level Floor Plan

Plan #331003

Dimensions: 68'8" W x 75' D

Levels: 2

Square Footage: 2,661

Main Level Sq. Ft.: 2,000

Upper Level Sq. Ft.: 660

Bedrooms: 4

Bathrooms: 3

Foundation: Basement, crawl space, or slab

Materials List Available: No

Price Category: F

Images provided by designer/architect.

Main Level Floor Plan

Upper Level Floor Plan

Copyright by designer/architect.

Plan #111048

Dimensions: 62' W x 65' D

Levels: 2

Square Footage: 2,665

Main Level Sq. Ft.: 1,916

Upper Level Sq. Ft.: 749

Bedrooms: 4

Bathrooms: 3

Foundation: Slab, optional crawl space

Materials List Available: No

Price Category: F

Images provided by designer/architect.

Main Level Floor Plan

Upper Level Floor Plan

Copyright by designer/architect.

Copyright by designer/architect.

Plan #321011

Dimensions: 83' W x 50'4" D
Levels: 1
Square Footage: 2,874
Bedrooms: 4
Bathrooms: 2½
Foundation: Basement
Materials List Available: Yes
Price Category: F

Images provided by designer/architect.

SMARTtip

Drilling for Kitchen Plumbing

Drill holes for plumbing and waste lines before installing the cabinets. It is easier to work when the cabinets are out in the middle of the floor, and there is no danger of knocking them out of alignment when creating the holes if they are not screwed to the wall studs or one another yet.

Plan #111001

Dimensions: 66'8" W x 76'11" D
Levels: 1
Square Footage: 2,832
Bedrooms: 4
Bathrooms: 2½
Foundation: Slab
Materials List Available: No
Price Category: F

Images provided by designer/architect.

Copyright by designer/architect.

Images provided by designer/architect.

Plan #241008

Dimensions: 65' W x 56'8" D
Levels: 1
Square Footage: 2,526
Bedrooms: 4
Bathrooms: 3
Foundation: Slab
Materials List Available: No
Price Category: E

A covered back porch—with access from the master suite and the breakfast area—makes this traditional home ideal for siting near a golf course or with a backyard pool.

Features:

- **Great Room:** From the foyer, guests enter this spacious and comfortable great room, which features a handsome fireplace.

- **Kitchen:** This kitchen—the hub of this family-oriented home—is a joy in which to work, thanks to abundant counter space, a pantry, a convenient eating bar, and an adjoining breakfast area and sunroom.

- **Master Suite:** Enjoy the quiet comfort of this coffered-ceiling master suite, which features dual vanities and separate walk-in closets.

- **Additional Bedrooms:** Two secondary bedrooms, which share a full bath, are located at the opposite end of the house from the master suite. Bedroom 4—in front of the house—can be converted into a study.

Copyright by designer/architect.

SMARTtip

Traditional-Style Kitchen Cabinetry

You can modify stock kitchen cabinetry to enjoy fine furniture-quality details. Prefabricated trims may be purchased at local lumber mills and home centers. For example, crown molding, applied to the top of stock cabinetry and stained or painted to match the door style, may be all you need. Likewise, you can replace hardware with reproduction polished-brass door and drawer knobs or pulls for a finishing touch.

Plan #101020

Dimensions: 55'8" W x 49'2" D
Levels: 2
Square Footage: 2,972
Main Level Sq. Ft.: 1,986
Upper Level Sq. Ft.: 986
Bedrooms: 4
Bathrooms: 3½
Foundation: Basement
Materials List Available: No
Price Category: F

Images provided by designer/architect.

This luxurious country home has an open-design main level that maximizes the use of space.

Features:

- Ceiling Height: 9 ft. unless otherwise noted.
- Foyer: Guests will be greeted by this grand two-story entry, with its graceful angled staircase.
- Dining Room: At nearly 12 ft. x 15 ft., this elegant dining room has plenty of room for large parties.
- Family Room: Everyone will be drawn to this 17-ft. x 19-ft. room, with its dramatic two-story ceiling and its handsome fireplace.
- Kitchen: This spacious kitchen is open to the family room and features a breakfast bar and built-in table in the cooktop island.
- Master Suite: This elegant retreat includes a bayed 18-ft.-5-in. x 14-ft.-9-in. bedroom and a beautiful corner his and her bath/closet arrangement.
- Secondary Bedrooms: Upstairs you'll find three spacious bathrooms, one with a private bath and two with access to a shared bath.

Main Level Floor Plan

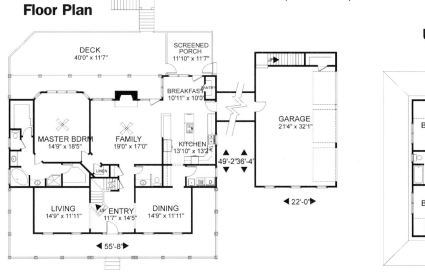

Upper Level Floor Plan

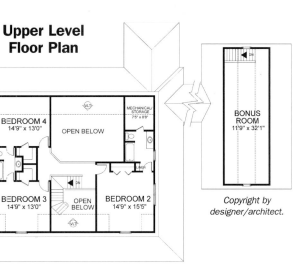

Copyright by designer/architect.

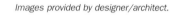

Plan #271054

Dimensions: 63' W x 49' D

Levels: 2

Square Footage: 2,654

Main Level Sq. Ft.: 1,384

Upper Level Sq. Ft.: 1,270

Bedrooms: 4

Bathrooms: 2½

Foundation: Daylight basement

Materials List Available: No

Price Category: F

Images provided by designer/architect.

This updated farmhouse attracts comments from passersby with its shuttered windows and welcoming wraparound porch.

Features:

- Great Room: This popular gathering spot includes a fireplace flanked by a media center and abundant shelves, and a wall of windows.

- Dining Room: This formal dining room is closed off with a pocket door for peace and quiet during meals. The bayed window facing the front is a nice touch.

- Kitchen: This thoroughly modern kitchen boasts an island with two sinks, a good-sized pantry, and a bayed dinette with sliding doors to the backyard.

- Sun Porch: Accessed via double doors from the dinette, this warm getaway spot flaunts a wood floor, ample angled windows, and a French door to the backyard.

- Owner's Suite: This master bedroom has a gorgeous tray ceiling in the sleeping chamber, plus a private bath with a corner whirlpool tub, a separate shower, and an endless walk-in closet.

Main Level Floor Plan

Upper Level Floor Plan

Copyright by designer/architect.

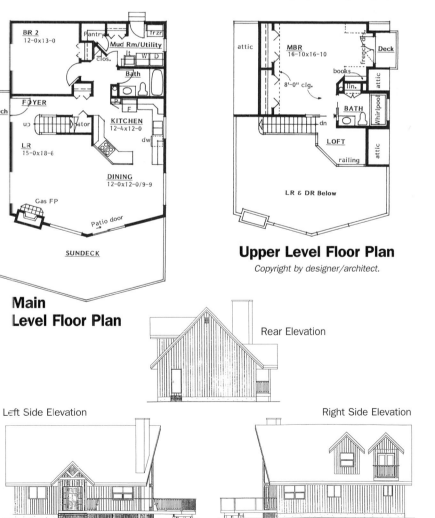

Plan #281014

Dimensions: 66' W x 49' D

Levels: 2

Square Footage: 2,904

Main Level Sq. Ft.: 1,494

Upper Level Sq. Ft.: 1,410

Bedrooms: 4

Bathrooms: 3

Foundation: Basement

Materials List Available: Yes

Price Category: F

You'll love the features that make this striking colonial design as gracious on the inside as it is on the outside.

Features:

- Porch: Use this wraparound porch as an extra room on fine days or when you're entertaining, and don't forget to add some potted plants.

- Foyer: The open staircase visible here announces the beauty of the home.

- Dining Room: This room is as appropriate for hosting formal dinner parties as it is for casual meals with the family.

- Kitchen: Designed to suit a gourmet chef, this kitchen will also please the smallest cooks in the family.

- Master Suite: Two walk-in closets, a double vanity, a whirlpool tub, and a separate shower make this lovely suite truly luxurious. The nearby bonus room can serve as an adjunct to the retreat.

Images provided by designer/architect.

Main Level Floor Plan

Upper Level Floor Plan

Copyright by designer/architect.

Rear Elevation

Left Side Elevation

Right Side Elevation

Plan #131027

Dimensions: 62'4" W x 53'6" D
Levels: 2
Square Footage: 2,567
Main Level Sq. Ft.: 2,017
Upper Level Sq. Ft.: 550
Bedrooms: 4
Bathrooms: 3
Foundation: Crawl space, slab, or basement
Materials List Available: Yes
Price Category: F

Images provided by designer/architect.

The features of this home are so good that you may have trouble imagining all of them at once.

Features:

- Great Room: Imagine a stepped ceiling, corner fireplace, built-media center, and wall of windows with a glass door to the backyard—in one room.

- Dining Room: A stepped ceiling and server with a sink add to the elegance of this formal room.

- Breakfast Room: Eat at the bar this room shares with the island kitchen, and admire the 12-ft. cathedral ceiling and bayed group of

8- and 9-ft. windows. Or go through the sliding glass door to the covered side porch.

- Master Suite: The bedroom has a tray ceiling and cozy sitting area, and a whirlpool tub, shower, and walk-in closet are in the skylighted bath.

- Optional Study: The private bath in bedroom 2 makes it ideal for a study or home office.

- Bonus Room: Enjoy the extra 300 sq. ft.

Breakfast Nook

Rear View

Great Room

Main Level Floor Plan

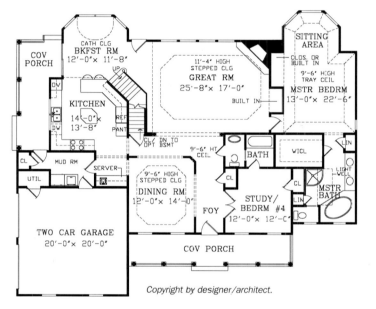

Copyright by designer/architect.

Upper Level Floor Plan

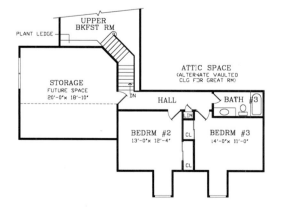

Painting Tips

As with any skill, there is a right and a wrong way to paint. There is a right way to hold a brush, a right way to maneuver a roller, a right way to spray a wall, etc. Follow these basic professional tips:

Brushing vs. Rolling. Some painters insist that only a brush-painted job looks right. However, most painters will "cut in" the edges with a brush, and then finish the main body of a wall or ceiling using a roller. Brushing alone can be time-consuming, and it is typically reserved for architectural woodwork.

Using the Right Brush. Use the largest brush with which you are comfortable. Professional painters seldom pick up anything smaller than a 4-inch brush. Most homeowners will achieve good results using a 4-inch brush for "cutting in" and for large surfaces, and an angled 2½- to 3-inch sash brush for trim around windows and doors. Be sure, also, to use brushes that are appropriate for the type of paint being applied. Oil-based paints require a natural bristle (also called "China bristles"), while water-based paints are applied with a synthetic bristle brush.

Handling a Brush. Many people grip a paintbrush as if they were shaking someone's hand. It is better to grip a brush more like a pencil, with the fingers and thumb wrapped around the metal ferrule. This grip provides the hand and wrist with a wider range of motion and therefore greater speed and precision. If your hand cramps, switch hands or switch temporarily to the handshake grip.

Wiping Rags. Before you begin painting, put a dust rag in your pocket. This is helpful for clearing away cobwebs and dust before painting. It is also handy for wiping off paint drips before they have a chance to dry.

Paint Hooks. When working on a ladder, use a good-quality paint hook to secure the paint bucket to your ladder. Avoid makeshift hooks made with wire or coat hangers. Paint hooks are inexpensive and available at virtually all paint and hardware stores.

Plan #141018

Dimensions: 45' W x 64' D

Levels: 2

Square Footage: 2,588

Main Level Sq. Ft.: 1,320

Upper Level Sq. Ft.: 1,268

Bedrooms: 4

Bathrooms: 2½

Foundation: Basement, crawl space, or slab

Materials List Available: Yes

Price Category: E

Images provided by designer/architect.

This country home features a large wraparound porch, along with many Victorian-style accents.

Features:

- Ceiling height: 9 ft.
- Formal Dining Room: Usher your dinner guests into this large formal dining room.
- Living Room: With a style to match the dining room, this is the perfect place to start an evening's entertainment.
- Family Room: With its handsome warming fireplace, this is the less-formal space where the family will go to unwind.
- Kitchen: Cooking will be a pleasure in this large, sunny kitchen.
- Breakfast Room: Located adjacent to the kitchen, this breakfast room is the perfect spot for informal family meals.
- Master Suite: This luxurious retreat offers a walk-in closet. The master bath has double vanities, a jet tub, and a separate shower.

Main Level Floor Plan

Double Garage
22-8 x 21-2

Opt. W/H for Slab Or Crawl Found.

Up / Stor.

Brkfst.
14-10 x 10-4

Lnd.

Sundeck
21-8 x 12-0

W/D / Lav.

Kit.
13-0 x 11-0

Family Rm.
21-4 x 13-6

Dining
13-0 x 11-6

Foyer
9-4 x 9-0

Living
15-6 x 11-6

Porch

64-0

45-0

Upper Level Floor Plan

Copyright by designer/architect.

Bonus Rm.
22-8 x 16-2

Flat Ceil. Line

Bdrm.2
12-10 x 11-2

Ks / Lin. / Seat

M.Bath

Bath 2

Ks

Bdrm.3
12-10 x 11-10

Bdrm.4
12-0 x 10-10

Master Bdrm.
12-10 x 16-6

Tray Ceil.

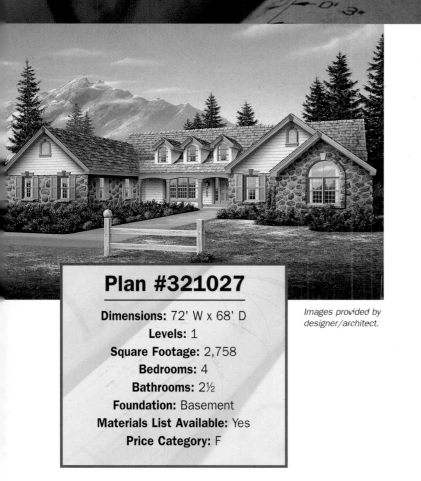

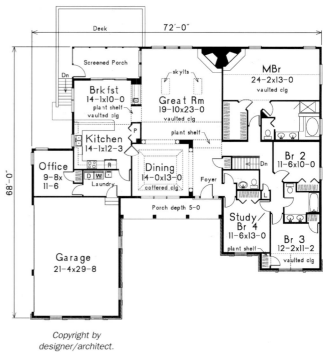

Images provided by designer/architect.

Plan #321027

Dimensions: 72' W x 68' D

Levels: 1

Square Footage: 2,758

Bedrooms: 4

Bathrooms: 2½

Foundation: Basement

Materials List Available: Yes

Price Category: F

Copyright by designer/architect.

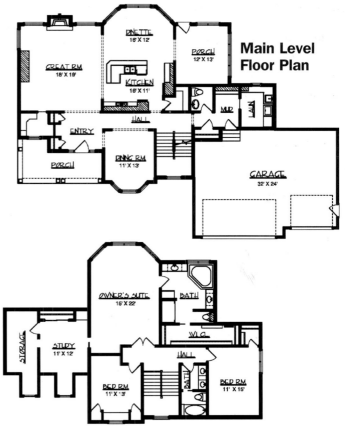

Images provided by designer/architect.

Main Level Floor Plan

Plan #271056

Dimensions: 73' W x 52' D

Levels: 2

Square Footage: 2,850

Main Level Sq. Ft.: 1,596

Upper Level Sq. Ft.: 1,254

Bedrooms: 3

Bathrooms: 2½

Foundation: Daylight basement

Materials List Available: No

Price Category: F

Upper Level Floor Plan

Copyright by designer/architect.

Plan #141036

Dimensions: 57' W x 41' D
Levels: 2
Square Footage: 2,527
Main Level Sq. Ft.: 1,236
Upper Level Sq. Ft.: 1,291
Bedrooms: 4
Bathrooms: 3
Foundation: Basement
Materials List Available: No
Price Category: E

Wood shakes and stone make the exterior of this home distinctive, and a fabulous layout and gorgeous features make the interior spectacular.

Features:

- **Living Room:** This spacious two-story room has a fireplace to make it cozy on chilly nights.

- **Guest Wing:** Guests will love having their own wing just beyond the computer command center.

- **Dining Room:** This room is ideal for entertaining or family dinner times.

- **Kitchen:** This step-saving design features an angled work area and a large pantry.

- **Breakfast Room:** The door to the patio makes this a perfect gathering place at any time of day.

- **Master Suite:** You'll love the stepped ceiling and hinged window seat in the bedroom, the walk-in closet, and the vaulted ceiling, tub, shower, and two vanities in the bath.

Images provided by designer/architect.

Copyright by designer/architect.

Living Room

Kitchen

Master Bedroom

Plan #151014

Dimensions: 70'2" W x 51'4" D

Levels: 2

Square Footage: 2,698

Main Level Sq. Ft.: 1,813

Upper Level Sq. Ft.: 885

Bedrooms: 5

Bathrooms: 3

Foundation: Crawl space, slab, optional basement for fee

Price Category: D

Images provided by designer/architect.

A comfortable front porch welcomes you into this home that features a balcony over the great room, a study, and a kitchen designed for gourmet cooks.

Features:

- Ceiling Height: 9 ft.
- Front Porch: Stately 12-in.-wide pillars form the entryway.
- Foyer: Open to upper story.
- Great Room: A fireplace, vaulted 9-ft. ceiling, and balcony from the second floor add character to this lovely room.
- Dining Room: Open to the kitchen for convenience.
- Kitchen: A large walk-in pantry, well-designed work areas, and eat-in bar make this room a treasure.
- Breakfast Room: Enjoy this spot that opens to both the kitchen and a large covered porch at the rear of the house.
- Study: This quiet room has French doors leading to the yard.
- Master Suite: This spacious area has cozy window seats as well as his and her walk-in closets. The master bathroom is fitted with a whirlpool tub, a glass shower, and his and her sinks.

Upper Level Floor Plan

Main Level Floor Plan

Copyright by designer/architect.

Country-Style Bathrooms

Call it pure Americana, English, Swedish, Italian, or French. The style is basic, casual, and warm—and every country has its own version. "Country" often implies a deeper connection with the outdoors and the simple life than other styles and uses an abundance of natural elements. For a Country bath, start with plain wood cabinetry stained a light maple, or add a distressed, crackled, or pickled finish. Door styles are usually framed, sometimes with a raised panel. Install a laminate countertop, and coordinate it with the tile you select for the room. Hand-painted tiles with a simple theme lend a custom touch.

For added Country charm, stencil a wall border or select a wallpaper pattern with a folk-art motif or floral prints. Checks and ticking stripes are also popular in a country-style room—on the wall, as a tile pattern, or on the shower-curtain fabric. If you feel creative, apply a painted finish to the wall. Otherwise, check out the many wallpaper designs on the market that emulate the look of sponging, ragging, combing, and other special painted effects.

Install a double-hung window in the room. (Casement windows look too contemporary in this setting.) Some window-treatment ideas include a balloon topper over miniblinds or shutters, for privacy, combined with a matching or contrasting lace café curtain. If you have a casement window in the bathroom that you do not want to change, install pop-in muntins to give the unit more of a traditional or old-fashioned look.

A skirted pedestal sink or pine chest-turned-vanity, along with reproduction faucets, will add a nostalgic charm to a Country bathroom. Bring a playful note to this informal design with whimsical hardware fabricated in wrought iron, brushed pewter, or porcelain. Hardware and fittings that are polished look too refined for this style.

Popular Country colors include red gingham and denim blue. Choose a checkerboard floor or a mosaic of broken tiles if hardwood is not available. Or consider laminate flooring that gives you the look of real wood without the maintenance. Some styles even come with a painted-floor design.

The Country bath is the type of room that begs for baskets, old bottles, and ceramic vases filled with wildflowers. Accessorize with these items or a collection of favorite things, and you've created a very personal space.

A yellow-and-white floor adds a dollop of sunshine underfoot, below.

A pedestal sink, opposite, is a hallmark of Country style.

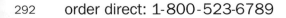

A Country Bath with Efficient Style

Although the ancient Greeks and Romans, along with other prosperous early civilizations, maintained luxurious public bathhouses, it was a long road to the private, plumbed-in tub with the toilet alongside that we know today. A relatively modern convenience, the bathroom typically packs lots of essential equipment into a small space, so it's in special need of old-fashioned details to become part of a welcoming country house.

In the 1790s the French produced shoe-shaped bathtubs; Benjamin Franklin brought one back to the United States so he could enjoy soaking, reading, and relaxing for hours.

But before the late nineteenth century, for most North Americans, bathing was utilitarian. Periodically, someone filled a portable tub with hand-pumped and stove-heated water from buckets, and each family member had a turn.

By the 1870s the houses of well-to-do North Americans had flush toilets, but only the wealthiest owned a plumbed-in tub in the same room. Most folks endured the inconvenience of chamber pots, water pitchers, and washbowls in their bedrooms. Finally, nearing the twentieth century, plumbing became increasingly common, and average homeowners carved out bathroom space from a bedroom. The old-fashioned claw-foot tub not only resembled formal furniture pieces but kept the often unreliable plumbing more accessible. Into the 1920s and '30s, closed-in tubs and crisp white tile became fashionable, celebrating thoroughly modern convenience.

Today's Typical Bathroom

Though the recent trend has been toward larger bathrooms, the standard is still focused on efficient use of space. This offers the decorator an unexpected side benefit, because even minor flourishes and ornamentation go a long way toward making the Country bathroom attractive and full of character. Follow the advice below to make this sometimes sterile room charming in a Country-style way.

Design It to Suit Its Use

Not only are we spoiled with indoor plumbing, we have come to expect more than one bathroom. With bathrooms in such abundance, each may be slanted toward a different role, with different decorating demands and possibilities.

The master bath is a private retreat,

Beadboard and Shaker-style pegs, opposite, provide a Country ambiance.

This Country-style bathroom, above, features a traditional floral wall treatment and light-colored cabinetry.

deserving some luxurious amenities, such as a makeup table, television and sound system, exercise equipment, or spa features. Space permitting, the bathroom can hold a piece or two of country furniture, such as a painted bench, an armoire, a wicker chair, or an added cabinet.

A family bathroom, on the other hand, may be where everyone showers or bathes—even the dog. It requires ample storage for toys, towels, and toiletries for kids and grownups. So keep an eye out for big baskets, quaint containers, shelves, and a capacious hamper for laundry. Because space is at often a premium, seek out useful shelves, towel bars, magazine racks, storage containers, and robe hooks styled with a bit of panache, whether in ceramic, brass, hand-painted finishes, or unusual materials. Everything should be water resistant and easy to clean, too.

Powder rooms are half-baths often located in the house's social or "public" areas. Because they're not subject to long, steamy showers or much of the morning get-up-and-go routine, durability and storage are less of an issue. Here you can indulge your decorating with delicate, eye-catching finishes, pretty collections, or displays that enhance the space.

Apply General Decorating Principles

Even if it's a small space, assess the room's strengths and weaknesses. A room's odd angles and small size can seem picturesque in lively, high-contrast finishes. Think about harmonies of scale, proportion, line, and color spiced with subtle differences. Because a bathroom tends toward slick modern surfaces, rough baskets and earthenware pots of ferns might be refreshing. Light finishes visually enlarge a small space, but wall-to-wall pastels can seem dull without a few bright notes.

Borrow Ideas from Other Rooms

Bathrooms can be too utilitarian, so have fun with unexpected elements, such as elaborate window treatments, handsome moldings, a slipper-chair, potted plants, and artwork, as long as the materials can hold up to dampness.

Fixtures

As in the kitchen, even bathrooms designed in the most authentic Country spirit can accommodate modern accoutrements. Consider a reproduction of a high-tank Victorian-style toilet, claw-foot tub, and classic gooseneck faucet with porcelain crosshandles.

Antique fixtures may be an attractive addition to your bathroom, but the inconvenience of future repairs may be a drawback.

Toilets

Many Country decorators choose standard, unobtrusive wares, often in versatile white or neutral, and concentrate their decorating efforts on elements and accessories that are easy to change, such as paint, wallpaper, linens, and rugs.

Basic two-piece toilets in white vitre-

"Brick" style ceramic tile is right at home in a Country scheme, opposite.

Use traditional fixtures, such as this crosshandle faucet set, above right, in a Country bathroom.

Period-furniture-style pieces, right, provide a distinct Country flavor.

ous china are unassuming features in a Country scheme, though more expensive, contemporary one-piece models may be your preference. New toilets feature a variety of internal mechanisms designed to meet a low-flush standard of using 1.6 gallons or less per flush. In addition to standard gravity-fed mechanisms, pressure-assisted systems use internal water pressure to compress air, which creates a more forceful flush.

Tubs and Showers

The tub and shower areas have the greatest visual weight in the room's design. Though they're most economical when combined (and a tub makes the most assuredly leakproof shower pan), the trend, especially in the master bath, is to separate the functions by creating separate fixtures for them. Tubs and shower enclosures can be found in a wide range of materials and styles. Cast-iron tubs are an attractive addition to any bathroom. However, the easier installation and lighter weight of modern plastics and ceramics make them more practical.

To keep the water contained, a clear glass shower door will do the job. A shower curtain, particularly if it consists of a waterproof liner combined with a frivolous fabric drapery, can add a soft, colorful, and easy-to-change touch amid all the hard surfaces. You can also pull it almost completely out of the way to show off any decorative tilework or handsome fittings within the tub alcove.

Country Sinks and Fittings

Bathroom sinks, which designers refer to as lavatories, can be made of vitreous china, cast iron, enameled steel, fiberglass, solid-surfacing material, stone, faux stone, or metal. Pedestal sinks or wall-mounted lavatories with metal or carved-wood legs encompass a variety of handsome vintage styles. Remember, today a beautiful fixture can stand alone as a piece of sculpture in the room.

Faucets. Faucets span a wide price range. In appearance, they can be considered as "jewelry" for the bathroom when fabricated in rich vintage styles, perhaps with china or bright crosshandles and a gooseneck spout. Brass is the traditional finish, but chrome can look at home fashioned after nostalgic styles. Single-lever controls, though undeniably modern, are convenient and easy to use.

Vanities

The vanity is often the keynote of a bathroom's country style because cabinetmaking is a venerable craft. An old but not valuable cabinet, small chest of drawers, or table can be converted into a charming vanity, though it must be carefully sealed against water. You'll also find vanities with evocative Country details made of rustic pine, smooth maple, or pickled oak, with planked or raised panel doors. Stock cabinetry often works well in standardized bathroom spaces. Custom cabinetry opens up more options and may offer accessories such as matching display shelves, moldings, or a bracket for a vase or candle.

Finishing Touches

Country bathrooms use many of the same practical finishing materials as Country kitchens. Wood instantly adds warmth and character and a "furnished" feeling. In the bath, consider softwoods such as fir, redwood, and pine or dense hardwoods like teak and maple for tongue-and-groove wainscoting, moldings, or furniture pieces.

Mirrors enhance a sense of space, albeit with a harder modern look. Downplay this by extending the mirror into a corner or framing it with molding.

Ceramic tile is a classic Country bathroom material, and it can be the decorative standout. There are some options to lend interest to a low-key background—for example, a play of different shapes, such as triangles, squares, and rectangles interlocked on a white wall. Or turn the square grid diagonally for an energetic diamond design. Try a stamped high-relief pattern or a heavy rope-molding trim to give a plain color more tactile appeal. Clay-colored tones and faux stone add a natural spirit to bare white walls and floors.

Lighting

In a room where people shave, put on makeup, remove splinters, and the like, good lighting, both natural and artificial, is essential.

Modern bathroom faucets, below left, can look like antique fixtures.

This bathroom, with its floral wallcovering and traditional faucet, below right, says "Country."

Use of a whirligig, opposite, reinforces the Country decor.

Just as in any room, windows add light and charm to a bath. Those with divided-light sash or projected bays add particular elegance. Skylights and clerestory windows can fetch sunlight with no worries about privacy.

All bathroom lighting fixtures should be suitable for damp areas. A ceiling-mounted fixture, perhaps a bowl-type pendant or a smaller chandelier, can cast a good general glow. Paired wall sconces alongside the mirror eliminate the shadows that can be cast by an overhead source.

Accessories

In limited space, every added object should be carefully chosen. Some fanciful touches with a Country sensibility might include a vintage sugar and creamer set to hold toothbrushes and cottonballs. An old teapot can be a charming planter or a place to store combs and brushes.

And don't forget the old model-home trick of displaying big fluffy towels to instantly make the room feel cozy and welcoming.

Plan #271072

Dimensions: 78' W x 38' D
Levels: 2
Square Footage: 3,081
Main Level Sq. Ft.: 1,358
Upper Level Sq. Ft.: 1,723
Bedrooms: 3
Bathrooms: 2½
Foundation: Basement, crawl space
Materials List Available: No
Price Category: G

This updated farmhouse design features a wraparound porch for savoring warm afternoons.

Features:

• Living Room: Striking columns invite visitors into this relaxing space. Double doors provide direct access to the casual family room beyond.

• Family Room: A focal-point fireplace warms this friendly space, while windows overlook impressive backyard vistas.

• Kitchen: An island cooktop and a menu desk simplify meal preparation here. A versatile dinette offers outdoor access through sliding glass doors.

• Dining Room: Neatly situated near the kitchen, this room will host important meals with style.

Images provided by designer/architect.

• Master Suite: Double doors and a tray ceiling make a good first impression. Two walk-in closets organize lots of clothes. A spa tub anchors the private bath.

• Bonus Room: A unique phone booth is found in this versatile room, which could serve as a playroom or an art studio.

Main Level Floor Plan

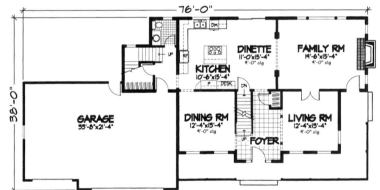

Upper Level Floor Plan

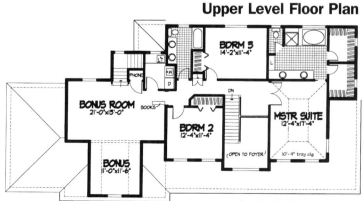

Copyright by designer/architect.

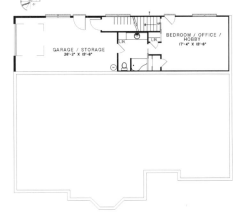

Plan #151022

Dimensions: 79' W x 77'8" D
Levels: 2
Square Footage: 3,059
Main Level Sq. Ft.: 2,650
Upper Level Sq. Ft.: 409
Bedrooms: 4
Bathrooms: 4
Foundation: Basement, crawl space, or slab
Materials List Available: Yes
Price Category: G

Images provided by designer/architect.

The two front porches, a rear covered porch, and a huge rear deck are your first clues to the comfort you'll enjoy in this home.

Features:

- Great Room: This versatile room with a 10-ft. ceiling has a gas fireplace, built-in shelves and entertainment center, a place for an optional staircase, and access to the rear covered porch.

- Dining Room: The 10-ft. ceiling lets you decorate for formal dining but still allows a casual feeling.

- Breakfast Room: This bright space is open to the kitchen, so you can enjoy it at any time of day.

- Hobby Room: Use this space just off the garage for almost any activity.

- Master Suite: Enjoy the 10-ft. boxed ceiling, built-in cabinets, and access to the rear covered porch. The split design gives privacy. The bath has a corner whirlpool tub, separate glass shower, and split vanities.

Main Level Floor Plan

Upper Level Floor Plan

Copyright by designer/architect.

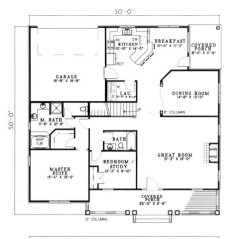

Main Level Floor Plan

Copyright by designer/architect.

Images provided by designer/architect.

Plan #151151

Dimensions: 50' W x 50' D

Levels: 1½

Square Footage: 3,002

Main Level Sq. Ft.: 1,733

Upper Level Sq. Ft.: 1,269

Bedrooms: 4

Bathrooms: 3

Foundation: Crawl space, slab

Materials List Available: Yes

Price Category: G

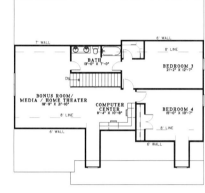

Upper Level Floor Plan

Main Level Floor Plan

Copyright by designer/architect.

Upper Level Floor Plan

Plan #151146

Dimensions: 113" W x 72" D

Levels: 2

Square Footage: 7,870

Finished Basement Sq. Ft.: 3,026

Main Level Sq. Ft.: 2,181

Upper Level Sq. Ft.: 2,663

Bedrooms: 6

Bathrooms: 5

Foundation: Walk out basement

Materials List Available: Yes

Price Category: I

Images provided by designer/architect.

Basement Level Floor Plan

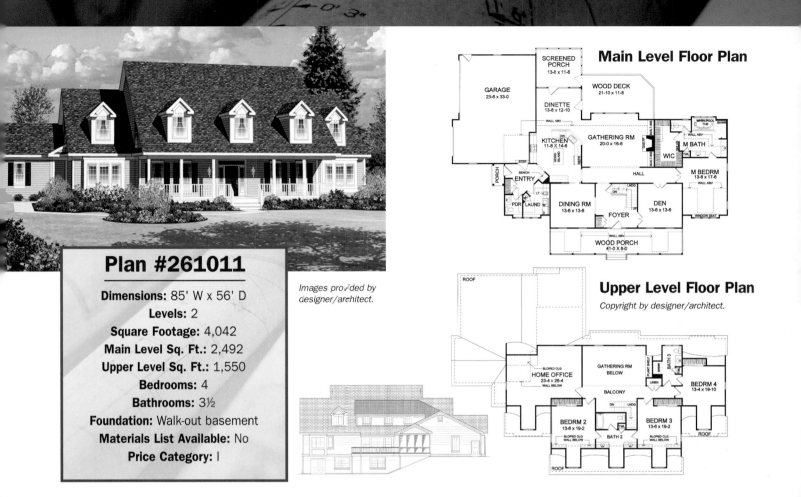

Main Level Floor Plan

Images provided by designer/architect.

Upper Level Floor Plan

Copyright by designer/architect.

Plan #261011

Dimensions: 85' W x 56' D

Levels: 2

Square Footage: 4,042

Main Level Sq. Ft.: 2,492

Upper Level Sq. Ft.: 1,550

Bedrooms: 4

Bathrooms: 3½

Foundation: Walk-out basement

Materials List Available: No

Price Category: I

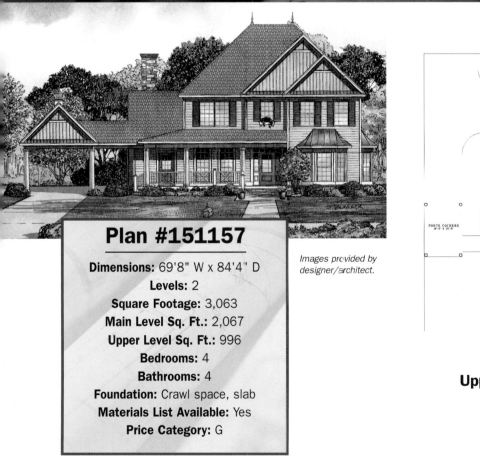

Plan #151157

Dimensions: 69'8" W x 84'4" D

Levels: 2

Square Footage: 3,063

Main Level Sq. Ft.: 2,067

Upper Level Sq. Ft.: 996

Bedrooms: 4

Bathrooms: 4

Foundation: Crawl space, slab

Materials List Available: Yes

Price Category: G

Images provided by designer/architect.

Main Level Floor Plan

Upper Level Floor Plan

Copyright by designer/architect.

Plan #331004

Dimensions: 81' W x 49'10" D

Levels: 2

Square Footage: 3,125

Main Level Sq. Ft.: 2,147

Upper Level Sq. Ft.: 978

Bedrooms: 4

Bathrooms: 3½

Foundation: Basement, crawl space, or slab

Materials List Available: No

Price Category: G

Images provided by designer/architect.

Main Level Floor Plan

Upper Level Floor Plan

Copyright by designer/architect.

Plan #341007

Dimensions: 87'7" W x 30' D

Levels: 2

Square Footage: 4,068

Main Level Sq. Ft.: 3,218

Upper Level Sq. Ft.: 850

Bedrooms: 4

Bathrooms: 2½

Foundation: Crawl space, slab, or basement

Materials List Available: Yes

Price Category: I

Images provided by designer/architect.

Main Level Floor Plan

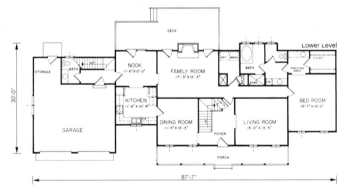

Upper Level Floor Plan

Copyright by designer/architect.

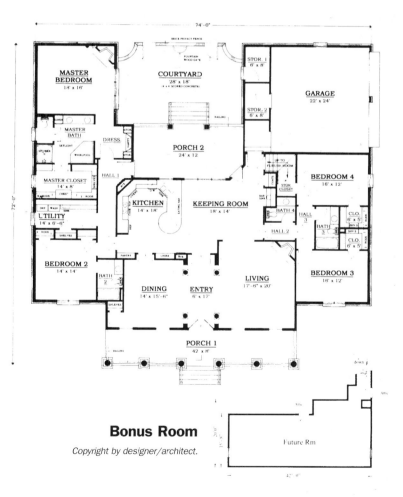

Plan #171013

Dimensions: 74' W x 72' D
Levels: 1
Square Footage: 3,084
Bedrooms: 4
Bathrooms: 3½
Foundation: Slab, crawl space
Materials List Available: Yes
Price Category: G

Images provided by designer/architect.

Impressive porch columns add to the country charm of this amenity-filled family home.

Features:

- **Ceiling Height:** 10 ft.

- **Foyer:** The sense of style continues from the front porch into this foyer, which opens to the formal dining room and the living room.

- **Dining Room:** Two handsome support columns accentuate the elegance of this dining room.

- **Living Room:** This living room features a cozy corner fireplace and plenty of room for the entire family to gather and relax.

- **Kitchen:** You'll be inspired to new culinary heights in this kitchen, which offers plenty of counter space, a snack bar, a built-in pantry, and a china closet.

- **Master Suite:** The bedroom of this master suite has a fireplace and overlooks a rear courtyard. The bath has two vanities a large walk-in closet, a deluxe tub, a walk-in shower, and a skylight.

Bonus Room

Copyright by designer/architect.

Main Level Floor Plan

Images provided by designer/architect.

Plan #151159

Dimensions: 80'6" W x 79'10" D

Levels: 2

Square Footage: 3,970

Main Level Sq. Ft.: 2,404

Upper Level Sq. Ft.: 1,566

Bedrooms: 4

Bathrooms: 3 Full, 2 Half

Foundation: Crawl space, slab

Materials List Available: Yes

Price Category: H

Upper Level Floor Plan

Copyright by designer/architect.

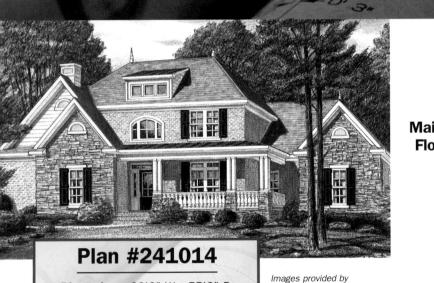

Main Level Floor Plan

Images provided by designer/architect.

Plan #241014

Dimensions: 66'6" W x 55'6" D

Levels: 2

Square Footage: 3,046

Main Level Sq. Ft.: 2,292

Upper Level Sq. Ft.: 754

Bedrooms: 4

Bathrooms: 3

Foundation: Slab

Materials List Available: No

Price Category: G

Upper Level Floor Plan

Copyright by designer/architect.

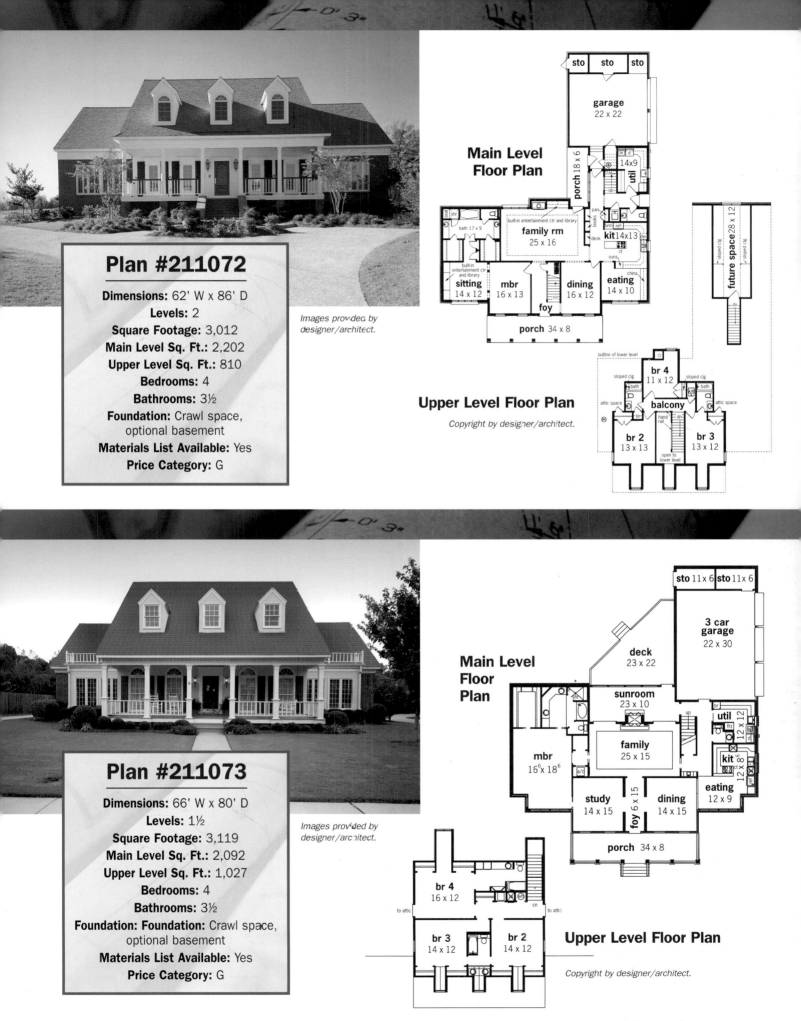

Plan #211072

Dimensions: 62' W x 86' D

Levels: 2

Square Footage: 3,012

Main Level Sq. Ft.: 2,202

Upper Level Sq. Ft.: 810

Bedrooms: 4

Bathrooms: 3½

Foundation: Crawl space, optional basement

Materials List Available: Yes

Price Category: G

Images provided by designer/architect.

Main Level Floor Plan

Upper Level Floor Plan

Copyright by designer/architect.

Plan #211073

Dimensions: 66' W x 80' D

Levels: 1½

Square Footage: 3,119

Main Level Sq. Ft.: 2,092

Upper Level Sq. Ft.: 1,027

Bedrooms: 4

Bathrooms: 3½

Foundation: Foundation: Crawl space, optional basement

Materials List Available: Yes

Price Category: G

Images provided by designer/architect.

Main Level Floor Plan

Upper Level Floor Plan

Copyright by designer/architect.

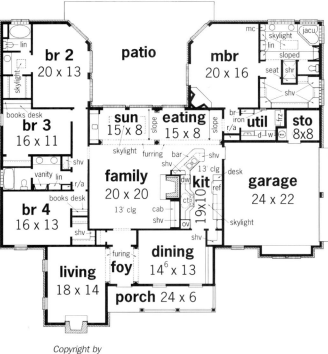

Images provided by designer/architect.

Plan #211065

Dimensions: 72' W x 70' D

Levels: 1

Square Footage: 3,158

Bedrooms: 4

Bathrooms: 3

Foundation: Crawl space

Materials List Available: Yes

Price Category: G

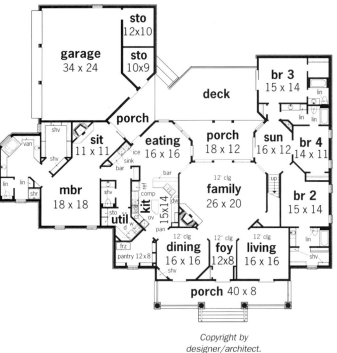

Images provided by designer/architect.

Plan #211067

Dimensions: 96' W x 90' D

Levels: 1

Square Footage: 4,038

Bedrooms: 4

Bathrooms: 4½

Foundation: Crawl space

Materials List Available: Yes

Price Category: I

Plan #131021

Dimensions: 60'0" W x 52'4" D
Levels: 2
Square Footage: 3,110
Main Level Sq. Ft.: 1,818
Upper Level Sq. Ft.: 1,292
Bedrooms: 5
Bathrooms: 2½
Foundation: Basement, crawl space, or slab
Materials List Available: Yes
Price Category: H

Amenities abound in this luxurious two-story beauty with a cozy gazebo on one corner of the spectacular wraparound front porch. Comfort, functionality, and spaciousness characterize this home.

Features:

- Ceiling Height: 8 ft.
- Foyer: This two-story high foyer is breathtaking.
- Family Room: Roomy with open views of the kitchen, the family room has a vaulted ceiling and boasts a functional fireplace and a built-in entertainment center.
- Dining Room: Formal yet comfortable, this spacious dining room is perfect for entertaining family and friends.
- Kitchen: Perfectly located with access to a breakfast room and the family room, this

U-shaped kitchen with large center island is charming as well as efficient.

- Master Suite: Enjoy this sizable room with a vaulted ceiling, two large walk-in closets, and a lovely compartmented bath.

Images provided by designer/architect.

Rear Elevation

Main Level Floor Plan

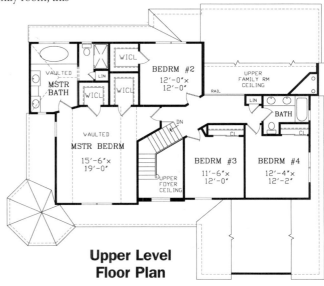

Upper Level Floor Plan

Copyright by designer/architect.

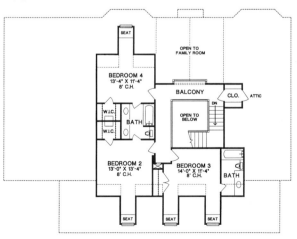

Plan #121047

Dimensions: 67'8" W x 57' D

Levels: 2

Square Footage: 3,072

Main Level Sq. Ft.: 2,116

Upper Level Sq. Ft.: 956

Bedrooms: 4

Bathrooms: 3½

Foundation: Slab

Materials List Available: Yes

Price Category: G

Images provided by designer/architect.

A long porch and a trio of roof dormers give this gracious home a sophisticated country look.

Features:

• Ceiling Height: 8 ft. unless otherwise noted.

• Balcony: This balcony overlooks the entry and the staircase hall.

• Dining Room: Columns and a cased opening lend elegance, making this the perfect venue for stylish dinner parties.

• Family Room: A cathedral ceiling gives this room a light and airy feel. The handsome fireplace framed by windows is sure to become a favorite family gathering place.

• Master Bedroom: This architecturally distinctive bedroom features a bayed sitting area and a tray ceiling.

• Bedrooms: One of the bedrooms enjoys a private bath, making it a perfect guest room. Other bedrooms feature walk-in closets.

Main Level Floor Plan

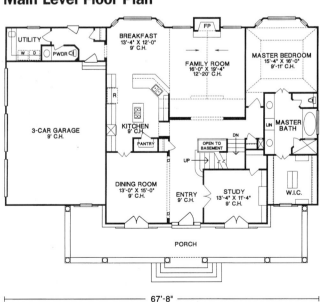

Upper Level Floor Plan

Copyright by designer/architect.

Let Us Help You
Plan Your
Dream Home

Whether you've always dreamed of building your own home or you can't find the right house from among the dozens you've toured, our collection of country and farmhouse home plans can help you achieve the home of your dreams. You could have an architect create a one-of-a-kind home for you, but the design services alone could end up costing up to 15 percent of the cost of construction—a hefty premium for any building project. Isn't it a better idea to select from among the hundreds of unique designs shown in our collection for a fraction of the cost?

What does Creative Homeowner Offer?

In this book, Creative Homeowner provides hundreds of home plans from the country's best architects and designers. Our designs are among the most popular available. Whether your taste runs from traditional to contemporary, Victorian to Colonial, you are sure to find the best house design for you and your family. Our plans packages include detailed drawings to help you or your builder construct your dream house. **(See page 312.)**

Can I Make Changes to the Plans?

Creative Homeowner offers three ways to help you achieve a truly unique home design. Our customizing service allows for extensive changes to our designs. **(See page 313.)** We also provide reverse images of our plans, or we can give you and your builder the tools for making minor changes on your own. **(See page 314.)**

Can You Help Me Stay on Budget?

Building a house is a large financial investment. To help you stay within your budget, Creative Homeowner can provide you with general construction costs based on your zip code. **(See page 314.)** Also, many of our plans come with the option of buying detailed materials lists to help you price out construction costs.

Is There Anything I Missed?

A typical construction crew consists of a number of skilled professionals. If you plan on doing all or part of the work yourself, or you want to keep tabs on your builder, we offer best-selling building and design books at attractive prices. Our book packages cover all phases of home construction, including framing and drywalling, interior decorating, kitchen and bath design, landscaping, and outdoor living. **(See pages 319–320.)**

Our Plans Packages Offer:

All of our home plans are the result of many hours of work by leading architects and professional designers. When you place an order for one of our home plans, you will receive the following.

Frontal Sheet

This artist's rendering of the front of the house gives you an idea of how the house will look once it is completed and the property landscaped.

Detailed Floor Plans

These plans show the size and layout of the rooms. They also provide the locations of doors, windows, fireplaces, closets, stairs, and electrical outlets and switches.

Foundation Plan

A foundation plan gives the dimensions of basements, walk-out basements, crawl spaces, pier foundations, and slab construction. Each house design lists the type of foundation included. If the plan you choose does not have the foundation type you require, our customer service department can help you customize the plan to meet your needs.

Roof Plan

In addition to providing the pitch of the roof, these plans also show the locations of dormers, skylights, and other elements.

Exterior Elevations

These drawings show the front, rear, and sides of the house as if you were looking at it head on. Elevations also provide information about architectural features and finish materials.

Interior Elevations and Details

Interior elevations show specific details of such elements as fireplaces, kitchen and bathroom cabinets, built-ins, and other unique features of the design.

Cross Sections

These show the structure as if it were sliced to reveal construction requirements, such as insulation, flooring, and roofing details.

Frontal Sheet

Floor Plan

Foundation Plan

Roof Plan

Cross Sections

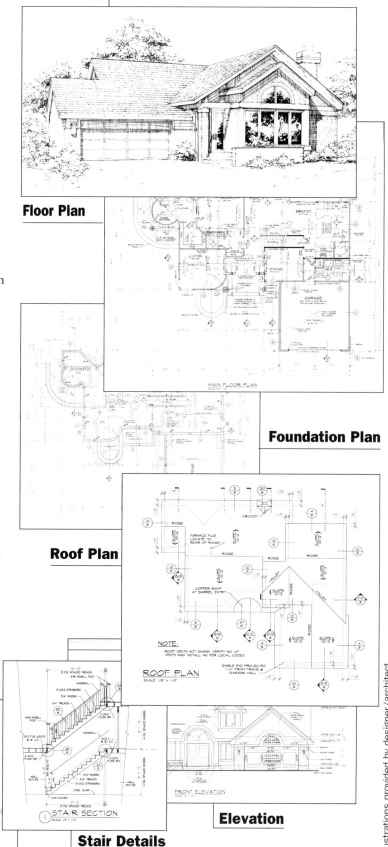

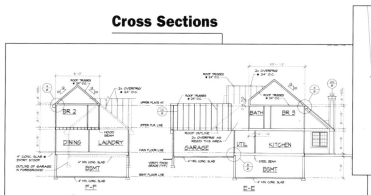

Stair Details

Elevation

Illustrations provided by designer/architect

Customize Your Plans in 4 Easy Steps

1 **Select the home plan** that most closely meets your needs. Purchase of a reproducible master is necessary in order to make changes to a plan.

2 **Call 1-800-523-6789 to place your order.** Tell our sales representative you are interested in customizing your plan. To receive your customization cost estimate, we will send you a checklist (via fax or email) for you to complete indicating the changes you would like to make to your plan. There is a $50 nonrefundable consultation fee for this service. If you decide to continue with the custom changes, the $50 fee is credited to the total amount charged.

3 **Fax the completed checklist** to 1-201-760-2431 or email it to us at customize@creativehomeowner.com. Within three business days of receipt of your checklist, a detailed cost estimate will be provided to you.

4 **Once you approve the estimate,** a 75% retainer fee is collected and customization work begins. Preliminary drawings typically take 10 to 15 business days. After approval, we will collect the balance of your customization order cost before shipping the completed plans. You will receive five sets of blueprints or a reproducible master, plus a customized materials list if desired.

Modification Pricing Guide

Categories	Average Cost From...	To
Add or remove living space	Quote required	
Bathroom layout redesign	$120	$280
Kitchen layout redesign	$120	$280
Garage: add or remove	$400	$680
Garage: front entry to side load or vice versa	Starting at $300	
Foundation changes	Starting at $220	
Exterior building materials change	Starting at $200	
Exterior openings: add, move, or remove	$55 per opening	
Roof line changes	$360	$630
Ceiling height adjustments	$280	$500
Fireplace: add or remove	$90	$200
Screened porch: add	$280	$600
Wall framing change from 2x4 to 2x6	Starting at $200	
Bearing and/or exterior walls changes	Quote required	
Non-bearing wall or room changes	$55 per room	
Metric conversion of home plan	$400	
Adjust plan for handicapped accessibility	Quote required	
Adapt plans for local building code requirements	Quote required	
Engineering stamping only	Quote required	
Any other engineering services	Quote required	
Interactive illustrations (choices of exterior materials)	Quote required	

Note: *Any home plan can be customized to accommodate your desired changes. The average prices above are provided only as examples of the most commonly requested changes, and are subject to change without notice. Prices for changes will vary according to the number of modifications requested, plan size, style, and method of design used by the original designer. To obtain a detailed cost estimate, please contact us.*

Architectural Seals

Because of differences in building codes, some cities and states now require an architect or engineer licensed in that state to review and "seal" a blueprint, or officially approve it, prior to construction. Delaware, Nevada, New Jersey, and New York require that all plans for houses built in those states be redrawn by an architect licensed in the state in which the home will be built.

Before Customization

After

Decide What Type of Plan Package You Need

How many Plans Should You Order?

Standard 8-Set Package. We've found that our 8-set package is the best value for someone who is ready to start building. Once the process begins, a number of people will require their own set of blueprints. The 8-set package provides plans for you, your builder, the subcontractors, mortgage lender, and the building department.
Minimum 4-Set Package. If you are in the bidding process, you may want to order only four sets for the bidding round and reorder additional sets as needed.
1-Set Study Package. The 1-set package allows you to review your home plan in detail. The plan will be marked as a study print, and it is illegal to build a house from a study print alone. It is a violation of copyright law to reproduce a blueprint without permission.

Buying Additional Sets

If you require additional copies of blueprints for your home construction, you can order additional sets within 60 days of the original order date at a reduced price. The cost is $45.00 for each additional set. For more information, contact customer service.

Reproducible Masters

If you plan to make minor changes to one of our home plans, you can purchase reproducible masters. Drawn on vellum paper, an erasable paper that you can reproduce in a copying machine, reproducible masters allow an architect, designer, or builder to alter our plans to give you a customized home design. This package also allows you to print as many copies of the modified plans as you need for construction.

Mirror-Reverse Sets

Plans can be printed in mirror-reverse—we can "flip" plans to create a mirror image of the design. This is useful when the house would fit your site or personal preferences if all the rooms were on the opposite side than shown. As the image is reversed, the lettering and dimensions will also be reversed, meaning they will read backwards. Therefore, when ordering mirror-reverse drawings, you must order at least one set of right-reading plans. A $50.00 fee per order will be charged for mirror-reverse (regardless of the number of mirror-reverse sets ordered).

Determine Your Construction Costs

EZ Quote: Home Cost Estimator

EZ Quote is our response to one of the most frequently asked questions we hear from customers: "How much will the house cost me to build?" EZ Quote: Home Cost Estimator will enable you to obtain a calculated building cost to construct your new home, based on labor rates and building material costs within your zip code area. This summary building cost report is particularly useful for first-time buyers who might be concerned with the total construction costs before purchasing sets of home plans. It will also provide a certain level of comfort when you begin soliciting bids from builders. The cost is $29.95 for the first EZ Quote and $14.95 for each additional EZ Quote.

Materials List

Available for most of our plans, the Materials List provides you an invaluable resource in planning and estimating the cost of your home. Each Materials List outlines the quantity, dimensions, and type of materials needed to build your home (with the exception of mechanical systems). You will get faster, more-accurate bids from your contractors and building suppliers—and avoid paying for unused materials. A Materials List may only be ordered with the purchase of a set of home plans.

Before You Order

Our Exchange Policy

Blueprints are nonrefundable. However, should you find that the plan you have purchased does not fit your needs, you may exchange that plan for another plan in our collection within 60 days from the date of your original order. The entire content of your original order must be returned before an exchange will be processed. You will be charged a processing fee of 20% of the amount of the original plan set, the cost difference between the new plan set and the original plan set (if applicable), and shipping costs for the new plans. Contact our customer service department for more information. Please note: reproducible masters may only be exchanged if the package is unopened.

Building Codes and Requirements

At the time of creation, our plans meet the building code requirements published by the Building Officials and Code Administrators International, the Southern Building Code Congress International, the International Conference of Building Officials, or the Council of American Building Officials. Because building codes vary from area to area, some drawing modifications and/or the assistance of a professional designer or architect may be necessary to comply with your local codes or to accommodate specific building site conditions. We strongly advise you to consult with your local building official for information regarding codes governing your area.

Blueprint Price Schedule

Price Code	1 Set	4 Sets	8 Sets	Reproducible Masters	Materials List
A	$275	$315	$365	$490	$60
B	$350	$390	$440	$555	$60
C	$400	$440	$490	$590	$60
D	$450	$490	$540	$630	$70
E	$500	$540	$590	$675	$70
F	$550	$590	$640	$725	$70
G	$600	$640	$690	$820	$70
H	$675	$715	$765	$865	$70
I	$780	$820	$870	$905	$80

Shipping & Handling

	1-4 Sets	5-7 Sets	8+ Sets or Reproducibles
US Regular (7–10 business days)	$15	$20	$25
US Priority (3–5 business days)	$25	$30	$35
US Express (1–2 business days)	$35	$40	$45
Canada Reg. (8–12 business days)	$25	$30	$35
Canada Exp. (3–5 business days)	$40	$40	$45

Overseas Shipping: Contact customer service for shipping costs.

Note: All delivery times are from date the blueprint and package is shipped.

- -

Order Form

Please send me the following:

Plan Number: _____

Price Code: _____ (see Plan Index)

Indicate Foundation Type: (see plan page for availability)
❑ Slab ❑ Crawl space ❑ Basement ❑ Walk-out basement

Basic Blueprint Package   **Cost**
❑ Reproducible Masters $_____
❑ 8-Set Plan Package $_____
❑ 4-Set Plan Package $_____
❑ 1-Set Study Package $_____

❑ Additional plan sets:
__ sets at $45.00 per set $_____
❑ Print in mirror-reverse: $50.00 per order $_____
__ sets printed in mirror-reverse

Important Extras
❑ Materials List $_____
❑ EZ Quote for Plan #_____ at $29.95 $_____
❑ Additional EZ Quotes for Plan #s_____
at $14.95 each $_____

Shipping (see chart above) $_____
SUBTOTAL $_____
Sales Tax (NJ residents add 6%) $_____

TOTAL $_____

Order Toll Free: 1-800-523-6789   By Fax: 201-760-2431
Creative Homeowner
24 Park Way
Upper Saddle River, NJ 07458

Name _____
(Please print or type)

Street _____
(Please do not use a P.O. Box)

City _____ State _____

Country _____ Zip _____

Daytime telephone ( )_____

Fax ( )_____
(Required for reproducible orders)

E-Mail _____

Payment ❑ Check/money order *Make checks payable to Creative Homeowner*

❑ VISA   ❑ MasterCard   ❑ American Express   ❑ DISCOVER

Credit card number _____

Expiration date (mm/yy) _____

Signature _____

Please check the appropriate box:
❑ Licensed builder/contractor   ❑ Homeowner   ❑ Renter

SOURCE CODE | CA500

www.ultimateplans.com   315

Index

order direct: 1-800-523-6789

Index

Plan #	Price Code	Page	Total Finished Area Square Feet	Materials List Available
151159	H	306	3970	Yes
151160	D	126	1845	Yes
151161	D	132	1915	Yes
151162	E	185	2231	Yes
151163	D	127	1832	Yes
151164	D	127	1848	Yes
151165	D	126	1927	Yes
151166	D	184	2140	Yes
151167	E	184	2286	Yes
161001	C	134	1782	Yes
161005	C	80	1593	Yes
161007	C	75	1611	Yes
171002	B	25	1458	Yes
171006	E	194	2296	Yes
171007	C	122	1650	Yes
171008	C	91	1652	Yes
171009	C	91	1771	Yes
171011	D	187	2069	Yes
171013	G	305	3084	Yes
171015	D	219	2089	Yes
171017	E	268	2558	Yes
181008	B	32	1106	Yes
181015	B	30	1176	Yes
181021	B	31	1124	Yes
181034	F	276	2687	Yes
181035	D	233	2129	Yes
181047	B	36	1458	Yes
181064	F	254	2802	Yes
181074	C	106	1760	Yes
181078	E	240	2292	Yes
181085	D	186	2183	Yes
181094	D	240	2099	Yes
181136	E	232	2426	Yes
181151	E	220	2283	Yes
181152	B	10	1339	Yes
181153	B	39	1478	Yes
181154	E	189	2406	Yes
181155	D	173	2118	Yes
181157	C	106	1795	Yes
181158	E	193	2391	Yes
181160	F	257	2768	Yes
191003	C	93	1785	No
191009	D	197	2172	No
191010	D	218	2189	No
191012	D	175	2123	No
191023	C	92	1785	No
191024	C	133	1700	No
191025	D	181	2052	No
191026	D	181	2052	No
191027	E	180	2354	No
191028	F	255	2669	No
191029	F	255	2726	No
191030	A	14	864	No
201002	B	48	1191	Yes
201003	B	48	1144	Yes
201004	B	49	1121	Yes
201005	B	49	1128	Yes
201006	B	33	1172	Yes
201012	B	12	1221	Yes
201014	B	50	1237	Yes
201015	B	19	1271	Yes
201016	B	45	1293	Yes
201017	B	50	1265	Yes
201018	B	45	1294	Yes
201022	B	10	1363	Yes
201025	B	38	1379	Yes
201027	B	33	1494	Yes
201031	C	102	1531	Yes
201034	C	143	1660	Yes
201038	C	75	1789	Yes
201045	D	70	1866	Yes
201051	D	143	1899	Yes
201056	D	71	1956	Yes
201071	A	26	984	Yes
201072	A	38	987	Yes
201073	C	74	1610	Yes
201079	D	103	1856	Yes
201084	D	179	2056	Yes
201086	C	99	1573	Yes
201096	D	237	2125	Yes
201099	E	190	2239	Yes
211016	B	13	1191	Yes
211018	B	16	1266	Yes
211019	B	24	1395	Yes
211021	B	19	1375	Yes
211022	B	22	1380	Yes
211024	B	22	1418	Yes
211025	B	23	1434	Yes
211029	C	90	1672	Yes
211030	C	98	1600	Yes
211032	C	81	1751	Yes
211036	D	84	1800	Yes
211037	D	98	1800	Yes
211038	D	100	1898	Yes
211042	D	81	1800	Yes
211046	D	70	1936	Yes
211047	D	212	2009	Yes
211048	D	196	2002	Yes
211051	D	224	2123	Yes
211054	E	193	2358	Yes
211055	E	224	2394	Yes
211065	G	308	3158	Yes
211067	I	308	4038	Yes
211069	C	146	1600	Yes
211070	C	117	1700	Yes
211072	G	307	3012	Yes
211073	G	307	3119	Yes
211084	B	36	1485	Yes
211089	D	101	1956	Yes
211090	D	84	1932	No
211103	F	275	2605	Yes
211108	F	273	2888	Yes
211129	D	119	1868	No
211130	E	180	2280	Yes
211131	E	260	2598	No
211132	E	257	2535	No
221016	B	26	1461	No
231013	F	264	2780	No

Index

Books To Help You Build

Creative Homeowner offers an extensive selection of leading how-to books.
Choose any of the book packages below to get started.

Home Building Package

Build and repair your home—inside and out—with these essential titles.

Retail Price: $74.80
Your Price: $65.95
Order #: 267095

Wiring: Complete Projects for the Home
Provides comprehensive information about the home electrical system. Over 750 color photos and 75 illustrations. 288 pages.

Plumbing: Basic, Intermediate & Advanced Projects
An overview of the plumbing system with code-compliant, step-by-step projects. Over 750 full-color photos, illustrations. 272 pages.

House Framing
Walks you through the framing basics, from assembling simple partitions to cutting compound angles for dormers. 500 full-color illustrations and photos. 208 pages.

Drywall: Pro Tips for Hanging and Finishing
Covers tools and materials, estimating, cutting, hanging, and finishing gypsum wallboard. 250 color photos and illustrations. 144 pages.

Kitchen & Bath Package

Learn to design and build kitchens and bathrooms like a pro.

Retail Price: $79.80
Your Price: $69.95
Order #267080

The *New* Smart Approach to Kitchen Design
Includes all the answers to help plan a project, hire a contractor, shop for appliances, and decorate like a design pro. More than 260 color photos. 208 pages.

Kitchens: Plan, Remodel, Build
A complete design and installation package, including design trends and step-by-step projects. More than 550 full-color photos and illustrations. 256 pages.

The *New* Smart Approach to Bath Design
The latest and best materials and products on the market for master baths, family baths, and powder rooms. More than 260 color photos. 208 pages.

Bathrooms: Plan, Remodel, Build
Includes step-by-step projects, storage options, products, materials, and lighting possibilities. Over 100 illustrations and 550 color photographs. 256 pages.

Landscaping Package

Create a yard you'll love with these comprehensive landscape guides.

Retail Price: $73.80
Your Price: $64.95
Order # 267075

Complete Home Landscaping
Covers everything from design principles to construction projects, from plant selection to plant care. More than 800 full-color photos and illustrations. 320 pages.

Trees, Shrubs & Hedges
Create a landscape, match plants to growing conditions, and learn to plant, transplant, and prune. Over 500 color photos and paintings. 208 pages.

Smart Guide: Ponds & Fountains
Plan, build, and maintain with projects and easy-to-understand text. Covers plant and fish selection. 175 color illustrations, 40 color photos. 80 pages.

Annuals, Perennials & Bulbs
Lavishly illustrated with portraits of over 100 flowering plants; filled with instructional techniques and tips. More than 500 color photos and illustrations. 208 pages.

Decks & Patios Package

Design and build decks and patios for your new home.

Retail Price$66.80
Your Price $55.95
Order # 267090

Decks: Planning, Designing, Building
Takes you through every step involved in designing and building a beautiful deck. 600 color photos and illustrations. 192 pages.

Deck Designs Plus Railings, Planters, Benches
The best plans from top deck designers. Includes planters, railings, benches, and trellises. 300 color photos and drawings. 192 pages.

Walks, Walls & Patios: Design, Plan & Build
Includes the ideas and how-to you'll need to integrate popular hardscape designs into a home landscape. Over 500 color photos and illustrations. 240 pages.

Design Ideas for Decks
Everything you'll need to create a beautiful deck for your home. Learn about the newest deck styles, designs, and patterns. More than 250 photos. 128 pages.

Decorating Package

Save money and design like a professional with these must-have decorating books.

Retail Price $65.85
Your Price $59.95
Order # 267085

The New Smart Approach to Home Decorating
Introduces the classic design theories, showcases interior design trends, and teaches how to make the most of any space. Over 440 color photos 288 pages.

Lyn Peterson's Real Life Decorating
Noted interior designer gives easy-to-live-with solutions to the most daunting decorating dilemmas. More than 300 color photos and illustrations. 304 pages.

Color in the American Home
Shows how the power of color can transform even the plainest room into a beauty. Over 200 color photos. 176 pages.

Outdoor Projects Package

Use these project guides to accessorize the largest room in your home—your yard.

Retail Price $51.85
Your Price $45.95
Order # 267060

Trellises & Arbors
Features inspiring photos, planning advice, design ideas, plant information, and 10 step-by-step trellis projects. Over 450 photos and illustrations. 160 pages.

Yard & Garden Furniture
Contains 20 step-by-step projects, from the comfortable lines of an Adirondack chair to the sturdy serviceability of a family picnic table. Over 600 color photos and illustrations. 208 pages.

Gazebos & Other Outdoor Structures
Design fundamentals, step-by-step building techniques, and custom options for the perfect gazebo, arbor, or pavilion. 480 color illustrations and photos. 160 pages.

Home Reference Package

Find it, fix it, design it, create it—
if it's in your home, it's in here.

Retail Price: $59.90
Your Cost: $49.95
Order # 267070

The Home Book
The largest, most complete home improvement book on the market—608 pages packed with over 2,300 photos, 800 drawings, and an understandable, practical text that covers your home top to bottom, inside and out. 608 pages.

The *New* Smart Approach to Home Decorating
Decorate every room in your home with the same confidence and flair as a professional designer. More than 440 color photos. 288 pages.

Family-Living Package

Start your home off right with these family-oriented ideas
for the home and garden.

Retail Price: $69.80
Your Cost: $59.95
Order # 267065

Lyn Peterson's Real Life Decorating
Noted interior designer gives easy-to-live-with solutions to the most daunting decorating dilemmas. More than 300 color photos and illustrations. 304 pages.

Smart Approach to Kids' Rooms
Ideas for decorating, furnishing, designing, and organizing space for children with practical design advice and safety tips. Over 200 color photos. 176 pages.

Build a Kids' Play Yard
How to build a swing set, monkey bars, balance beam, playhouse, and more. Over 200 color photos and drawings. 144 pages.

National Wildlife Federation®
Attracting Birds, Butterflies and Other Backyard Wildlife
Wildlife-friendly gardening, landscape designs, and family projects from the National Wildlife Federation. Over 200 color photos and illustrations. 128 pages.

Order Form for Books to Help Complete Your Home

Qty.	Description	Order #	Price	Cost
Book Packages:				
___	Home Building Package	267095	$65.95	___
___	Kitchen & Bath Package	267080	69.95	___
___	Landscaping Package	267075	64.95	___
___	Decks & Patios Package	267090	55.95	___
___	Decorating Package	267085	59.95	___
___	Outdoor Projects Package	267060	45.95	___
___	Home Reference Package	267070	49.95	___
___	Family-Living Package	267065	59.95	___
Individual Titles from Creative Homeowner:				
___	Wiring: Basic and Advanced Projects	278237	$19.95	___
___	Plumbing: Basic, Intermediate & Advanced Projects	278210	19.95	___
___	House Framing	277655	19.95	___
___	Drywall: Pro Tips for Hanging and Finishing	278315	14.95	___
___	The New Smart Approach to Kitchen Design	279946	19.95	___
___	Kitchens: Plan, Remodel, Build	277061	19.95	___
___	The New Smart Approach to Bath Design	279234	19.95	___
___	Bathrooms: Plan, Remodel, Build	278627	19.95	___
___	Complete Home Landscaping	274615	24.95	___
___	Trees, Shrubs & Hedges	274238	19.95	___
___	Smart Guide: Ponds & Fountains	274643	8.95	___
___	Annuals, Perennials & Bulbs	274032	19.95	___
___	The New Smart Approach to Home Decorating	279672	24.95	___
___	Lyn Peterson's Real Life Decorating	279382	21.95	___
___	Color in the American Home	287264	19.95	___
___	Decks: Planning, Designing, Building	277162	16.95	___
___	Deck Designs	277369	16.95	___
___	Walks, Walls & Patios	277997	19.95	___
___	Design Ideas for Decks	277155	12.95	___
___	Trellises & Arbors	274804	16.95	___

Qty.	Description	Order #	Price	Cost
Individual Titles from Creative Homeowner:				
___	Yard & Garden Furniture	277462	$19.95	___
___	Gazebos & Other Outdoor Structures	277138	14.95	___
___	The Home Book	267855	34.95	___
___	The Smart Approach to Kids' Rooms	279473	19.95	___
___	Build a Kids' Play Yard	277662	14.95	___
___	Attracting Birds, Butterflies & and Other Backyard Wildlife	274955	12.95	___

Shipping* ___

SUBTOTAL ___

Sales Tax (NJ residents add 6%) ___

TOTAL ___

*Shipping Costs:
For book packages: $5.95 per package
For individual titles: $4.75 for first book
$1.75 for each additional book

Make check payable to Creative Homeowner
To order, send form to:
Creative Homeowner
P.O. Box 38
24 Park Way
Upper Saddle River, NJ 07458

Or call
1-800-523-6789

SHIP TO:

Name _____
(Please print)

Address _____

City _____ State:____ Zip:_____ Phone # _____